Copyright © 2019 Meteoor bvba

THE ULTIMATE GRANNY SQUARE SOURCEBOOK
100 contemporary motifs to mix and match

**Share your creations with
#grannysquaresourcebook**

Fourth print run: March 2021

First published November 2019 by
Meteoor Books, Antwerp, Belgium
www.meteoorbooks.com
hello@meteoorbooks.com

Text and images
© 2019 Meteoor bvba and designers

Pictures by Sophie Peirsman, sophiepeirsman.be
Printed and bound by Grafistar

ISBN 9789491643293
D/2019/13.030/5

A catalogue record for this book is available from the
Royal Library of Belgium.

THE ULTIMATE

GRANNY SQUARE SOURCEBOOK

100 CONTEMPORARY MOTIFS TO MIX AND MATCH

METEOOR BOOKS

CONTENTS

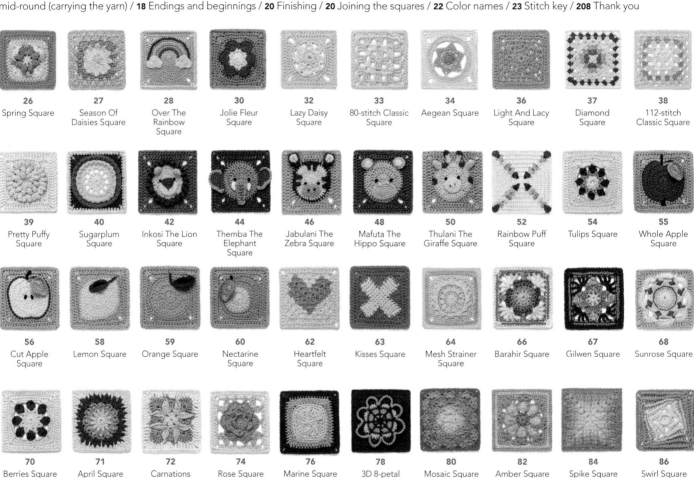

FOREWORD

Gather your hooks and yarns, pour yourself a drink and flex your fingers, because we're making 100 gorgeous granny squares!

Traditional or modern, vibrant or subtle, the possibilities of granny squares are endless! They captivate tones and lines much like a yarn canvas and come together as snuggly blankets, soft cushions, smart garments and much more.

This unique granny square collection combines the styles of 23 creative designers from all over the world, who each bring their best game to the table. With ample suggestions for captivating combinations, written instructions as well as clear graphs for every square in the book, stitch tutorials and techniques for blocking and joining, this sourcebook goes above and beyond to show you the endless possibilities of granny square crochet.

These squares have been selected from the Granny Square Design Contest on *www.allcrochetpatterns.net*. You'll discover basic beginner-friendly squares (the 'classic' granny square) as well as elaborate layered squares for the more experienced crocheter to create stunning pieces.

All motifs match in both size and stitch count, so they can easily be combined into stunning combinations, bringing you the best of this unbeaten crochet classic!

Making granny squares is satisfying in many ways. It's a great way to use up small remnants of yarn, the perfect crochet project to take along when you're on-the-go, it's a quick make that gives an instant result and it's perfect to take your mind off your everyday worries for a moment.

We hope this book will cast a new light on the beloved granny square and adds a dash of inspiration to your crochet practice.

Enjoy crocheting!

Share your creations with #grannysquaresourcebook.

The list of colors used by the designer. You can find info on the color names on page 22. We use Yarn A, Yarn B,... so you can easily replace colors and not get confused by color-specific instructions in the pattern.

An image of the blocked square (in colors chosen by the designer) shows you the end result.

The skill level gives a rough guide to difficulty. Details on skill level can be found on page 11.

All squares in this book have either 80 stitches (green label) or 112 stitches (red label) in the final round.

A note gives additional info about the round you are about to start or have just finished.

100 different squares by 23 creative designers from all around the world make up this Granny Square sourcebook. Written instructions and visual charts help you to create a wide variety of designs, from beginner-friendly to extra advanced.

Details of this square's designer.

Special stitches used in this pattern, this gives you a more detailed idea of the skill level.

Pattern-specific special stitches are not explained at the front of the book. The full explanation can be found here.

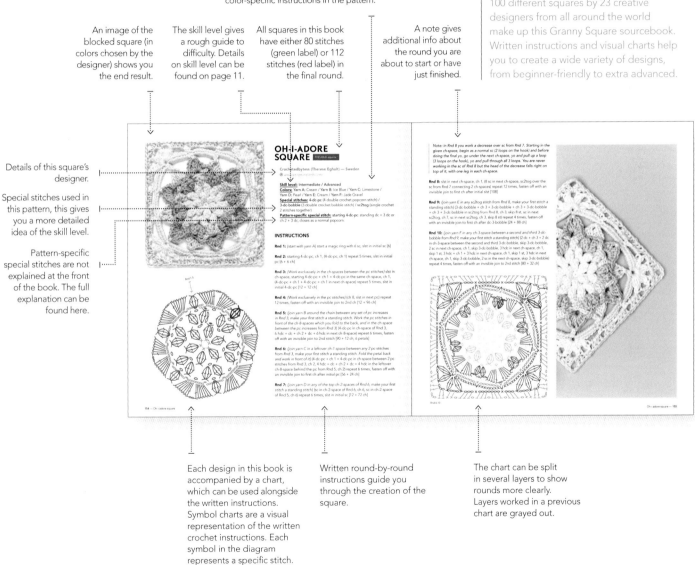

Each design in this book is accompanied by a chart, which can be used alongside the written instructions. Symbol charts are a visual representation of the written crochet instructions. Each symbol in the diagram represents a specific stitch. Find more info on reading charts on page 11.

Written round-by-round instructions guide you through the creation of the square.

The chart can be split in several layers to show rounds more clearly. Layers worked in a previous chart are grayed out.

MATERIALS

When you're standing in front of a yarn display, you'll easily find yourself overwhelmed by all the gorgeous yarns in different weights, colors and fibers. Finding your absolute favorite yarn might take a lifetime, but with the help of the guide below, we'll try to make the search a bit easier.

YARN

All samples in this book have been made with Yarn and Colors Must Have, which is a 100% mercerized cotton, fine / sport weight yarn. Don't feel tied to the choice of yarn though, as any weight of cotton, acrylic or wool can be used as a substitute, provided you use the appropriately-sized crochet hook.

There are different thicknesses of yarn. Thickness is called weight. You can find the weight of the yarn on its label, indicated by a number between 1 and 7. Most crocheters work granny squares with a yarn in the range between fine / sport weight (2) and medium / worsted weight (4). If you want to make a large blanket and work it up quickly, you can use a light worsted (3) or worsted weight yarn (4). If you plan on making a smaller project with lots of details, like a handbag or a scarf, try your hand at a sport weight yarn (2).

You'll want to consider the fiber content before starting a project. A different fiber will give a different drape. The three most common yarn fibers are wool, acrylic and cotton.

- **Wool** is a soft, natural and durable fiber, but wool allergies and the higher price can be potential drawbacks.

- **Cotton** can be challenging for beginners as it's a little stiff to work with, but the stitch definition is very clear. The resulting fabric is durable, but will be less flexible. Although less warm, cotton is a popular summer fiber choice.

- **Acrylic** is a popular and very affordable synthetic fiber. It's washable, strong and lightweight. Projects made with acrylic yarn can lose their shape over time, though.

Yarns with a combination of fibers often combine the best of worlds.

💡 *Tip:* **In general, yarns with a smooth texture and a tight twist are easier to work with.**

Before starting a large project, it's best to test one square with the yarn of your choice, wash it according to the instructions on the yarn label and block it into shape to check if you're happy with the outcome.

The patterns in this book don't give the yarn quantity. The quantities per square are rather small and will vary according to how loosely or tightly you crochet. You could use some of the remnants from other projects or start with a new ball of yarn.

💡 *Tip:* **It can be challenging to see your stitches when you work with yarns in dark colors.**

HOOKS

Hooks as well as yarn come in a range of sizes, according to their diameter. You typically match your crochet hook size to your yarn weight, which is usually on the yarn label. In the table below you will find the standard hook size recommended for each yarn weight.

NUMBER (SYMBOL)	1	2	3	4
CATEGORY NAME	super fine	fine	light	medium
UK YARN TYPE	3 ply	4 ply	double knitting (DK)	aran
US YARN TYPE	fingering	sport	light worsted	worsted
RECOMMENDED HOOK IN US SIZE	B-1 to E-4	E-4 to 7	7 to I-9	I-9 to K-10 1/2
RECOMMENDED HOOK IN METRIC SIZE	2.25 to 3.5mm	3.5 to 4.5mm	4.5 to 5.5mm	5.5 to 6.5mm

You may find that your work is too tight or loose using this hook size. Try different hook sizes until you're happy with the fabric feel and drape of the completed square. Size down to make your work more stiff and firm. Go up a size to make it more drapeable and flexible.

Hooks are usually made from aluminum or steel. Metal hooks tend to slip between the stitches more easily. Choose a crochet hook with a rubber or ergonomic handle for comfort.

ACCESSORIES

In addition to yarn and hook, there are only a few other tools you'll need to get started. Use a tape measure or ruler to calculate the gauge, a sharp pair of scissors to cut your yarn, stitch markers to mark a specific part in your crochet work, and a tapestry or yarn needle to weave in the yarn ends. A blocking board and pins will come in handy if you want to block your squares (page 20).

HOW TO READ A PATTERN

With a little explanation, even a daunting-looking pattern, becomes clear. Abbreviations and symbols may vary from one source to another, so make sure to check that you understand the system used in this book before starting a pattern.

DECODING INSTRUCTIONS

At the beginning of each line you will find 'Rnd + a number' to indicate which round you are in.

At the end of each line you will find the total number of stitches you should have, contained in square brackets, split up between stitches and chains. Slip stitches to join rounds are not counted in the total stitch count as these are generally worked on top of the starting stitch of the round.

Example: [72 + 8 ch]. In this example you have 72 stitches and 8 chains

☀️ *Tip:* **When in doubt, take a moment to check your total stitch count.**

When a chain start is counted as a stitch in the total stitch count, we add this information in gray between rounded brackets, after the chain start.

Example: *{start with yarn D}* start a magic ring with ch 2 (count as hdc), 11 hdc, fasten off with an invisible join to first true hdc [12]

Instructions on how to start a round are placed in italics between accolades after the round number.

Example: *{join yarn C in any 3-dc-bobble in Rnd 3 at the back of the flower, make your first stitch a standing stitch}* (slst in 3-dc-bobble, ch 3) repeat 8 times [8 + 24 ch]

☀️ *Tip:* **More info on deciphering standing stitch instructions can be found on page 18.**

When multiple stitches are worked in the same stitch or space, we join them with a + symbol.

Example: 4 tr + ch 2 + 4 tr in next ch-space.

If you need to skip stitches or chain spaces, it will be stated in the pattern.

Example: skip next 2 st.

If you work in rounds other than the previous round, it will be referred to with the round number. If no round is stated, you work in the previous round only.

Example: {work behind the petals of Rnd 3} ch 1, (BPsc around hdc of Rnd 3, ch 3) repeat 6 times, slst in initial BPsc [6 + 18 ch]

PATTERN REPEATS

The crochet patterns in this book are written as groups of stitches that are repeated a number of times in a round. We do this to shorten the pattern and make it less cluttered. When part of the instructions repeats throughout the round, we place it between rounded brackets, followed by the number of times this part should be worked. Occasionally you will see a repeat within a repeat. In this case the inner repeat will use rounded brackets while the outer repeat uses square brackets.

Example: (sc in next 2 st, 2 sc in next st) repeat 12 times [48]

In this example you work the stitches between the rounded brackets a total of 12 times.

Example: ch 1, [(sc in next 2 st, 2 sc in next st) repeat 3 times, sc in next 2 st, hdc in next st, 2 hdc in next st, dc in next st, 2 tr in next st, dc in next st, 2 hdc in next st, hdc in next st] repeat 2 times [48]

In this example you work the part between square brackets a total of 2 times. Within this repeat, you work the part between rounded brackets a total of 3 times.

WORKING IN COLOR

We state the colors used in the sample in the pattern introduction. In the pattern instructions we use Yarn A, B, C and so on. This will make it less confusing for you to use alternative colors of your choice. You can write down your yarn choices if this makes it easier for you.

NOTES, SPECIAL STITCHES AND TIPS

If there is anything unusual about a pattern that needs extra attention, or if a pattern-specific stitch is used, it will be explained at the top of the pattern.

HOW TO READ A CHART

Each design in this book is accompanied by a chart, which can be used alongside the written instructions. Symbol charts are a visual representation of the written crochet instructions. Each symbol in the diagram represents a specific stitch. You can find a helpful stitch key on page 23.

Charts are read counterclockwise, unless a round is worked on the wrong side (WS). Then an arrow indicates the change in direction.

The charts are worked in 3 colors to make it easier for you to track the rounds visually as you go. These colors do not reflect the colors used in the sample square.

When a chart is complex and has multiple layers of stitches crossing each other, we split it up in multiple parts to make it clearer. The stitches already worked are shown in gray in the follow-up chart, so you can clearly see where the stitches of the new round go.

When a round starts with a standing stitch (page 18), we put this symbol in bold, so you can immediately spot the start of the round.

💡 *Tip:* **Charts do not distinguish between working into a chain stitch or into the space created by the chain stitch. You will need to refer to the written pattern for details.**

SKILL LEVELS

- **Beginner:** basic stitches only, working in stitches and ch-spaces of the previous round only, simple repetition, no color changes within the round.
- **Intermediate:** more advanced stitches and techniques, working in stitches and ch-spaces of one or more rounds below, color changes within the round.
- **Advanced:** complex stitches and techniques, complex repetition, a large variation of positions to insert the hook.
- **Extra Advanced:** challenging repetitions and positions of the hook, patterns for experienced crocheters.

MATCHING THE SIZE OF SQUARES

All squares in this book have either 80 or 112 stitches in the final round. However, this doesn't always result in the same size squares. Variations in stitch height, yarn fiber and personal crochet style can result in major differences in size. If you want to combine two or more squares in a project, make sure to crochet a sample in your preferred yarn to check if the sizes match. If they don't match, you can size up or down a hook for one of both squares. Always change the hook size to get the proper square size, rather than trying to work tighter or looser. Squares that generally turn out bigger or smaller than others in this book have been marked.
When squares are more or less the same size, blocking (page 20) will even out little differences.

The sample squares in this book, worked in sport weight yarn with a 3 mm hook, are generally
- 3.5 inch / 9 cm for 80 stitches squares
- 4.75 inch / 12 cm for 112 stitches squares

When worked in light worsted weight yarn with a 4.5 mm hook, the squares will approximately be
- 4.5 inch / 11.5 cm for 80 stitches squares
- 6.5 inch / 16.5 cm for 112 stitches squares

When worked in worsted weight yarn with a 5.5 mm hook, the squares will approximately be
- 5.75 inch / 14.5 cm for 80 stitches squares
- 8 inch / 20 cm for 112 stitches squares

BASIC STITCHES

SLIP KNOT

A slip knot is not a stitch, but the first step in putting yarn on the hook. Create a loop with the yarn. Insert the hook through the center of the loop and pull up the end attached to the ball (1). Pull the free yarn end to tighten the loop on the hook (2).

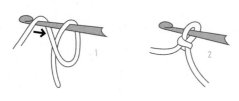

CHAIN (abbreviation: ch)

Wrap the yarn over the hook from back to front. Pull the hook, carrying the yarn, through the loop already on the hook. One chain stitch completed.

SLIP STITCH (abbreviation: slst)

A slip stitch is used to move across one or more stitches at once or to finish a piece. Insert hook in indicated stitch or space (1). Wrap the yarn over the hook and draw through both loops at once (2). One slip stitch completed.

SINGLE CROCHET (abbreviation: sc)

Insert the hook in indicated stitch or space (1) and wrap the yarn over the hook. Draw the yarn through the stitch (2). You will see that there are now two loops on the hook. Wrap the yarn over the hook again and draw it through both loops at once (3). One single crochet stitch completed (4).

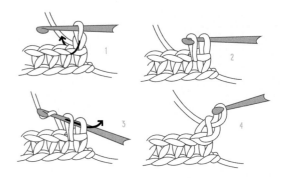

EXTENDED SINGLE CROCHET (abbreviation: esc)

Insert the hook in indicated stitch or space (1) Wrap the yarn over the hook and draw the yarn through the stitch. You now have two loops on the hook (2). Wrap the yarn over the hook again and pull it through the first loop only (3). Wrap the yarn over the hook again and pull it through both loops on the hook (4). One extended single crochet stitch completed (5).

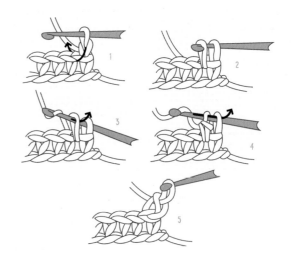

HALF DOUBLE CROCHET (abbreviation: hdc)

Bring the yarn over the hook from back to front before placing the hook in indicated stitch or space (1). Wrap the yarn over the hook and draw the yarn through the stitch. You now have three loops on the hook (2). Wrap the yarn over the hook again and pull it through all three loops on the hook (3). One half double crochet stitch completed (4).

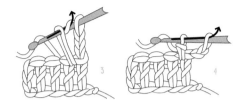

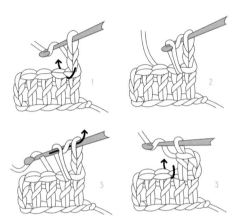

DOUBLE CROCHET (abbreviation: dc)

Bring the yarn over the hook from back to front before placing the hook in indicated stitch or space (1). Wrap the yarn over the hook and draw the yarn through the stitch. You now have three loops on the hook (2). Wrap the yarn over the hook again and pull it through the first two loops on the hook (3). You now have two loops on the hook. Wrap the yarn over the hook one last time and pull it through both loops on the hook (4). One double crochet stitch completed.

EXTENDED DOUBLE CROCHET (abbreviation: edc)

Bring your yarn over the hook from back to front before placing the hook in indicated stitch or space (1). Wrap the yarn over the hook and draw the yarn through the stitch (2). You now have three loops on the hook. Wrap the yarn over the hook again and pull it through the first loop on the hook (3). You now have three loops on the hook. Wrap the yarn over the hook again and pull it through the first two loops on the hook (4). You now have two loops on the hook. Wrap the yarn over the hook one last time and pull it through both loops on the hook (5). One extended double crochet stitch completed.

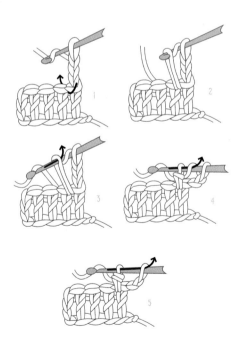

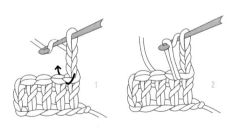

HALF TREBLE CROCHET (abbreviation: htr)

Bring the yarn over the hook two times before placing the hook in the indicated stitch or space (1). Wrap the yarn over the hook and draw the yarn through the stitch (2). You now have four loops on the hook. Wrap the yarn over the hook again and pull it through the first two loops on the hook (3). You now have three loops on the hook. Wrap the yarn over the hook one last time and pull it through the remaining loops on the hook (4). One half treble crochet stitch completed.

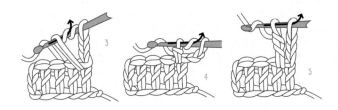

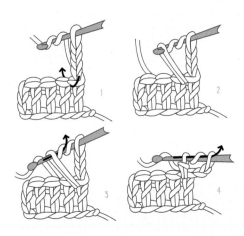

TREBLE CROCHET (abbreviation: tr)

Bring the yarn over the hook two times before placing the hook in the indicated stitch or space (1). Wrap the yarn over the hook and draw the yarn through the stitch (2). Wrap the yarn over the hook again and pull it through the first two loops on the hook (3). Repeat this last step two times (4, 5). One treble crochet stitch completed.

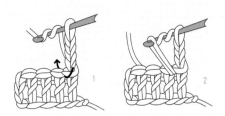

EXTENDED TREBLE CROCHET (abbreviation: etr)

Bring the yarn over the hook two times before placing the hook in the indicated stitch or space (1). Wrap the yarn over the hook and draw the yarn through the stitch (2). Wrap the yarn over the hook and pull it through the first loop on the hook (3). Wrap the yarn over the hook again and pull it through the first two loops on the hook (4). Repeat this last step two times (5, 6). One extended treble crochet stitch completed.

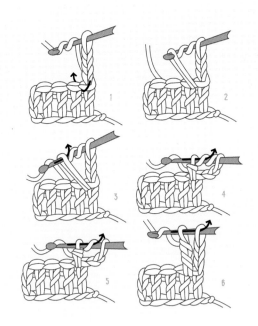

DOUBLE TREBLE CROCHET (abbreviation: dtr)

Bring the yarn over the hook three times before placing the hook in the indicated stitch or space. Wrap the yarn over the hook and draw the yarn through the stitch. Wrap the yarn over the hook again and pull it through the first 2 loops on the hook. Repeat this last step 3 times until there is one leftover loop on the hook. One double treble crochet stitch completed.

TRIPLE TREBLE CROCHET (abbreviation: trtr)

Bring your yarn over the hook four times and place the hook in the indicated stitch or space. Wrap the yarn over the hook and draw the yarn through the stitch. Wrap the yarn over the hook again and pull it through the first 2 loops on the hook. Repeat this last step 4 times until there is one leftover loop on the hook. One triple treble crochet stitch completed.

POSITION OF STITCHES

When you crochet a stitch, you automatically create a set of loops at the top of the stitch. If the pattern doesn't state otherwise, stitches are worked through both of these loops. However, there are several techniques to create different textures by working the same stitch in a different location.

- **BLO (back loops only)**: Insert the hook under the back loop, away from you, at the top of the stitch. Leave the front loop untouched.
- **FLO (front loops only)**: Insert the hook under the front loop, facing you, at the top of the stitch. Leave the back loop untouched.
- **third loop:** The third loop is found right down below the back loop. Slightly tilt the stitch you will be working into forwards so you can see the horizontal bar to the back of the stitch.
- **BP (back post):** The post of the stitch is the main vertical portion of the stitch. Insert the hook from right to left and from back to front to back around the vertical post of the stitch.
- **FP (front post):** Insert the hook from right to left and from front to back to front around the vertical post of the next stitch.
- **between stitches:** Insert the hook underneath all horizontal threads of the stitch and between the posts of two crochet stitches.
- **crossed stitch:** Skip a stitch in the round and work in the next stitch(es). Go back to the skipped st and work the crossed stitch in the skipped stitch, above the previously worked stitch.
- **work in the ring:** Insert the hook into the center of the (magic) ring, instead of into the next stitch.
- **back stitch:** Fold the work towards you. Insert the hook into the inverted "V" of the stitch one round below, from back to front and move around the base of the stitch.

DECREASES

Decrease stitches are made by starting several individual stitches into consecutive stitches or spaces and joining them together so they count as one stitch. There are several variations, using stitches of different height.

- **sc-x-tog:** [insert hook in next st, yo and pull up a loop] repeat x times, yo and draw through all remaining loops on hook.
- **hdc-x-tog:** [yo, insert hook in next st, yo and pull up a loop] repeat x times, yo and draw through all remaining loops on hook.
- **dc-x-tog:** [yo, insert hook in next st, yo and pull up a loop, yo and draw through 2 loops] repeat x times, yo and draw through all remaining loops on hook.
- **tr-x-tog:** [yo two times, insert hook in next st, yo and pull up a loop, (yo and draw through 2 loops) repeat 2 times] repeat x times, yo and draw through all remaining loops on hook.

CLUSTER STITCHES

Cluster stitches are made by working several stitches into one space or stitch and then finishing them together so that they count as one stitch. There's several techniques, each with their own kind of texture.

BOBBLE STITCH WITH DOUBLE OR TREBLE CROCHET STITCHES

A bobble stitch is also referred to as a basic cluster stitch. It creates a soft dimensional bobble by crocheting several incomplete tall stitches in the same stitch and then joining them together at the top.

- **2-dc-bobble:** (yo, insert hook in st or space, yo and pull up a loop, yo and draw through 2 loops) repeat 2 times, yo and pull through remaining 3 loops on hook.
- **3-dc-bobble:** (yo, insert hook in st or space, yo and pull up a loop, yo and draw through 2 loops) repeat 3 times, yo and pull through remaining 4 loops on hook.
- **4-dc-bobble:** (yo, insert hook in st or space, yo and pull up a loop, yo and draw through 2 loops) repeat 4 times, yo and pull through remaining 5 loops on hook.
- **2-tr-bobble:** [yo two times, insert hook in st or space, yo and pull up a loop, (yo and draw through 2 loops) repeat 2 times] repeat 2 times, yo and pull through remaining 3 loops on hook.
- **3-tr-bobble:** [yo two times, insert hook in st or space, yo and pull up a loop, (yo and draw through 2 loops) repeat 2 times] repeat 3 times, yo and pull through remaining 4 loops on hook.
- **4-tr-bobble:** [yo two times, insert hook in st or space, yo and pull up a loop, (yo and draw through 2 loops) repeat 2 times] repeat 4 times, yo and pull through remaining 5 loops on hook.

POPCORN STITCH

A popcorn stitch consists of several fully completed stitches, worked into the same stitch. To close, you join together the first and last stitches at the top with a chain stitch. Popcorn stitches in this book are made from any number of dc stitches.

- **3-dc-pc:** Make 3 dc stitches in the same st. Remove the hook from the last dc and insert it into both loops of the first dc. Grab the last dc with the hook and pull it through the first dc.
- **4-dc-pc:** Make 4 dc stitches in the same st. Remove your hook from the last dc and insert it into both loops of the first dc. Grab the last dc with the hook and pull it through the first dc.
- **5-dc-pc:** Make 5 dc stitches in the same st. Remove the hook from the last dc and insert it into both loops of the first dc. Grab the last dc with the hook and pull it through the first dc.

PUFF STITCH

A puff stitch resembles a bobble stitch, but instead of working with incomplete double or treble crochet stitches in the same stitch, the puff stitch is always made with half-finished half double crochet stitches.

(Yo, insert hook in st or space and pull up a loop) repeat x times, yo and pull through all loops on hook.

 Tip: **When you have made all wraps around your hook, hold them together at the base as you yarn over and pull through all loops, to help prevent them from slipping.**

The puff stitch generally closes with a ch 1. This chain is mentioned in the pattern and diagram.

SHELL STITCH

When working a shell stitch you usually skip a number of stitches and work multiple stitches into the next stitch. This will cause the stitches to fan out and create a shell shape.

Examples:
- 5 dc in indicated stitch or space
- 2 dc + ch 2 + 2 dc in indicated stitch or space
- **v-stitch:** dc + ch 2 + dc in indicated stitch or space
- **tall v-stitch:** tr + ch 2 + tr in indicated stitch or space

MAGIC RING

A magic ring is a method to start crocheting in the round. You start by crocheting over an adjustable loop and finally pull the loop tight when you have finished the required number of stitches. The advantage of this method is that there's no hole left in the middle of your starting round. In the following example we describe a magic ring starting with a single crochet stitch. Of course a magic ring can be worked with stitches of different height, as described in the pattern.
Start with the yarn crossed to form a circle (1). Draw up a loop with your hook but don't pull it tight (2). Hold the circle with your index finger and thumb and wrap the working yarn over your middle finger (3). Make one chain stitch by wrapping the yarn over the hook and pulling it through the loop on your hook (4, 5).
Now insert your hook into the loop and underneath the tail. Wrap the yarn over the hook and draw up a loop (6). Wrap the yarn over the hook again (7) and draw it through both loops on your hook. You have now completed your first single crochet stitch (8). Continue to crochet (repeating step 6, 7, 8) until you have the required number of stitches as mentioned in the pattern.

Now grab the yarn tail and pull to draw the center of the ring tightly closed (9, 10). You can now begin your second round by crocheting into the first stitch of the magic ring.

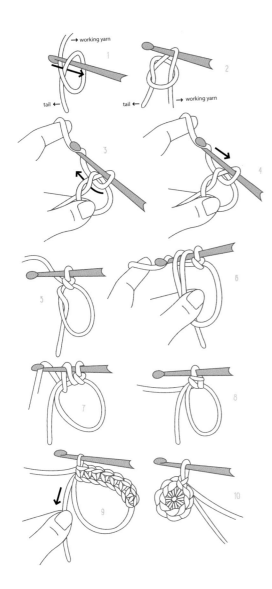

ALTERNATIVE METHOD

If you don't prefer the magic ring, you can start each piece using the following technique: ch 2, x stitches into the second chain from the hook – where x is the stitches you would make in your magic ring.

SPECIAL STITCHES

PICOT STITCH
(abbreviation: ch-2-picot / ch-3-picot / ch-4-picot)

Picots are created by working the number of chains mentioned in the pattern and then working a slip stitch in the first chain stitch you made.

SPIKE STITCH (spike-hdc / -dc / -sc)

Instead of working into the two top loops of the next stitch, work into the corresponding stitch in the round below (1). Wrap the yarn over the hook and draw it through the stitch. You now have two loops on your hook. Wrap the yarn over the hook once more and pull it through both loops on your hook (2). You have now completed one spike-hdc stitch.

LONG STITCH (abbreviation: long sc / hdc / dc / tr / puff)

The long stitch is very similar to a regular stitch. The difference is that the loop you pull through the stitch at the beginning is drawn to a longer height so it levels with your other working stitches.

> **Example: long dc:** yo, insert hook in next st or space, yo, pull up a loop to the height of the previous stitch, (yo, draw through 2 loops on hook) repeat 2 times.

BROOM STITCH

In this book we use the broom stitch, which is a derivative of the more commonly known broomstick lace stitch. Make a tight slip stitch in the next st and pull up a long loop. Take your hook out of the stitch. Insert your hook in the next stitch, yarn over and pull up a loop. Repeat as instructed in the pattern. You can thread the loops onto a pencil or knitting needle while working. The loops will be secured by working into them in the next round.

HERRINGBONE STITCH (abbreviation: HBdc)

The herringbone stitch causes the stitch to lean forward and gives it a slanted appearance. In this book we use the herringbone double crochet stitch.

> **HBdc:** yo, insert hook in next st or space, yo and pull through stitch and first loop on hook, yo and pull through one loop on the hook, yo and pull through both loops on hook.

> 💡 *Note:* **Special stitches used in a single pattern will be explained on that pattern's page.**

EMBELLISHMENT TECHNIQUES

SURFACE SLIP STITCH

The surface slip stitch is an embellishment of slip stitches worked on top of the fabric of your crochet work. Insert the hook from the right side to the wrong side where you want your line of slip stitches to start, now wrap the yarn over the hook and draw it through the stitch. Insert the hook in the next stitch, wrap the yarn over the hook and pull it through the stitch and the loop on the hook. This is the start of your line of surface slip stitches. Repeat this to the end of your crochet work or in any shape you like.

FRENCH KNOT

The French knot is an embroidery stitch. Insert a threaded embroidery needle from the back to the front through the stitch where you want the knot to show. Keep the tip of the needle flat against your crochetwork and wrap the yarn around your needle two times. Carefully pull the needle through these loops so that you end up with a double knot. Insert the needle in the crochet stitch next to the knot – not in the same stitch, as this will make the knot disappear – and fasten at the back.

CHANGING COLOR MID-ROUND (CARRYING THE YARN)

Use this method for a neat join between colors in the middle of a round. Do not fasten off your original color. Work up to the final "yarn over, pull through" of the last stitch in the original color. Wrap the new color around your hook and use it to complete the stitch. Lay your original color on top of your work and crochet over it as you go.

ENDINGS AND BEGINNINGS

JOINING YARN

As granny squares are worked in joined rounds each round starts with a number of chain stitches, or alternatively a standing stitch, to gain height.

Ch-start (when continuing in the same color)

We use the classical ch-start for rounds that do not require a color change. If you continue working in the same color, you close the previous round with a slst in the first stitch and start the new round with a number of starting chains:

- Rounds starting with a single crochet stitch do not have a ch-start, as the jump from a slip stitch to a single crochet stitch needs no additional height.
- A half double crochet stitch requires a ch-start of 2 chain stitches.
- A double crochet stitch requires a ch-start of 3 chain stitches.
- A treble crochet stitch requires a ch-start of 4 chain stitches.

  Example: ch 3 (count as dc) + 2 dc in corner-space,…

These starting chains are usually counted as a stitch, which is mentioned in gray between rounded brackets after the ch-start.

Standing stitch start (when continuing with a new color)

The squares in this book are all very colorful, as playing with colors is one of the fun ways to personalize a granny square. When changing colors, the standing stitch start is our preferred way to begin a round. Fasten off the previous round and begin the next round with a chainless start. Attach your new yarn color to your hook with a slip knot. Insert your hook into the designated stitch or space and pull up a loop. Then work the stitch as you would normally do.
When starting with a standing stitch, you will find these instructions at the start of your round:

  Example: {join yarn B in any ch-space, make your first stitch a standing stitch} (3 dc + ch 2 in ch-space) repeat 4 times, fasten off with an invisible join to 2nd stitch [12 + 8 ch]

In this example your first dc stitch will be a standing dc. You then continue with the leftover 2 dc and ch 2. In the next repeat, you will work 3 regular double crochet stitches as the standing stitch instructions refer to the start of the round only.

  Example: {join yarn G in the first sc after ch-2-space, make your first stitch a standing stitch} (BPsc around next 19 st, ch 2 behind ch 2 corner space from Rnd 6) repeat 4 times, ch 2, fasten off, fasten off with an invisible join to 2nd stitch [76 + 8 ch]

In this example your first BPsc stitch will be a standing BPsc. You then continue with the leftover 18 BPsc and ch 2. In the next repeat, you will work 19 BPsc as the standing stitch instructions refer to the start of the round only.

> 💡 *Note:* **The advantage of a standing stitch start is having an invisible start, leaving no trail of ch-starts. The disadvantage is having two yarn ends to weave in at the same place, one at the start and one at the end of each round.**

- **standing sc:** make a slip knot on your hook, insert hook in indicated stitch or space, yo, pull up a loop, yo, pull through both loops on hook.
- **standing hdc:** make a slip knot on your hook, wrap the yarn around your hook (hold loops on your hook with your finger until the stitch is completed), insert hook in indicated stitch or space, yo, pull up a loop, yo, pull through 3 loops on hook.
- **standing dc:** make a slip knot on your hook, wrap the yarn around your hook (hold loops on your hook with your finger until the stitch is completed), insert hook in indicated stitch or space, yo, pull up a loop, yo, pull through 2 loops on hook, yo, pull through 2 loops on hook.
- **standing tr:** make a slip knot on your hook, wrap the yarn around your hook two times (hold loops on your hook with your finger until the stitch is completed), insert hook in indicated stitch or space, yo, pull up a loop, yo, pull through 2 loops on hook, yo, pull through 2 loops on hook, yo, pull through 2 loops on hook.
- **standing pc:** work 1 standing dc, work 3 regular dc in the same st, close as a regular popcorn stitch.
- **standing bobble:** make a slip knot on your hook, wrap the yarn around your hook (hold loops on your hook with your finger until the stitch is completed), insert hook in indicated stitch or space, yo, pull up a loop, yo, pull through 2 loops on hook, (yo, insert hook in st, yo and pull up a loop, yo and draw through 2 loops) repeat x times, yo and pull through all remaining loops on hook.
- **standing puff:** make a slip knot on your hook, pull loop on hook up to roughly the height of a double crochet stitch; (yo, insert hook in indicated stitch or space and pull up a loop) repeat x times, yo and pull through all loops on hook.

If you do not prefer this method, the standing stitch start can be replaced by a classical ch-start. Simply replace the first stitch of your round by the number of ch-stitches corresponding with the stitch height.

> 💡 *Note:* **The standing stitch has no standard abbreviation. In our diagrams it is marked with a more dense symbol, so it pops out.**

CLOSING A ROUND

We use two methods for closing a round, depending on whether the next round is worked in a different color or not.

Slst join

The most common join involves working a slip stitch into the beginning chain or beginning stitch of the round. In this book the slst join is used when working consecutive rounds in the same color.

Invisible join

We fasten off each round before a color change with an invisible join, so you can rejoin with a new color and weave in your yarn tail neatly as you go – or leave it to weave in later. Finish with the last stitch and do not join to the beginning with a slip stitch. Cut your yarn, leaving a length of 5"/12 cm.
Pull the yarn tail all the way through the stitch. Take the yarn tail on your tapestry needle. Insert your needle underneath both loops of the second stitch of the round, from back to front. Then insert it into the back loop only of the last stitch you made. Pull the tail to the back of the work and weave in the yarn end.
You will see that your invisible join covers the first stitch of the round.

> 💡 *Tip:* **Tip: Count your stitches after every round and check if you have the correct number of stitches before continuing.**

- **invisible join over standing stitch**
  Cut your yarn, leaving a length of 5"/12 cm. Pull the yarn tail all the way through the stitch. Take the yarn tail on your tapestry needle. Take the starting yarn tail of your standing stitch and hold it down by the side of your standing stitch. Insert your needle underneath both loops of the second stitch of the round. Then insert into the back loop and third loop of the last stitch you made. Pull the yarn through. Next, insert your needle in the top of the standing stitch and go down to the bottom of the stitch. Weave in the yarn end.

- **invisible join when 2nd stitch is a chain stitch**
  Cut your yarn, leaving a length of 5"/12 cm. Pull the yarn tail all the way through the stitch. Take the yarn tail on your tapestry needle. Insert your needle underneath the top two loops of the chain, making sure the third loop goes underneath your needle. Then insert your needle into the back loop of the last stitch you made. Pull the yarn through. Next, insert your needle in the top of the standing stitch and go down to the bottom of the stitch. Weave in the yarn end.

FINISHING

WORKING IN THE ENDS

If you want your piece to last a long time, you need to properly weave in your yarn tails, whether at the end of a project or at a yarn join in the middle. Weaving in yarn tails on a colorful lacy square may be a bit intimidating because gaps in the fabric make hiding the tails more difficult. Crocheting over yarn tails in the next round would allow the tails to show through the open work stitches. Instead, take your yarn tail on a tapestry needle and weave your needle through the tops of the stitches to hide the tail, following the flow of your crochet work for at least 1" / 2.5 cm. After working the yarn tail through the stitches, come back the opposite way. Pull the end gently and cut the leftover tail, allowing the yarn to ease back into the stitches.

Tip: ***If working with multiple colors, weave the yarn ends through the stitches with the same color to keep them invisible.***

BLOCKING SQUARES

Blocking is crucial to neaten up the shape of your square and give it a nice symmetrical form and crisp corners. You can also use it to make sure that each square is exactly the same size, which makes joining them easier.

Take your finished, unblocked squares, a set of rust-proof straight pins, a spray bottle with cold water and a blocking mat (an ironing board or foam board does the trick). Decide on the size you want your square to be. Pin your granny square in place. Start by pinning two opposite corners. Once the corners are done, straighten out the edges of the squares, using as many pins as you need. Lightly spray the square, it should not be soaking wet. Give your granny square plenty of time to dry completely. Don't remove the pins from your blocking mat until your square is dry.

If your squares are made with acrylic yarn, or a blend of acrylic and natural fibers, you might need to steam block your square for the best result. Hold the iron carefully over the granny square, a few centimeters from the surface, allowing the steam to plume onto the yarn for 15 seconds. Do not put the iron directly on the granny square, as it will melt the acrylic yarn. Allow the square to dry.

Tip: ***Remember to weave in the yarn ends before you block your square.***

JOINING THE SQUARES

If you're planning on making a blanket, garment or other project using multiple granny squares, you will need to join them together. There are several ways to join granny squares to each other. We will show you 4 methods, either using a tapestry needle or crocheting them together, so you have a few options to choose from.

Tip: ***Use the same yarn (fiber and weight) as used for the granny squares to avoid problems when washing.***

WHIPSTITCH SEAM (tapestry needle)

Place two squares side by side, with the wrong sides facing up. Align the stitches of the outer round. Insert your tapestry needle through the top loops of the corresponding stitches, pull through and repeat in the same direction. This method creates a decorative ridge on the right side of your work.

WOVEN SEAM (tapestry needle)

Place two squares side by side, with the wrong sides facing up. Insert your needle from left to right through the top loops of the corresponding stitches, pull through and continue in the other direction, going from right to left. Repeat throughout. This method creates a flat seam on the right side.

SINGLE CROCHET SEAM (crochet hook)

You can choose to work a single crochet join on the wrong or on the right side of your square. Working on the wrong side is ideal for same color squares, since this method creates a flat seam on the right side. The ridge on the back is hardly noticeable. Working on the right side is ideal for different color squares, as you create a decorative ridge.

Hold the squares together (wrong or right sides facing, as you prefer) and align the stitches of the outer round. Insert your hook through the corresponding stitch of both sides to work a single crochet stitch. Continue along.

Tip: ***Start with a standing single crochet to make a neat start.***

SLIP STITCH SEAM (crochet hook)

A slip stitch join is preferably worked on the front of your square.

Hold the squares together, with the wrong sides facing each other and align the stitches of the outer round. Insert your hook through the back loops only of the corresponding stitch of both sides to work a slip stitch. Continue along.

MIX AND MATCH 80- AND 112-STITCH SQUARES – HOW TO JOIN THEM MATHEMATICALLY

Joining two 80-stitch squares or two 112-stitch squares is easy, as you will have an equal number of stitches on each side of both squares.
If you want to combine both 112-stitch squares and 80-stitch squares in a project, you'll have to calculate the arrangement of the motifs so the total stitch count of the squares match both in length and width. The basic calculation is:

Seven 80-stitch squares in a row have the same length as five 112-stitch squares.

$80 \times 7 = 560 \ / \ 112 \times 5 = 560$

You can combine them in projects, provided you use the same size squares in a row and use multiples of 7 (for 80-stitch squares) and 5 (for 112 stitch squares).

These colors (and more) are available in the Yarn And Colors Must-Have (mini) range.

Cream	Ecru	Birch	Clay	Limestone	Vanilla	Golden Glow	Sunflower	Mustard	Cantaloupe	Papaya
Sorbus	Chestnut	Brownie	Satay	Burgundy	Cardinal	Raspberry	Girly Pink	Cotton Candy	Peony Pink	Salmon
Pink Sand	Peach	Pearl	Pastel Pink	Old Pink	Antique Pink	Fuchsia	Purple Bordeaux	Plum	Grape	Lavender
Navy Blue	Denim	Larimar	Ice Blue	Nordic Blue	Turquoise	Blue Lake	Pacific Blue	Petrol Blue	Petroleum	Riverside
Glass	Jade Gravel	Opaline Glass	Green Ice	Mint	Green Beryl	Aventurine	Eucalyptus	Lettuce	Grass	Peridot
Pistachio	Amazon	Forest	Olive	Pea Green	Cold Green	Silver	Soft Grey	Shark Grey	Graphite	Black

SYMBOL	STITCH	ABBREVIATION
⌒	magic ring	magic ring
○	chain	ch
●	slip stitch	slst
×	single crochet	sc
⊥	extended single crochet	esc
T	half double crochet	hdc
T	double crochet	dc
T	extended double crochet	edc
T	half treble crochet	htr
T	treble crochet	tr
T	extended treble crochet	etr
T	double treble crochet	dtr
T	triple treble crochet	trtr
T	herringbone double crochet	HBdc
T T V	spike stitch	spike-dc, spike-hdc, spike-sc,...
popcorn stitch	popcorn stitch	x-dc-pc
bobble	bobble stitch with double crochet stitches	x-dc-bobble
bobble	bobble stitch with treble crochet stitches	x-tr-bobble
puff	puff stitch	3-puff, 4-puff,...
⋏ ⋏	single crochet 2 stitches together	sc2tog
⋏	single crochet 3 stitches together	sc3tog
⋔	double crochet 3 stitches together	dc3tog
⊕	picot stitch	ch-3-picot,...
⋁	v-stitch	v-stitch
⋁	tall v-stitch	tall v-stitch

SYMBOL	STITCH	ABBREVIATION
⌒	back loops only	BLO
⌣	front loops only	FLO
c	back post	BP
ɔ	front post	FP
⌄	crochet in third loop	in third loop
‹	crochet in back stitch	in back stitch
ɔ	surface slip stitch	surface slst
Ɛ	back post single crochet	BPsc
Ƨ	front post single crochet	FPsc
X	single crochet in back loops only	BLO sc
X	single crochet in front loops only	FLO sc
ʃ	back post half double crochet	BPhdc
ʃ	front post half double crochet	FPhdc
T	half double crochet in back loops only	BLO hdc
T	half double crochet in front loops only	FLO hdc
ʃ	back post double crochet	BPdc
ʃ	front post double crochet	FPdc
T	double crochet in back loops only	BLO dc
T	double crochet in front loops only	FLO dc
ʃ	back post treble crochet	BPtr
ʃ	front post treble crochet	FPtr
T	treble crochet in back loops only	BLO tr
T	treble crochet in front loops only	FLO tr
⌒	invisible join	invisible join
T T ×	standing stitch	standing dc, hdc,...
	round	Rnd
	right side	RS
	wrong side	WS
	stitch / stitches	st
	yarn over	yo

PATTERNS

SPRING SQUARE `80 stitch square`

Conmismanoss (Susana Villalobos) — Argentina
@conmismanoss f hilandosuenoss

Skill level: Beginner
Colors: Yarn A: Sunflower / Yarn B: Pink Sand / Yarn C: Cream /
Yarn D: Grass / Yarn E: Peach
Special stitches: 5-dc-pc (popcorn stitch with 5 dc) / 4-dc-pc (popcorn
stitch with 4 dc)

INSTRUCTIONS

Rnd 1: *{start with yarn A}* start a magic ring with (hdc + ch 2) repeat 8
times, fasten off with an invisible join to first ch after initial hdc [8 + 16 ch]

Rnd 2: *{join yarn B in any ch-space, make your first stitch a standing
stitch}* (5-dc-pc + ch 3) repeat 8 times, fasten off with an invisible join to
first ch after initial 5-dc-pc [8 + 24 ch / 8 petals]

Rnd 3: *{join yarn C in any ch-space, make your first stitch a standing
stitch}* (3 dc + ch 2 + 3 dc in ch-space, *{Change to yarn D}* 4-dc-pc in
next ch-space *{Change to yarn C}*) repeat 4 times, fasten off with an
invisible join to 2nd stitch [28 + 8 ch]

Rnd 4: *{join yarn E in any ch-space, make your first stitch a standing
stitch}* (2 dc + ch 2 + 2 dc in ch-space, dc in next 7 st) repeat 4 times,
fasten off with an invisible join to 2nd stitch [44 + 8 ch]

Rnd 5: *{join yarn B in any ch-space, make your first stitch a standing
stitch}* (2 hdc + ch 2 + 2 hdc in ch-space, hdc in next 11 st) repeat 4 times,
slst in first hdc [60 + 8 ch]

Rnd 6: slst in next st, slst in next ch-space, ch 2 (count as hdc), hdc +
ch 1 + 2 hdc in ch-space, hdc in next 15 st, (2 hdc + ch 1 + 2 hdc in
ch-space, hdc in next 15 st) repeat 4 times, fasten off with an invisible
join to first true hdc [76 + 4 ch]

SEASON OF DAISIES SQUARE `80 stitch square`

Conmismanoss (Susana Villalobos) — Argentina
@conmismanoss f hilandosuenoss

Skill level: Beginner
Colors: **Yarn A:** Sunflower / **Yarn B:** Cream / **Yarn C:** Peridot /
Yarn D: Ecru
Special stitches: Work in third loop

INSTRUCTIONS

Rnd 1: *{start with yarn A}* start a magic ring with 6 hdc, fasten off with
an invisible join [6]

Rnd 2: *{join yarn B in any st, make your first stitch a standing stitch}*
(slst in next st, ch 11, slst in same st, ch 11) repeat 6 times, fasten off
with an invisible join to first ch after initial slst [12 petals]

> *Note: Chain loosely in Rnd 3, or ch 3 if it feels too tight.*

Rnd 3: *{join yarn C in the third loop of the sixth chain of a petal, make
your first stitch a standing stitch. In this round we catch the petals in
the crochet work}* (sc in the third loop of the sixth chain of a petal, ch 2)
repeat 12 times, slst in initial sc [12 + 24 ch]

Rnd 4: *{work this round in the ch-spaces only}* slst in next ch-space,
ch 3 (count as dc) + 2 dc + ch 2 + 3 dc in first ch-space, 3 dc in next 2
ch-spaces, (3 dc + ch 2 + 3 dc in next ch-space, 3 dc in next 2 ch-spaces)
repeat 3 times, fasten off with an invisible join to first true dc [48 + 8 ch]

Rnd 5: *{join yarn D in any corner-space, make your first stitch a standing
stitch}* [3 dc + ch 2 + 3 dc in corner-space, (3 dc in the gap between next
2 dc-groups) repeat 3 times] repeat 4 times, slst in initial dc [60 + 8 ch]

Rnd 6: slst in next 2 st, slst in next ch-space, ch 3 (count as dc) + 2 dc +
ch 2 + 3 dc in next corner-space, (3 dc in the gap between next 2 dc-groups)
repeat 4 times, [3 dc + ch 2 + 3 dc in next corner-space, (3 dc in the gap
between next 2 dc-groups) repeat 4 times] repeat 3 times, fasten off with an
invisible join to first true dc [72 + 8 ch]

OVER THE RAINBOW SQUARE `112 stitch square`

Crafty CC (Celine Semaan) — Australia
@crafty_cc ⊕ www.craftycc.com

Skill level: Beginner
Colors: Yarn A: Silver / Yarn B: Plum / Yarn C: Turquoise / Yarn D: Peridot / Yarn E: Sunflower / Yarn F: Papaya / Yarn G: Cardinal / Yarn H: Cream
Special stitches: BPsc (Back post single crochet) / Change color mid-round

INSTRUCTIONS

Rnd 1: {start with yarn A} start a magic ring with ch 3 (count as dc), 11 dc, slst in 3rd ch of initial ch 3 [12]

Rnd 2: ch 2 (count as hdc), hdc in same st, 2 hdc in next 11 st [24]

Rnd 3: {work in continuous rounds} hdc in all 24 st [24]

Rnd 4: {work in continuous rounds. Continue working with yarn A. Join yarn B by using it to complete hdc before the color change. Carry yarn A when not in use} 2 hdc in next st, hdc in next st, 2 hdc in next st, {Change to yarn B} (hdc in next st, 2 hdc in next st) repeat 7 times, hdc in next st, {Cut yarn B, change to yarn A} (2 hdc in next st, hdc in next st) repeat 3 times [36]

Note: From Rnd 5 on, the rainbow is worked in BLO.

Rnd 5: {work in continuous rounds. Continue working with yarn A. Join yarn C by using it to complete hdc before the color change. Carry yarn A when not in use} hdc in next 5 st, {Change to yarn C} BLO hdc in next 22 st, {Cut yarn C, change to yarn A} hdc in next 9 st [36]

Rnd 6: {work in continuous rounds. Continue working with yarn A. Join yarn D by using it to complete hdc before the color change. Carry yarn A when not in use} (2 hdc in next st, hdc in next 2 st) repeat 2 times {Change to yarn D} (BLO 2 hdc in next st, BLO hdc in next 2 st) repeat 7 times, {Cut yarn D, change to yarn A} (2 hdc in next st, hdc in next 2 st) repeat 3 times [48]

Rnd 7: {work in continuous rounds. Continue working with yarn A. Join yarn E by using it to complete hdc before the color change. Carry yarn A when not in use} hdc in next 9 st, {Change to yarn E} BLO hdc in next 27 st, {Cut yarn E, change to yarn A} hdc in next 12 st [48]

Rnd 8: {work in continuous rounds. Continue working with yarn A. Join yarn F by using it to complete hdc before the color change. Carry yarn A

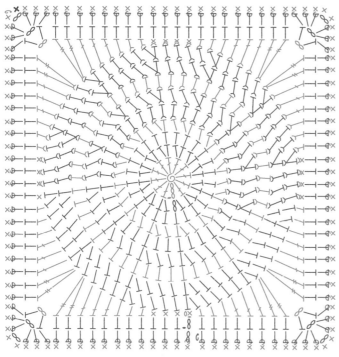

when not in use} (2 hdc in next st, hdc in next 3 st) repeat 2 times, 2 hdc in next st, *{Change to yarn F}* (BLO hdc in next 3 st, BLO 2 hdc in next st) repeat 6 times, BLO hdc in next 3 st, *{Cut yarn F, change to yarn A}* (2 hdc in next st, hdc in next 3 st) repeat 3 times [60]

Rnd 9: *{work in continuous rounds. Continue working with yarn A. Join yarn G by using it to complete hdc before the color change. Carry yarn A when not in use}* (2 hdc in next st, hdc in next 4 st) repeat 2 times, 2 hdc in next st, hdc in next st, *{Change to yarn G}* BLO hdc in next 3 st, (BLO 2 hdc in next st, BLO hdc in next 4 st) repeat 6 times, *{Cut yarn G, change to yarn A}* (2 hdc in next st, hdc in next 4 st) repeat 3 times, slst in first hdc [72]

Rnd 10: ch 1, sc in same st, hdc in next 3 st, dc in next 3 st, 2 tr in next st, ch 2, 2 tr in next st, dc in next 3 st, hdc in next 3 st, (BLO sc in next 4 st, BLO hdc in next 3 st, BLO dc in next 3 st, BLO 2 tr in next st, ch 2, BLO 2 tr in next st, BLO dc in next 3 st, hdc in next 3 st) repeat 2 times, BLO sc in next 3 st, sc in next st, hdc in next 3 st, dc in next 3 st, 2 tr in next st, ch 2, 2 tr in next st, dc in next 3 st, hdc in next 3 st, sc in next 3 st, slst in initial sc [80 + 8 ch]

Rnd 11: ch 2 (count as hdc), hdc in next 8 st, (hdc + ch 2 + hdc in ch-space, hdc in next 20 st) repeat 3 times, hdc + ch 2 + hdc in ch-space, hdc in next 11 st, slst in 2nd ch of initial ch 2 [88 + 8 ch]

Rnd 12: ch 2 (count as hdc), hdc in next 9 st, (2 hdc + ch 2 + 2 hdc in next ch-space, hdc in next 22 st) repeat 3 times, 2 hdc + ch 2 + 2 hdc in next ch-space, hdc in next 12 st, fasten off with an invisible join to first true hdc [104 + 8 ch]

Rnd 13: *{join yarn H in any corner-space, make your first stitch a standing stitch}* (2 sc in corner-space, BPsc around next 26 st) repeat 4 times, fasten off with an invisible join to 2nd stitch [112]

Cloud (make 2)

Rnd 1: *{start with yarn H}* ch 4, sc in 2nd ch from hook, sc in next ch, 3 sc in next ch. Continue working on the other side of the foundation chain, sc in next st, 2 sc in next st [8]

Rnd 2: *{work in continuous rounds}* 3 sc in next st, (sc in next st, 2 sc in next st) repeat 3 times, sc in next st [13]

Rnd 3: *{work in continuous rounds}* slst in next 2 st, ch 3, 5 dc in next st, skip 1 st, slst in next st, skip 1 st, 5 hdc in next st, skip 1 st, slst in next 5 st, slst in next 2 slst, fasten off with an invisible join to third ch of initial ch 3 [19 + 3 ch] Sew the clouds to the square.

cloud |┄┄┄┄>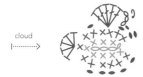

JOLIE FLEUR SQUARE 80 stitch square

Marie et ses jolies choses (Marie Orhon) — France
@marie_et_ses_jolies_choses f Marie et ses jolies choses

Skill level: Beginner
Colors: Yarn A: Pearl / Yarn B: Cardinal / Yarn C: Green Beryl

INSTRUCTIONS

Rnd 1: {start with yarn A} start a magic ring with ch 3 (count as dc), 11 dc, slst in 3rd ch of initial ch 3 [12]

Rnd 2: 2 sc in all 12 st, fasten off with an invisible join to 2nd stitch [24]

Rnd 3: {join yarn B in any st, make your first stitch a standing stitch} (5 dc in next st, skip 1 st, slst in next st, skip 1 st) repeat 6 times, slst in initial dc [36]

Rnd 4: ch 2 (count as hdc), hdc in next st, 2 hdc in next st, hdc in next 2 st, slst in Rnd 2 over the slst of Rnd 3, (hdc in next 2 st, 2 hdc in next st, hdc in next 2 st, slst in Rnd 2 over the slst of Rnd 3) repeat 5 times, fasten off with an invisible join to first true hdc [42]

Rnd 5: {join yarn C in any 2nd hdc of a petal, make your first stitch a standing stitch} (sc in next 4 st, hdc in next st, 2 hdc in next slst, hdc in next st) repeat 6 times, slst in initial sc [48]

Rnd 6: sc in next 4 st, hdc in next 3 st, 2 dc + ch 2 + 2 dc in next st, hdc in next 3 st, (sc in next 5 st, hdc in next 3 st, 2 dc + ch 2 + 2 dc in next st, hdc in next 3 st) repeat 3 times, sc in next st, slst in initial sc [60 + 8 ch]

Rnd 7: sc in next 6 st, hdc in next 2 st, hdc + ch 2 + hdc in next ch-space, (hdc in next 2 st, sc in next 11 st, hdc in next 2 st, hdc + ch 2 + hdc in next ch-space) repeat 3 times, hdc in next 2 st, sc in next 5 st, slst in initial sc [68 + 8 ch]

Rnd 8: sc in next 8 st, sc + ch 2 + sc in next ch-space, skip 1 (hidden) st, (sc in next 16 st, sc + ch 2 + sc in next ch-space, skip 1 (hidden) st) repeat 3 times, sc in next 8 st, fasten off with an invisible join to 2nd stitch [72 + 8 ch]

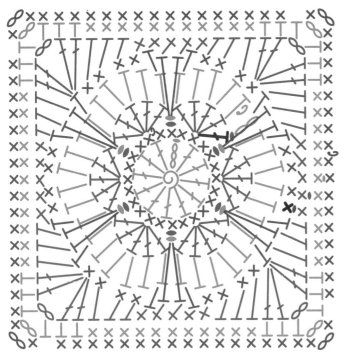

LAZY DAISY SQUARE `80 stitch square`

RedAgape (Mandy O'Sullivan) — Australia
@ @crochetbyredagape ⊕ www.redagapeblog.com **f** redagapeblog

Skill level: Beginner
Colors: Yarn A: Golden Glow / Yarn B: Cream / **Yarn C:** Opaline Glass
Special stitches: 3-dc-bobble (3 double crochet bobble stitch) /
5-tr-bobble (5 treble crochet bobble stitch)

This square generally turns out smaller than other 80-stitch squares
in this book. You might want to change the hook size to make sizes
match if you're planning to combine squares in a project.

INSTRUCTIONS

Rnd 1: *{start with yarn A}* start a magic ring with ch 2 + 2-dc-bobble
(count as 3-dc-bobble), ch 1, (3-dc-bobble, ch 1) repeat 7 times, fasten off
with an invisible join to ch 1 after initial bobble [8 + 8 ch]

Rnd 2: *{join yarn B in any ch-space, make your first stitch a standing
stitch}* (5-tr-bobble in ch-space, ch 4) repeat 8 times, fasten off with an
invisible join to first ch after initial 5-tr-bobble [8 + 32 ch]

Rnd 3: *{join yarn C with a slst in any ch-space}* 6 sc in all 8 ch-spaces,
slst in initial sc [48]

Rnd 4: ch 4 (count as tr), tr in next st, dc in next st, hdc in next 6 st, dc in
next st, tr in next 2 st, ch 2, (tr in next 2 st, dc in next st, hdc in next 6 st,
dc in next st, tr in next 2 st, ch 2) repeat 3 times, slst in 4th ch of initial
ch 4 [48 + 8 ch]

Rnd 5: ch 3 (count as dc), dc in next 11 st, 3 dc + ch 2 + 3 dc in ch-space,
(dc in next 12 st, 3 dc + ch 2 + 3 dc in ch-space) repeat 3 times, fasten off
with an invisible join to first true dc [72 + 8 ch]

*This Lazy Daisy Square combines beautifully with Pretty Puffy
Square on page 39 or Spring Square on page 26.*

80-STITCH CLASSIC SQUARE `80 stitch square`

RedAgape (Mandy O'Sullivan) — Australia
@crochetbyredagape ⊕ www.redagapeblog.com f redagapeblog

Skill level: Beginner
Colors: Yarn A: Opaline Glass / Yarn B: Cream / Yarn C: Pastel Pink /
Yarn D: Golden Glow

INSTRUCTIONS

Rnd 1: *{start with yarn A}* start a magic ring with ch 4 (count as tr), 2 tr, ch 3, (3 tr, ch 3) repeat 3 times, fasten off with an invisible join to first true tr [12 + 12 ch]

Rnd 2: *{join yarn B in any ch-space, make your first stitch a standing stitch}* (3 dc + ch 2 + 3 dc + ch 1 in ch-space) repeat 4 times, fasten off with an invisible join to 2nd stitch [24 + 12 ch]

Rnd 3: *{join yarn C in any ch-2-space, make your first stitch a standing stitch}* (3 tr + ch 3 + 3 tr + ch 1 in ch-2-space, 3 tr + ch 1 in ch-1-space) repeat 4 times, fasten off with an invisible join to 2nd stitch [36 + 20 ch]

Rnd 4: *{join yarn D in any ch-3-space, make your first stitch a standing stitch}* (3 dc + ch 2 + 3 dc + ch 1 in ch-3-space, 3 dc + ch 1 in next 2 ch-1-spaces) repeat 4 times, slst in initial dc [48 + 20 ch]

Rnd 5: slst in next 2 st, (2 sc + ch 1 + 2 sc in corner space, sc in each st and space along the side) repeat 4 times, fasten off with an invisible join to 2nd sc [76 + 4 ch]

The classic granny square is the quintessential crochet project. This iconic and beautiful classic has endless possibilities, and can be combined with all other 80-stitch squares in this book.

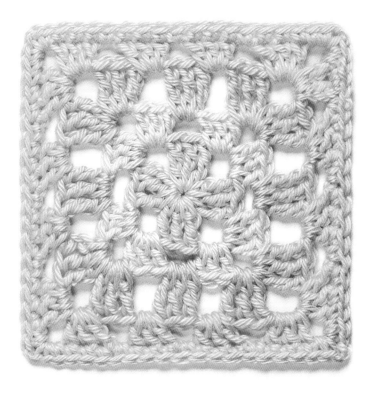

AEGEAN SQUARE `112 stitch square`

Spincushions (Shelley Husband) — Australia
⊛ www.spincushions.com ⊙ @spincushions **f** Spincushions

Skill level: Beginner
Colors: Yarn A: Blue Lake / Yarn B: Turquoise / Yarn C: Opaline Glass / Yarn D: Cream

INSTRUCTIONS

Rnd 1: {start with yarn A} start a magic ring with ch 3 (count as dc), 11 dc, fasten off with an invisible join to first true dc [12]

Rnd 2: {join yarn B in any st, make your first stitch a standing stitch} (sc in next st, ch 3, skip 1 st) repeat 6 times, slst in initial sc [6 + 18 ch]

Rnd 3: ch 5 (count as dc + ch 2), sc in next ch-space, ch 2, (dc in next st, ch 2, sc in next ch-space, ch 2) repeat 5 times, slst in 3rd ch of initial ch 5 [12 + 24 ch]

Rnd 4: ch 5 (count as dc + ch 2) + dc in same st, (hdc + sc in ch-space, skip next st, sc + hdc in ch-space, dc + ch 2 + dc in next st) repeat 5 times, hdc + sc in ch-space, skip next st, sc + hdc in ch-space, fasten off with an invisible join to 4th ch [36 + 12 ch]

Rnd 5: {join yarn C in any ch-2-space, make your first stitch a standing stitch} (sc in ch-space, ch 8, skip 6 st) repeat 6 times, slst in initial sc [6 + 48 ch]

Rnd 6: ch 3 (count as dc), (9 dc in ch-space, dc in next st) repeat 5 times, 9 dc in ch-space, fasten off with an invisible join to first true dc [60]

Rnd 7: {join Yarn D to a stitch located above a star point, make your first stitch a standing stitch} tr in this st, (dc in next 2 st, hdc in next 3 st, sc in next 4 st, hdc in next 3 st, dc in next 2 st, tr + ch 3 + tr in next st) repeat 3 times, dc in next 2 st, hdc in next 3 st, sc in next 4 st, hdc in next 3 st, dc in next 2 st, tr in same st as initial tr, ch 1, hdc in initial tr [64 st + 8 ch]

Note: You start Rnd 8, 9 and 10 by working over the joining stitch. Treat the joining stitch as a chain loop and work over it, covering it entirely.

Rnd 8: 2 sc over joining hdc, (sc in next 16 st, 2 sc + ch 2 + 2 sc in next ch-space) repeat 3 times, sc in next 16 st, 2 sc same ch-space as first st, ch 1, sc in initial sc [80 + 8 ch]

Rnd 9: 2 sc over joining sc, (sc in next 20 st, 2 sc + ch 2 + 2 sc in next ch-space) repeat 3 times, sc in next 20 st, 2 sc in same ch-space as first st, ch 1, sc in initial sc [96 + 8 ch]

Rnd 10: sc over joining sc, (sc in next 24 st, sc + ch 2 + sc in next ch space) repeat 3 times, sc in next 24 st, sc in same ch-space as initial sc, ch 2, fasten off with an invisible join to 2nd stitch [104 +8 ch]

Designer Spincushions named several of her square designs after seas and oceans of the world. She looks out at the sea every day and loves the dreamy calm blues. The Aegean (a bay in the Mediterranean Sea) Square looks gorgeous in her favorite turquoise-blue color scheme, but of course you can use any color combination you like.

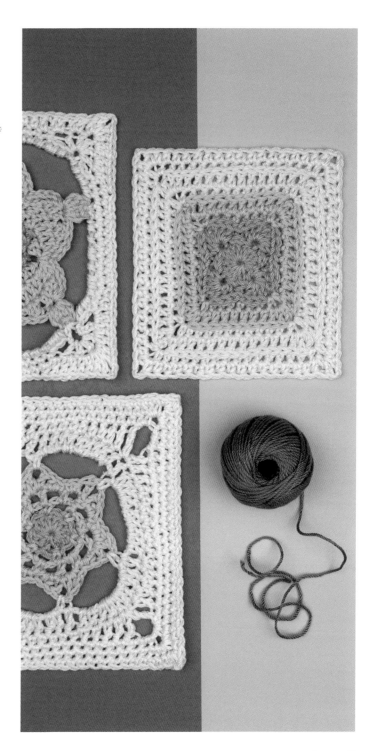

LIGHT AND LACY SQUARE `80 stitch square`

RedAgape (Mandy O'Sullivan) — Australia
@crochetbyredagape ⊗ www.redagapeblog.com f redagapeblog

Skill level: Beginner
Colors: Yarn A: Peony Pink
Special stitches: 3-dc-bobble (3 double crochet bobble stitch)

INSTRUCTIONS

Rnd 1: {start with yarn A} ch 4, slst to first ch to form a ring [4]

Rnd 2: {work in the ring} ch 2 + 2-dc-bobble (count as 3-dc-bobble), ch 1, (3-dc-bobble, ch 1) repeat 7 times, slst in initial 3-dc-bobble [8 + 8 ch]

Rnd 3: slst in next ch-space, ch 5 (count as dc + ch 2) + dc + ch 1 in same ch-space, (dc + ch 2 + dc + ch 1 in next ch-space) repeat 7 times, slst in 3rd ch of initial ch 5 [16 + 24 ch]

Rnd 4: slst in next ch-space, ch 2 + 2-dc-bobble (count as 3-dc-bobble) + ch 3 + 3-dc-bobble + ch 1 in same ch-space, dc + ch 1 in next 3 ch-spaces, (3-dc-bobble + ch 3 + 3-dc-bobble + ch 1 in next ch-space, dc + ch 1 in next 3 ch-spaces) repeat 3 times, slst in initial 3-dc-bobble [20 + 28 ch]

Rnd 5: slst in next corner-space, sc + ch 4 + sc + ch 3 in same space, sc + ch 3 in next 4 ch-spaces, (sc + ch 4 + sc + ch 3 in next corner-space, sc + ch 3 in next 4 ch-spaces) repeat 4 times, slst in initial sc [24 + 76 ch]

Rnd 6: (2 sc + ch 2 + 2 sc in next corner-space, 2 sc in next 5 ch-spaces) repeat 4 times, slst in initial sc [56 + 8 ch]

Rnd 7: ch 3 (count as dc), dc in next st, 2 dc + ch 2 + 2 dc in corner-space, (dc in next 14 st, 2 dc + ch 2 + 2 dc in corner-space) repeat 3 times, dc in next 12 st, fasten off with an invisible join to first true dc [72 + 8 ch]

Make Light And Lacy Square in a single color or try multiple colors for a surprising effect.

DIAMOND SQUARE `112 stitch square`

Crafty CC (Celine Semaan) — Australia
@crafty_cc ⊕ www.craftycc.com

Skill level: Beginner
Colors: **Yarn A:** Pastel Pink / **Yarn B:** Girly Pink / **Yarn C:** Papaya /
Yarn D: Sunflower / **Yarn E:** Pistachio / **Yarn F:** Opaline Glass /
Yarn G: Plum / **Yarn H:** Cream

INSTRUCTIONS

Rnd 1: *{start with yarn A}* start a magic ring with ch 3 (count as dc), 2 dc, ch 2, (3 dc, ch 2) repeat 3 times, fasten off with an invisible join to first true dc [12 + 8 ch]

Rnd 2: *{join yarn B in any ch-space, make your first stitch a standing stitch}* 3 dc + ch 2 + 3 dc in all 4 ch-spaces, fasten off with an invisible join to 2nd stitch [24 + 8 ch]

Rnd 3: *{join yarn C in any ch-space, make your first stitch a standing stitch}* (3 dc + ch 2 + 3 dc in ch-space, 3 dc in next gap between 3-dc-groups) repeat 4 times, fasten off with an invisible join to 2nd stitch [36 + 8 ch]

Rnd 4: *{join yarn D in any ch-space, make your first stitch a standing stitch}* (3 dc + ch 2 + 3 dc in ch-space, 3 dc in next 2 gaps between 3-dc-groups) repeat 4 times, fasten off with an invisible join to 2nd stitch [48 + 8 ch]

Rnd 5: *{join yarn E in any ch-space, make your first stitch a standing stitch. All stitches in this round are made in BLO}* (slst in ch-space, sc in next 2 st, hdc in next st, ch 1, hdc in next st, dc in next 2 st, tr + ch 2 + tr in gap between 3-dc-groups from Rnd 4, dc in next 2 st, hdc in next st, ch 1, hdc in next st, sc in next 2 st) repeat 4 times, fasten off with an invisible join to 2nd stitch [60 + 16 ch]

Rnd 6: *{join yarn F in any ch-2-space, make your first stitch a standing stitch}* (3 tr + ch 2 + 3 tr in ch-space, 3 dc in next ch-space, 3 dc in ch-2-space from Rnd 4 working over slst from Rnd 5, 3 dc in next ch-space) repeat 4 times, fasten off with an invisible join to 2nd stitch [60 + 8 ch]

Rnd 7: *{join yarn G in any ch-space, make your first stitch a standing stitch}* (3 dc + ch 2 + 3 dc in ch-space, 3 dc in next 4 gaps between 3-dc-groups) repeat 4 times, fasten off with an invisible join to 2nd stitch [72 + 8 ch]

Rnd 8: *{join yarn H in any ch-space, make your first stitch a standing stitch}* (3 dc + ch 2 + 3 dc in ch-space, 4 dc in next 5 gaps between 3-dc-groups) repeat 4 times, fasten off with an invisible join to 2nd stitch [104 + 8 ch]

112-STITCH SQUARE

112-STITCH CLASSIC SQUARE `112 stitch square`

RedAgape (Mandy O'Sullivan) — Australia

@crochetbyredagape ⊕ www.redagapeblog.com f redagapeblog

Skill level: Beginner
Colors: Yarn A: Golden Glow / **Yarn B:** Cream / **Yarn C:** Pastel Pink /
Yarn D: Peony Pink / **Yarn E:** Peach / **Yarn F:** Opaline Glass

INSTRUCTIONS

Rnd 1: *{start with yarn A}* start a magic ring with ch 4 (count as tr), 2 tr, ch 3, (3 tr + ch 3) repeat 3 times, fasten off with an invisible join to first true tr [12 + 12 ch]

Rnd 2: *{join yarn B in any ch-space, make your first stitch a standing stitch}* (3 dc + ch 2 + 3 dc + ch 1 in next ch-space) repeat 4 times, fasten off with an invisible join to 2nd stitch [24 + 12 ch]

Rnd 3: *{join yarn C in any ch-2-space, make your first stitch a standing stitch}* (3 tr + ch 3 + 3 tr + ch 1 in ch-2-space, 3 tr + ch 1 in next ch-1-space) repeat 4 times, fasten off with an invisible join to 2nd stitch [36 + 20 ch]

Rnd 4: *{join yarn D in any ch-3-space, make your first stitch a standing stitch}* (3 dc + ch 2 + 3 dc + ch 1 in ch-3-space, 3 dc + ch 1 in next 2 ch-1-spaces) repeat 4 times, fasten off with an invisible join to 2nd stitch [48 + 20 ch]

Rnd 5: *{join yarn E in any ch-2-space, make your first stitch a standing stitch}* (3 dc + ch 2 + 3 dc + ch 1 in ch-2-space, 3 dc + ch 1 in next 3 ch-1-spaces) repeat 4 times, fasten off with an invisible join to 2nd stitch [60 + 24 ch]

Rnd 6: {join yarn F in any ch-2-space, make your first stitch a standing stitch} (3 dc + ch 2 + 3 dc + ch 1 in ch-2-space, 3 dc + ch 1 in next 4 ch-1-spaces) repeat 4 times, slst in initial dc [72 + 28 ch]

Rnd 7: slst in next 2 st, [2 sc + ch 1 + 2 sc in corner space, (sc in next 3 st, sc in next ch-space) repeat 5 times, sc in next 3 st] repeat 4 times, fasten off with an invisible join to 2nd sc [108 + 4 ch]

The classic granny square is the quintessential crochet project. This iconic and beautiful classic has endless possibilities, and can be combined with all other 112-stitch squares in this book.

PRETTY PUFFY SQUARE

RedAgape (Mandy O'Sullivan) — Australia
@crochetbyredagape www.redagapeblog.com f redagapeblog

Skill level: Beginner
Colors: Yarn A: Peach / Yarn B: Pastel Pink / Yarn C: Opaline Glass /
Yarn D: Cream
Special stitches: 5-dc-pc (5 double crochet popcorn stitch)

INSTRUCTIONS

Rnd 1: {start with yarn A} start 6 sc in a magic ring, slst in the initial sc [6]

Rnd 2: ch 3 (count as dc) + 4 dc (form first pc with these 5 st) + ch 1 in next st, (5-dc-pc + ch 1 in next st) repeat 5 times, fasten off with an invisible join to first ch after initial pc [12]

Rnd 3: {join yarn B in any ch-space, make your first stitch a standing stitch} (5-dc-pc + ch 1 + 5-dc-pc + ch 1 in ch-space) repeat 6 times, fasten off with an invisible join to first ch after initial pc [12 + 12 ch]

Rnd 4: {join yarn C in any ch-space, make your first stitch a standing stitch} (5-dc-pc + ch 1 + 5-dc-pc + ch 1 in ch-space) repeat 12 times, fasten off with an invisible join to first ch after initial pc [24 + 24 ch]

Rnd 5: {join yarn D in any ch-space, make your first stitch a standing stitch} (hdc + dc + ch 2 + dc + hdc in ch-space, 2 hdc in next ch-space, 2 sc in next 3 ch-spaces, 2 hdc in next ch-space) repeat 4 times, slst in initial hdc [76 + 8 ch]

Rnd 6: ch 4 (count as tr), tr in next st, 2 tr + ch 2 + 2 tr in corner-space, (tr in next 14 st, 2 tr + ch 2 + 2 tr in corner-space) repeat 3 times, tr in next 12 st, fasten off with an invisible join to first true tr [72 + 8 ch]

This Pretty Puffy Square can add a nice 3D touch to a blanket. Combine it with the 80-stitch Classic Square on page 33 or Season Of Daisies Square on page 27 for a vintage look.

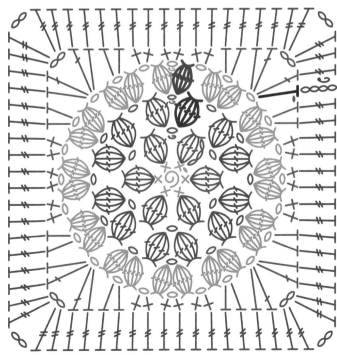

SUGARPLUM SQUARE 80 stitch square

Yarn Blossom Boutique (Melissa Bradley) — USA
@yarnblossomboutique f yarnblossomboutique

Skill level: Beginner
Colors: Yarn A: Cream / **Yarn B:** Pastel Pink / **Yarn C:** Fuchsia /
Yarn D: Grape

INSTRUCTIONS

Rnd 1: {*start with yarn A*} start a magic ring with ch 4 (count as dc + ch 1), (dc, ch 1) repeat 11 times, slst 3rd ch of initial ch 4 [12 + 12 ch]

Rnd 2: slst in next ch-space, ch 5 (count as dc + ch 2), (dc + ch 2 in next ch-space) repeat 11 times, fasten off with an invisible join to 4th ch [12 + 24 ch]

Rnd 3: {*join yarn B in any ch-space, make your first stitch a standing stitch*} 4 dc in all 12 ch-spaces, slst in initial dc [48]

Rnd 4: {*work this round in FLO*} (sc in next st, ch 2, skip next st) repeat 24 times, fasten off with an invisible join to first ch after initial sc [24 + 48 ch]

Rnd 5: {*join yarn C in any leftover back loop of a dc stitch in Rnd 3, make your first stitch a standing stitch. Work this round in BLO of the stitches in Rnd 3*} (dc in next 5 st, 2 dc in next st) repeat 8 times, slst in initial dc [56]

Rnd 6: {*work this round in FLO*} (sc in next st, ch 2, skip next st) repeat 28 times, fasten off with an invisible join in first ch after initial sc [28 + 56 ch]

Rnd 7: {*join yarn D in any leftover back loop of a dc stitch in Rnd 5, make your first stitch a standing stitch. Work this round in BLO of the stitches in Rnd 5*} (sc in next 2 st, hdc in next 2 st, dc in next 2 st, 2 tr in next st, ch 2, 2 tr in next st, dc in next 2 st, hdc in next 2 st, sc in next 2 st) repeat 4 times, fasten off with an invisible join to 2nd stitch [64 + 8 ch]

Rnd 8: {*Join Yarn A in any tr after a ch-space, make your first stitch a standing stitch*} (hdc in next 16 st, hdc + ch 2 + hdc in next ch-space) repeat 4 times, fasten off with an invisible join to 2nd stitch [72 + 8 ch]

INKOSI THE LION SQUARE 80 stitch square

Thoresby Cottage (Caitie Moore) — South Africa
⊗ thoresbycottage.com 🅾 @thoresbycottage f thoresbycottage

Skill level: Beginner
Colors: Yarn A: Sunflower / Yarn B: Pacific blue / Yarn C: Chestnut /
Yarn D: Cream / Yarn E: Satay / Yarn F: Black
Special stitches: French knot

INSTRUCTIONS

*Note: Some parts of this pattern are worked in continuous rounds,
do not join the rounds unless instructed to do so.*

BASE SQUARE

Rnd 1: {start with yarn A} start a magic ring with 6 sc, slst in initial sc [6]

Rnd 2: ch 3 (count as dc), 3 dc in next 5 st, 2 dc in last st, slst in 3rd ch of initial ch 3 [18]

Rnd 3: ch 3 (count as dc), dc in next st, (dc in next st, 2 dc in next st) repeat 8 times, slst in 3rd ch of initial ch 3 [26]

Rnd 4: ch 3 (count as dc), (2 dc in next 2 st, dc in next st) repeat 8 times, 3 dc in next st, fasten off with an invisible join to first true dc [44]

Rnd 5: {join yarn B in any st, make your first stitch a standing stitch} (tr in next st, dc in next st, hdc in next st, sc in next 4 st, hdc in next st, dc in next st, tr in next st, tr + ch 3 + tr in next st) repeat 4 times, slst in initial tr [48 + 12 ch]

Rnd 6: ch 3 (count as dc), dc in next 10 st, 2 dc + ch 2 + 2 dc in next ch-space, (dc in next 12 st, 2 dc + ch 2 + 2 dc in next ch-space) repeat 3 times, dc in last st, slst in 3rd ch of initial ch 3 [64 + 8 ch]

Rnd 7: ch 2 (count as hdc), hdc in next 12 st, hdc + ch 2 + hdc in next ch-space, (hdc in next 16 st, hdc + ch 2 + hdc in next ch-space) repeat 3 times, hdc in next 3 st, fasten off with an invisible join to first true hdc [72 + 8 ch]

MANE

Note: work the dc stitches of the mane around the post of the dc in Rnd 4 rather than into the top of the stitch. There is a bit more space there.

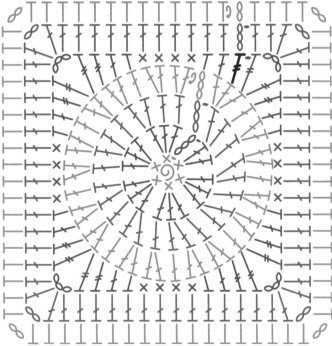

Rnd 1: {join yarn C in any st on the outer edge of Rnd 4, make your first stitch a standing stitch} (slst in next st, 4 dc in next st) repeat 22 times, fasten off with an invisible join in 2nd stitch [110]

EAR (MAKE 2)

Rnd 1: {start with yarn A, work in continuous rounds} start a magic ring with 5 sc [5]
Rnd 2: sc in next st, 2 sc in next 2 st, sc in next 2 st [7]
Rnd 3: sc in all 7 st [7] Slst in next st. Fasten off, leaving a tail for sewing.

MUZZLE

Rnd 1: {start with yarn D, work in continuous rounds} start a magic ring with 6 sc [6]
Rnd 2: 2 sc in all 6 st [12]
Rnd 3: (sc in next st, 2 sc in next st) repeat 6 times [18]
Rnd 4: sc in all 18 st [18] Fasten off, leaving a tail for sewing.

NOSE

Row 1: {start with yarn E} ch 3, sc in 2nd ch from hook, 2 sc in last st, ch 1, turn [3]
Row 2: sc in next 2 st, 2 sc in next st, ch 1, turn [4]
Row 3: sc in next 3 st, 2 sc in next st [5] Fasten off, leaving a tail for sewing.

ASSEMBLY AND DETAILS

1. Sew the nose to the muzzle. Embroider the muzzle detail using yarn E (the stitch spans 2 sc, from the point of the nose).
2. Sew the muzzle to the square. The bottom of the muzzle should be lined up with the outer edge of Rnd 3.
3. Using the leftover yarn tail, sew the ears to the outer edge of Rnd 4, approximately 8 stitches apart, in line with the ch-space from Rnd 5.
4. Using yarn F, embroider eyes on either side of the nose, approximately 7 stitches apart. This can be done either with a whip stitch, or a French knot. Make sure to use a large yarn needle so that your knots will be big enough. You can secure the knots in place by whip stitching all the way around the edge of the knot using matching sewing thread.

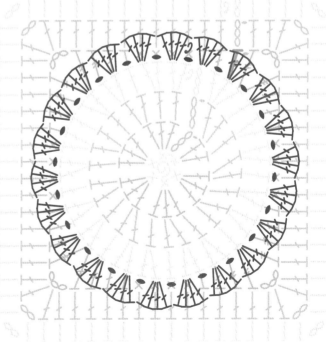

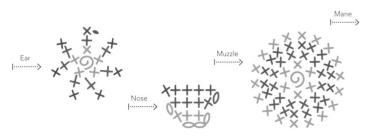

THEMBA THE ELEPHANT SQUARE 80 stitch square

Thoresby Cottage (Caitie Moore) — South Africa
⊗ thoresbycottage.com ⊙ @thoresbycottage f thoresbycottage

Skill level: Beginner
Colors: Yarn A: Shark grey / Yarn B: Burgundy / Yarn C: Graphite / Yarn D: Cream / Yarn E: Black

INSTRUCTIONS

Note: Some parts of this pattern are worked in continuous rounds, do not join the rounds unless instructed to do so.

BASE SQUARE

Rnd 1: *{start with yarn A}* start a magic ring with 6 sc, slst in initial sc [6]

Rnd 2: ch 3 (count as dc), 3 dc in next 5 st, 2 dc in last st, slst in 3rd ch of initial ch 3 [18]

Rnd 3: ch 3 (count as dc), dc in next st, (dc in next st, 2 dc in next st) repeat 8 times, slst in 3rd ch of initial ch 3 [26]

Rnd 4: ch 3 (count as dc), (2 dc in next 2 st, dc in next st) repeat 8 times, 3 dc in next st, fasten off with an invisible join to first true dc [44]

Rnd 5: *{join yarn B in any st, make your first stitch a standing stitch}* (tr in next st, dc in next st, hdc in next st, sc in next 4 st, hdc in next st, dc in next st, tr in next st, tr + ch 3 + tr in next st) repeat 4 times, slst in initial tr [48 + 12 ch]

Rnd 6: ch 3 (count as dc), dc in next 10 st, 2 dc + ch 2 + 2 dc in next ch-space, (dc in next 12 st, 2 dc + ch 2 + 2 dc in next ch-space) repeat 3 times, dc in last st, slst in 3rd ch of initial ch 3 [64 + 8 ch]

Rnd 7: ch 2 (count as hdc), hdc in next 12 st, hdc + ch 2 + hdc in next ch-space, (hdc in next 16 st, hdc + ch 2 + hdc in next ch-space) repeat 3 times, hdc in next 3 st, fasten off with an invisible join to first true hdc [72 + 8 ch]

TRUNK

Row 1: *{start with yarn A}* ch 6, work back on the ch, skip 1 ch, sc in next 5 ch, ch 1, turn [5]
Row 2: sc in next 5 st, ch 1, turn [5]

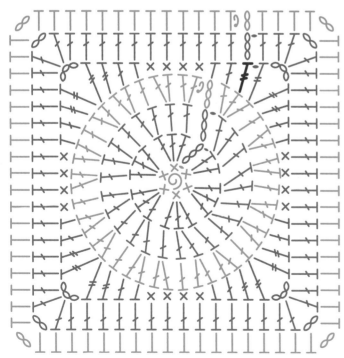

Row 3: sc2tog, sc in next 3 st, ch 1, turn [4]
Row 4: sc in next 4 st, ch 1, turn [4]
Row 5: sc2tog, sc in next 2 st, ch 1, turn [3]
Row 6 - 8: sc in next 3 st, ch 1, turn [3]
Row 9: sc2tog, slst in next st [2] fasten off, leaving a tail for sewing.
Using yarn C, embroider 6 bars evenly down the length of the trunk, starting after Row 2.

RIGHT EAR

Rnd 1: *{start with yarn C, work in continuous rounds}* start a magic ring with 5 sc [5]
Rnd 2: 2 sc in all 5 st [10]
Rnd 3: (sc in next st, 2 sc in next st) repeat 5 times [15]
Rnd 4: ch 2, 3 hdc in 2nd ch from hook, slst in next st, fasten off.
Rnd 5: *{join yarn A in 3rd st after slst, make your first stitch a standing stitch}* sc in next 10 st, 2 sc in next st, sc in next st, 2 sc in next st [16] Slst in next st. Do not finish this round. Fasten off, leaving a tail for sewing.

LEFT EAR

Rnd 1-4: *{start with yarn C}* repeat Rnd 1-4 of the right ear
Rnd 5: *{join yarn A with a standing stitch to first hdc of previous round}* 2 sc in this st, sc in next st, 2 sc in next st, sc in next 10 st [16] Slst in next st. Do not finish this round. Fasten off, leaving a tail for sewing.

TUSK (MAKE 2)

Rnd 1: *{start with yarn D}* ch 4, sc in 2nd ch from hook *{this is the side of the tusk that gets attached to the trunk}*, slst in next 2 st. Fasten off, leaving a tail for sewing.

ASSEMBLY AND DETAILS

1. Sew the ears to either side of the outer edge of Rnd 4 of the base square. If you want the ears to flap, then do not sew all the way around.
2. Sew the trunk to the center of the base square.
3. Using yarn E, embroider eyes to either side of the trunk, approximately 8 stitches apart. This can be done either with a whip stitch, or a French knot. Make sure to use a large yarn needle so that your knots will be big enough. You can secure the knots in place by whip stitching all the way around the edge of the knot using matching sewing thread.
4. Sew the tusks to either side of the trunk, just below the eyes.

Tusk
|············>

Right ear
|············>

Left ear
|············>

Trunk
|············>

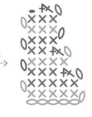

JABULANI THE ZEBRA SQUARE 80 stitch square

Thoresby Cottage (Caitie Moore) — South Africa
🌐 thoresbycottage.com 📷 @thoresbycottage **f** thoresbycottage

Skill level: Beginner
Colors: Yarn A: Cream / Yarn B: Graphite / Yarn C: Nordic Blue /
Yarn D: Soft Grey / Yarn E: Pearl / Yarn F: Black

INSTRUCTIONS

Note: Some parts of this pattern are worked in continuous rounds, do not join the rounds unless instructed to do so.

BASE SQUARE

Rnd 1: *{start with yarn A}* start a magic ring with 6 sc, slst in initial sc [6]

Rnd 2: ch 3 (count as dc), 3 dc in next 5 st, 2 dc in last st, slst in 3rd ch of initial ch 3 [18]

Rnd 3: ch 3 (count as dc), dc in next st, (dc in next st, 2 dc in next st) repeat 8 times, slst in 3rd ch of initial ch 3 [26]

Rnd 4: ch 3 (count as dc), (2 dc in next 2 st, dc in next st) repeat 8 times, 3 dc in next st, fasten off with an invisible join to first true dc [44]

Rnd 5: *{join yarn B in any st, make your first stitch a standing stitch}* sc in all 44 st, fasten off with an invisible join to 2nd stitch [44]

Rnd 6: *{join yarn C in any st, make your first stitch a standing stitch}* (tr in next st, dc in next st, hdc in next st, sc in next 4 st, hdc in next st, dc in next st, tr in next st, tr + ch 3 + tr in next st) repeat 4 times, slst in initial tr [48 + 12 ch]

Rnd 7: ch 3 (count as dc), dc in next 10 st, 2 dc + ch 2 + 2 dc in next ch-space, (dc in next 12 st, 2 dc + ch 2 + 2 dc in next ch-space) repeat 3 times, dc in last st, slst in 3rd ch of initial ch 3 [64 + 8 ch]

Rnd 8: ch 2 (count as hdc), hdc in next 12 st, hdc + ch 2 + hdc in next ch-space, (hdc in next 16 st, hdc + ch 2 + hdc in next ch-space) repeat 3 times, hdc in next 3 st, fasten off with an invisible join to first true hdc [72 + 8 ch]

PICOT / STRIPES

The stripes are worked in the outer edge of Rnd 5 as a series of picots around the circular part of the base square. The picots are then stitched down to form the stripes.

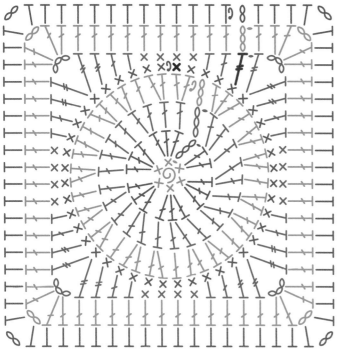

Rnd 1: *{join yarn B}* (slst into sc (see chart for placement), ch 5, work back down the ch: slst in 2nd ch from hook, slst in next ch, sc in next 2 ch, skip 2 st on the base Rnd 5 and slst in next st) repeat 2 times [2 stripes] Fasten off, fold the picot downwards towards the center of the square and use the yarn tail to tack the picots into place. Repeat two more times so that there are two stripes on either side of the face and two stripes on top of the head between the ears.

EAR INNER (MAKE 2)

Rnd 1: *{start with yarn E, work in continuous rounds}* start a magic ring with 6 sc [6]
Rnd 2: 2 sc in all 6 st [12] Slst in next st. Fasten off, leaving a tail for sewing.

EAR OUTER (MAKE 2)

Rnd 1: *{start with yarn B, work in continuous rounds}* start a magic ring with 6 sc [6]
Rnd 2: 2 sc in all 6 st [12]
Rnd 3: (sc in next st, 2 sc in next st) repeat 6 times [18] Slst in next st. Fasten off, leaving a tail for sewing.

SNOUT

Rnd 1: *{start with yarn D, work in continuous rounds}* ch 5, work back on the ch, skip first ch, sc in next 3 ch, 3 sc in last ch, continue on other side of the starting chain, sc in next 3 ch, 3 sc in next ch [12]
Rnd 2: sc in next 4 st, 2 sc in next 2 st, sc in next 4 st, 2 sc in next 2 st [16]
Rnd 3: sc in next 6 st, slst in next st [7] Do not finish this round. Fasten off, leaving a tail for sewing.

ASSEMBLY AND DETAILS

1. Assemble the ears. Place an inner ear and outer ear wrong sides together. Sew the inner ear to the outer ear using the leftover yarn E yarn tail. Then, pinch the circles closed, with the inner ear on the inside. Using the yarn B tail, sew together approximately 3 st, through 2 layers of the outer ear to form a cone shape. Repeat for the second ear. Sew the ears to the base square, lining them up with the ch-space from Rnd 6.
2. Using yarn B, embroider 2 nostrils onto the middle of the snout, approximately 3 stitches apart. Sew the snout to the base square. The top of the snout should sit just below Rnd 1 and the bottom of the snout should sit just above Rnd 5.
3. Using yarn F, embroider eyes above the snout, along the outer edge of Rnd 2 of the base square, approximately 6 stitches apart. This can be done either with a whip stitch, or a French knot. Make sure to use a large yarn needle so that your knots will be big enough. You can secure the knots in place by whip stitching all the way around the edge of the knot using matching sewing thread.

Jabulani (jah-boo-la-ni) is the Xhosa word for "rejoice and be glad"; a perfect name for this wonderfully quirky and joyful animal.

Stripes

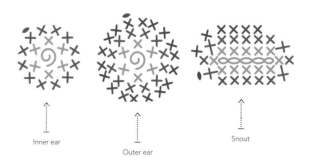

Inner ear

Outer ear

Snout

MAFUTA THE HIPPO SQUARE `80 stitch square`

Thoresby Cottage (Caitie Moore) — South Africa
🌐 thoresbycottage.com 📷 @thoresbycottage f thoresbycottage

Skill level: Beginner
Colors: Yarn A: Soft grey / Yarn B: Plum / Yarn C: Pearl /
Yarn D: Old Pink / Yarn E: Black
Special stitch: French knot

INSTRUCTIONS

Note: Some parts of this pattern are worked in continuous rounds, do not join the rounds unless instructed to do so.

BASE SQUARE

Rnd 1: *{start with yarn A}* start a magic ring with 6 sc, slst in initial sc [6]

Rnd 2: ch 3 (count as dc), 3 dc in next 5 st, 2 dc in last st, slst in 3rd ch of initial ch 3 [18]

Rnd 3: ch 3 (count as dc), dc in next st, (dc in next st, 2 dc in next st) repeat 8 times, slst in 3rd ch of initial ch 3 [26]

Rnd 4: ch 3 (count as dc), (2 dc in next 2 st, dc in next st) repeat 8 times, 3 dc in next st, fasten off with an invisible join to first true dc [44]

Rnd 5: *{join yarn B in any st, make your first stitch a standing stitch}* (tr in next st, dc in next st, hdc in next st, sc in next 4 st, hdc in next st, dc in next st, tr in next st, tr + ch 3 + tr in next st) repeat 4 times, slst in initial tr [48 + 12 ch]

Rnd 6: ch 3 (count as dc), dc in next 10 st, 2 dc + ch 2 + 2 dc in next ch-space, (dc in next 12 st, 2 dc + ch 2 + 2 dc in next ch-space) repeat 3 times, dc in last st, slst in 3rd ch of initial ch 3 [64 + 8 ch]

Rnd 7: ch 2 (count as hdc), hdc in next 12 st, hdc + ch 2 + hdc in next ch-space, (hdc in next 16 st, hdc + ch 2 + hdc in next ch-space) repeat 3 times, hdc in next 3 st, fasten off with an invisible join to first true hdc [72 + 8 ch]

INNER EAR (MAKE 2)

Rnd 1: *{start with yarn C}* start a magic ring with 6 sc [6] Fasten off, leaving a tail for sewing.

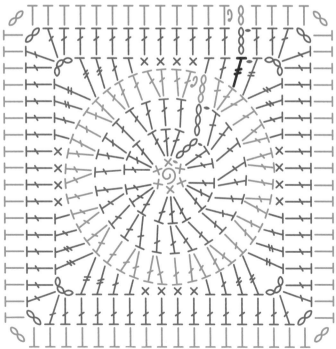

OUTER EAR (MAKE 2)

Rnd 1: {start with yarn A, work in continuous rounds} start a magic ring with 6 sc [6]
Rnd 2: 2 sc in all 6 st [12] Slst in next st. Fasten off, leaving a tail for sewing.

SNOUT

Rnd 1: {start with yarn A, work in continuous rounds} ch 7, work back on the chain, start in second ch from hook, sc in next 5 ch, 3 sc in last ch, continue on other side of the starting chain, sc in next 5 ch, 3 sc in next ch [16]
Rnd 2: sc in next 6 st, 2 sc in next 2 st, sc in next 6 st, 2 sc in next 2 st [20]
Rnd 3: sc in next 6 st, 2 sc in next 2 st, sc in next 3 st, ch-3-picot, sc in next 3 st, ch-3-picot, slst in next st [17 + 2 ch-3-loops] Fasten off, leaving a tail for sewing.

ASSEMBLY AND DETAILS

1. Assemble the ears by sewing an inner ear on top of an outer ear with right sides facing outwards. Place the ear inner slightly off center and sew down using the leftover yarn tail. Use the outer ear yarn tail to sew the ears in place on the base square, about 9 stitches apart, in line with the ch-space from Rnd 5.
2. With the nostrils at the top of the snout, sew on the mouth using yarn D. The mouth should be placed 2 rounds inwards from the outer edge of the snout and worked over 3 stitches from the center working towards the outer edge.
3. Using yarn C, sew on the center of the nostrils. This can be done either with a whip stitch, or a French knot. Make sure to use a large yarn needle so that your knots will be big enough. You can secure the knots in place by whip stitching all the way around the edge of the knot using matching sewing thread.
4. Sew the snout to the base square, making sure the bottom of the snout is lined up with the outer edge of Rnd 4 of your base square.
5. Using yarn E, embroider eyes above the nostrils, along the outer edge of Rnd 2 of the base square, approx. 7 stitches apart. This can be done either with a whip stitch, or a French knot. Make sure to use a large yarn needle so that your knots will be big enough. You can secure the knots in place by whip stitching all the way around the edge of the knot using matching sewing thread.

Inner ear

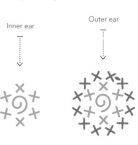

Outer ear

Snout

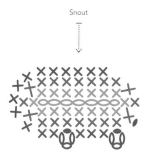

THULANI THE GIRAFFE SQUARE `80 stitch square`

Thoresby Cottage (Caitie Moore) — South Africa
🌐 thoresbycottage.com 📷 @thoresbycottage 𝐟 thoresbycottage

Skill level: Beginner
Colors: Yarn A: Sunflower / Yarn B: Peridot / Yarn C: Cream /
Yarn D: Satay / Yarn E: Black
Special stitch: French knot

INSTRUCTIONS

Note: Some parts of this pattern are worked in continuous rounds, do not join the rounds unless instructed to do so.

BASE SQUARE

Rnd 1: *{start with yarn A}* start a magic ring with 6 sc, slst in initial sc [6]

Rnd 2: ch 3 (count as dc), 3 dc in next 5 st, 2 dc in last st, slst in 3rd ch of initial ch 3 [18]

Rnd 3: ch 3 (count as dc), dc in next st, (dc in next st, 2 dc in next st) repeat 8 times, slst in 3rd ch of initial ch 3 [26]

Rnd 4: ch 3 (count as dc), (2 dc in next 2 st, dc in next st) repeat 8 times, 3 dc in next st, fasten off with an invisible join to first true dc [44]

Rnd 5: *{join yarn B in any st, make your first stitch a standing stitch}* tr in next st, dc in next st, hdc in next st, sc in next 4 st, hdc in next st, dc in next st, tr in next st, tr + ch 3 + tr in next st) repeat 4 times, slst in initial tr [48 + 12 ch]

Rnd 6: ch 3 (count as dc), dc in next 10 st, 2 dc + ch 2 + 2 dc in next ch-space, (dc in next 12 st, 2 dc + ch 2 + 2 dc in next ch-space) repeat 3 times, dc in last st, slst in 3rd ch of initial ch 3 [64 + 8 ch]

Rnd 7: ch 2 (count as hdc), hdc in next 12 st, hdc + ch 2 + hdc in next ch-space, (hdc in next 16 st, hdc + ch 2 + hdc in next ch-space) repeat 3 times, hdc in next 3 st, fasten off with an invisible join to first true hdc [72 + 8 ch]

SNOUT

Rnd 1: *{start with yarn C, work in continuous rounds}* start a magic ring with 6 sc [6]
Rnd 2: (2 sc in next 2 st, 3 sc in next st) repeat 2 times [14]
Rnd 3: (sc in next 6 st, 3 sc in next st) repeat 2 times [18] Slst in next st.

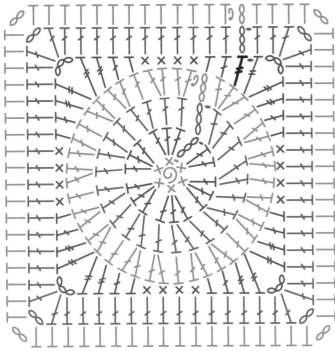

Fasten off, leaving a tail for sewing.

EAR (MAKE 2)

Rnd 1: *{start with yarn A, work in continuous rounds}* start a magic ring with 5 sc [5]
Rnd 2 – 4: sc in all 5 st [5]
Slst in next st. Fasten off, leaving a tail for sewing.

SPOT (MAKE 4)

Rnd 1: *{start with yarn D}* start a magic ring with 3 sc [3] Do not slst to join the round. Fasten off, leaving a tail for sewing.

HORN (MAKE 2)

Rnd 1: *{start with yarn D}* start a magic ring with 5 sc, fasten off with an invisible join [5]
Rnd 2: *{join yarn A in any st, make your first stitch a standing stitch}* slst in first st, ch 4, work back on the ch, skip 1 ch, sc in next 3 ch, slst in next st on the magic ring. Fasten off, leaving a tail for sewing.

ASSEMBLY AND DETAILS

1. Sew the ears to either side of the head along the outer edge of Rnd 4 of the base square, approximately 10 stitches apart, in line with the ch-space from Rnd 5.
2. Sew the horns to the top of the head, 2 stitches apart.
3. Using yarn D, embroider the nostrils.
4. Sew the snout to the base square, lining up the bottom of the snout with the outer edge of Rnd 3.
5. Sew the spots in place; one on either side of the head, below the ears, and one on either side of the horns. The flat part of the half circle should be on the outer edge of Rnd 4 of the base square.
6. Using yarn E, embroider eyes above the snout, along the outer edge of Rnd 2 of the base square, approximately 8 stitches apart. This can be done either with a whip stitch, or a French knot. Make sure to use a large yarn needle so that your knots will be big enough. You can secure the knots in place by whip stitching all the way around the edge of the knot using matching sewing thread.

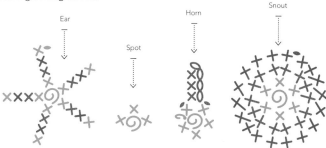

Ear   Spot   Horn   Snout

RAINBOW PUFF SQUARE 112 stitch square

Crafty CC (Celine Semaan) — Australia
@crafty_cc · www.craftycc.com

Skill level: Beginner / Intermediate
Colors: Yarn A: Cream / Yarn B: Grape / Yarn C: Turquoise / Yarn D: Perido / Yarn E: Sunflower / Yarn F: Papaya / Yarn G: Cardinal
Special stitches: 4-puff (Puff stitch with 4 loops) / changing color mid-round

INSTRUCTIONS

Note: Apart from Rnd 1, you'll be working with two colors at a time.

Rnd 1: *{start with yarn A}* start a magic ring with ch 5 (count as dc + ch 2), (3 dc, ch 2) repeat 3 times, 2 dc, slst in 3rd ch of initial ch 5 [12 + 8 ch]

Rnd 2: *{continue working with Yarn A. Use yarn B for each 4-puff + ch 3 + 4-puff in this round. Join yarn B by using it to finish dc before puff. Carry yarn B when not in use}* ch 3 (count as dc), (dc + 4-puff + ch 3 + 4-puff + ch 1 + dc in ch-space, dc in next 3 st) repeat 3 times, dc + 4-puff + ch 3 + 4-puff + ch 1 + dc in ch-space, dc in next 2 st, slst in 3rd ch of initial ch 3 [28 + 8 ch] Fasten off yarn B.

Rnd 3: *{continue working with Yarn A. Use yarn C for each 4-puff + ch 3 + 4-puff in this round. Join yarn C by using it to finish dc before puff. Carry yarn C when not in use}* slst in next 2 st, ch 3 (count as dc), (dc + 4-puff + ch 3 + 4-puff + ch 1 + dc in ch-space, dc in next 7 st) repeat 3 times, dc + 4-puff + ch 3 + 4-puff + ch 1 + dc in ch-space, dc in next 6 st, slst in 3rd ch of initial ch 3 [44 + 8 ch] Fasten off yarn C.

Rnd 4: *{continue working with Yarn A. Use yarn D for each 4-puff + ch 3 + 4-puff in this round. Join yarn D by using it to finish dc before puff. Carry color D when not in use}* slst in next 2 st, ch 3 (count as dc), (dc + 4-puff + ch 3 + 4-puff + ch 1 + dc in ch-space, dc in next 11 st) repeat 3 times, dc + 4-puff + ch 3 + 4-puff + ch 1 + dc in ch-space, dc in next 10 st, slst in 3rd ch of initial ch 3 [60 + 8 ch] Fasten off yarn D.

Rnd 5: *{continue working with Yarn A. Use yarn E for each 4-puff + ch 3 + 4-puff in this round. Join yarn E by using it to finish dc before puff. Carry yarn E when not in use}* slst in next 2 st, ch 3 (count as dc), (dc + 4-puff + ch 3 + 4-puff + ch 1 + dc into ch-space, dc in next 15 st) repeat 3 times, dc + 4-puff + ch 3 + 4-puff + ch 1 + dc into ch-space, dc in next 14 st, slst in 3rd ch of initial ch 3 [76 + 8 ch] Fasten off yarn E.

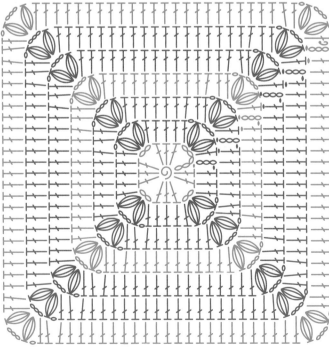

Rnd 6: *{continue working with Yarn A. Use yarn F for each 4-puff + ch 3 + 4-puff in this round. Join yarn F by using it to finish dc before puff. Carry yarn F when not in use}* slst in next 2 st, ch 3 (count as dc), (dc + 4-puff + ch 3 + 4-puff + ch 1 + dc in ch-space, dc in next 19 st) repeat 3 times, dc + 4-puff + ch 3 + 4-puff + ch 1 + dc in ch-space, dc in next 18 st, slst in 3rd ch of initial ch 3 [92 + 8 ch] Fasten off yarn F.

Rnd 7: *{continue working with Yarn A. Use yarn G for each 4-puff + ch 3 + 4-puff in this round. Join yarn G by using it to finish dc before puff. Carry yarn G when not in use}* slst in next 2 st, ch 3 (count as dc), (dc + 4-puff + ch 2 + 4-puff + ch 1 + dc in ch-space, dc in next 23 st) repeat 4 times, fasten off with an invisible join to first true dc [108 + 4 ch]

Rainbow Puff Square makes a beautiful combination with the other rainbow squares by Crafty CC, like the Rainbow Blossom Square on page 108, Over The Rainbow Square on page 28 and Diamond Square on page 37.

TULIPS SQUARE `80 stitch square`

Ms.Eni (Simone Conrad) — Germany
 @ms.eni   ms.eni.handmade

Skill level: Beginner
Colors: Yarn A: Cream / Yarn B: Peridot / Yarn C: Grape
Special stitches: Work in the ring / 5-dc-bobble (5 double crochet bobble stitch)

INSTRUCTIONS

Rnd 1: *{start with yarn A}* ch 8, close the ring with a slst [8]

Rnd 2: ch 2 (count as hdc), 15 hdc into the ring, fasten off with an invisible join in first true hdc [16]

Rnd 3: *{join yarn B in any st, make your first stitch a standing stitch}* dc in first st, (skip 1 st, dc + ch 1 + dc in next st) repeat 7 times, skip 1 st, dc in next st, ch 1, fasten off with an invisible join in 2nd stitch [16 + 8 ch]

Rnd 4: *{join yarn C in any ch-space between 2 dc, make your first stitch a standing stitch}* (5-dc-bobble in ch-space, ch 3) repeat 8 times, fasten off with an invisible join in first ch after initial 5-dc-bobble [8 flowers]

Rnd 5: *{join yarn A in any ch-space, make your first stitch a standing stitch}* 8 hdc in all 8 ch-spaces, slst in initial hdc [64]

Rnd 6: ch 1 (count as sc), sc in next 4 st, skip 3 st, 3 dc + ch 1 + 3 dc in next st, skip 3 st, (sc in next 9 st, skip 3 st, 3 dc + ch 1 + 3 dc in next st, skip 3 st) repeat 3 times, sc in next 4 st, slst in initial ch 1 [60 + 4 ch]

Rnd 7: ch 2 (count as hdc), hdc in next 7 st, (hdc + ch 1 + hdc in next ch-space, hdc in next 15 st) repeat 3 times, hdc + ch 1 + hdc in next ch-space, hdc in next 7 st, slst in 2nd ch of initial ch 2 [68 + 4 ch]

Rnd 8: ch 3 (count as dc), dc in next 8 st, (3 dc in next ch-space, dc in next 17 st) repeat 3 times, 3 dc in next ch-space, dc in next 8 st, fasten off with an invisible join to first true dc [80]

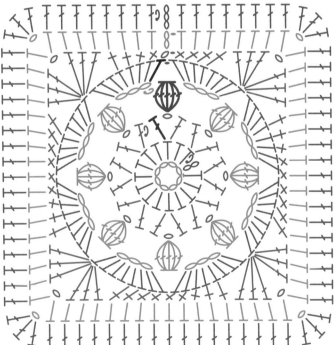

WHOLE APPLE SQUARE 80 stitch square

Irene Strange — United Kingdom

@irenestrange www.irenestrange.co.uk

Skill level: Intermediate
Colors: Yarn A: Peridot / Yarn B: Birch / Yarn C: Amazon /
Yarn D: Brownie
Special stitches: hdc2tog (half double crochet 2 stitches together)

INSTRUCTIONS

Rnd 1: {start with yarn A} start a magic ring with ch 3 (count as dc),
11 dc, slst in 3rd ch of initial ch 3 [12]

Rnd 2: ch 3 (count as dc), dc in same st, 2 dc in in next 11 st, slst in 3rd ch
of initial ch 3 [24]

Rnd 3: ch 3 (count as dc), 2 dc in next st, (dc in next st, 2 dc in next st)
repeat 11 times, slst in 3rd ch of initial ch 3 [36]

Rnd 4: slst in next st, ch 1, sc + hdc in next st, (2 dc in next st, dc in next
st) repeat 3 times, (2 hdc in next st, hdc in next 2 st) repeat 2 times, 2 hdc
in next st, hdc in next st, sc in next st, slst in next 2 st, sc in next st, hdc
in next st, (2 hdc in next st, hdc in next 2 st) repeat 2 times, 2 hdc in next
st, (dc in next st, 2 dc in next st) repeat 3 times, hdc + sc in next st, slst in
next st [50] fasten off.

Rnd 5: {join yarn B in the first slst of Rnd 4, make your first stitch a standing stitch} hdc2tog worked over the first slst and sc from Rnd 4, hdc in
next st, sc in next 2 st, hdc in next st, 2 dc in next st, ch 2, 2 dc in next st,
hdc in next st, sc in next 7 st, hdc in next 2 st, 2 dc in next st, ch 2,
2 dc in next st, hdc in next st, sc in next 2 st, hdc in next st, dc in next
2 st, hdc in next st, sc in next 2 st, hdc in next st, 2 dc in next st, ch 2,
2 dc in next st, hdc in next 2 st, sc in next 7 st, hdc in next st, 2 dc in next st,
ch 2, 2 dc in next st, hdc in next st, sc in next 2 st, hdc in next st, hdc2tog
worked over the last sc and last slst from Rnd 4, slst in initial hdc2tog [64]

Rnd 6: ch 2 (count as hdc), hdc in next 6 st, 2 hdc + ch 1 + 2 hdc in next
ch-space, (hdc in next 14 st, 2 hdc + ch 1 + 2 hdc in next ch-space) repeat 3
times, hdc in next 7 st, slst in 2nd ch of initial ch 2 [72 + 4 ch]

Rnd 7: ch 1, sc in same st, sc in next 8 st, (sc + ch 1 in next ch-space,
sc in next 18 st) repeat 3 times, sc + ch 1 in next ch-space, sc in next 9 st,
fasten off with an invisible join to 2nd stitch [76 + 4 ch]

LEAF
Follow instructions and diagram on page 57 (Cut Apple Square).

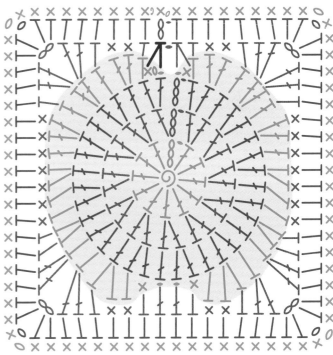

CUT APPLE SQUARE 80 stitch square

Irene Strange — United Kingdom
@irenestrange ⊕ www.irenestrange.co.uk

Skill level: Intermediate
Colors: Yarn A: Cream / Yarn B: Cold Green / Yarn C: Peridot /
Yarn D: Brownie / Yarn E: Cardinal
Special stitches: Surface slst (Surface slip stitch) / hdc2tog (half
double crochet 2 stitches together)

INSTRUCTIONS

Rnd 1: {start with yarn A} start a magic ring with ch 3 (count as dc), 11 dc,
slst in 3rd ch of initial ch 3 [12]

Rnd 2: ch 3 (count as dc), dc in same st, 2 dc in in next 11 st, slst in 3rd ch
of initial ch 3 [24]

Rnd 3: ch 3 (count as dc), 2 dc in next st, (dc in next st, 2 dc in next st)
repeat 11 times, slst in 3rd ch of initial ch 3 [36]

Rnd 4: slst in next st, ch 1, sc + hdc in next st, (2 dc in next st, dc in next
st) repeat 3 times, (2 hdc in next st, hdc in next 2 st) repeat 2 times, 2 hdc
in next st, hdc in next st, sc in next st, slst in next 2 st, sc in next st, hdc
in next st, (2 hdc in next st, hdc in next 2 st) repeat 2 times, 2 hdc in next
st, (dc in next st, 2 dc in next st) repeat 3 times, hdc + sc in next st, slst in
next st [50] fasten off.

Rnd 5: {join yarn B in the first slst of Rnd 4, make your first stitch a
standing stitch} hdc2tog worked over the first slst and sc from Rnd 4,
hdc in next st, sc in next 2 st, hdc in next st, 2 dc in next st, ch 2, 2 dc in
next st, hdc in next st, sc in next 7 st, hdc in next 2 st, 2 dc in next st, ch 2,
2 dc in next st, hdc in next st, sc in next 2 st, hdc in next st, dc in next
2 st, hdc in next st, sc in next 2 st, hdc in next st, 2 dc in next st, ch 2,
2 dc in next st, hdc in next 2 st, sc in next 7 st, hdc in next st, 2 dc in
next st, ch 2, 2 dc in next st, hdc in next st, sc in next 2 st, hdc in next st,
hdc2tog worked over the last sc and last slst from Rnd 4, slst in initial
hdc2tog [64]

Rnd 6: ch 2 (count as hdc), hdc in next 6 st, 2 hdc + ch 1 + 2 hdc in next
ch-space, (hdc in next 14 st, 2 hdc + ch 1 + 2 hdc in next ch-space) repeat
3 times, hdc in next 7 st, slst in 2nd ch of initial ch 2 [72 + 4 ch]

Rnd 7: ch 1, sc in same st, sc in next 8 st, (sc + 1 ch in next ch-space,
sc in next 18 st) repeat 3 times, sc + 1 ch in next ch-space, sc in next 9 st,
fasten off with an invisible join to 2nd stitch [76 + 4 ch]

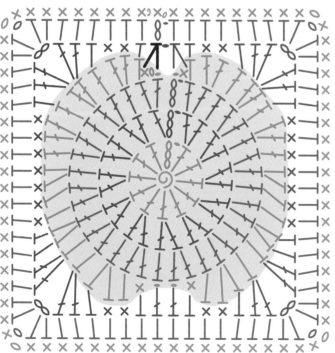

APPLE EDGE

Rnd 1: *{pull up a loop of yarn E along the apple shape, where the color changes}* surface slst all around the yarn A apple shape [50] Fasten off.

LEAF

Rnd 1: *{start with yarn C}* ch 6, hdc in 2nd ch from hook, 3 dc in next ch, hdc in next 2 ch, 3 sc in next ch, continue on the other side of the starting ch, hdc in next 2 ch, 3 dc in next ch, hdc in next ch, turn [15]

Rnd 2: ch 1, sc in next st, 2 sc in next 3 st, sc in next 3 st, 3 sc in next st, sc in next 3 st, 2 sc in next 3 st, sc in next st, slst in initial ch, ch 5 [29] Fasten off, leaving a tail for sewing. Sew the leaf to the square using the yarn tail. Using yarn D, embroider little apple pips in the center and a stalk on top.

You can combine the Cut Apple pattern with the Whole Apple pattern on page 55 in a super cute baby blanket. Make green and red apples for more variation.

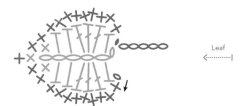

Leaf
<----------|

LEMON SQUARE `80 stitch square`

Irene Strange — United Kingdom
@irenestrange www.irenestrange.co.uk

Skill level: Beginner
Colors: Yarn A: Golden Glow / Yarn B: Cold Green / Yarn C: Amazon

INSTRUCTIONS

Rnd 1: {start with yarn A} start a magic ring with ch 3 (count as dc), 11 dc, slst in 3rd ch of initial ch 3 [12]

Rnd 2: ch 3 (count as dc), dc in same st, 2 dc in in next 11 st, slst in 3rd ch of initial ch 3 [24]

Rnd 3: ch 3 (count as dc), 2 dc in next st, (dc in next st, 2 dc in next st) repeat 11 times, slst in 3rd ch of initial ch 3 [36]

Rnd 4: ch 1, [(sc in next 2 st, 2 sc in next st) repeat 3 times, sc in next 2 st, hdc in next st, 2 hdc in next st, dc in next st, 2 tr in next st, dc in next st, 2 hdc in next st, hdc in next st] repeat 2 times, fasten off with an invisible join to 2nd sc [48]

Rnd 5: {join yarn B in last dc, make your first stitch a standing stitch} (sc in next 2 st, hdc in next 5 st, dc in next 3 st, 2 tr in next st, ch 2, 2 tr in next st, dc in next 3 st, hdc in next 5 st, sc in next 2 st, 2 sc in next st, ch 2, 2 sc in next st) repeat 2 times, slst in initial sc [64]

Rnd 6: ch 2 (count as hdc), hdc in next 11 st, 2 hdc + ch 1 + 2 hdc in next ch-space, (hdc in next 14 st, 2 hdc + ch 1 + 2 hdc in next ch-space) repeat 3 times, hdc in next 2 st, slst in 2nd ch of initial ch 2 [72 + 4 ch]

Rnd 7: ch 1, sc in same st, sc in next 13 st, sc + ch 1 in next ch-space, (sc in next 18 st, sc + ch 1 in next ch-space) repeat 3 times, sc in next 4 st, fasten off with an invisible join to 2nd sc [76 + 4 ch]

LEAF

Follow instructions and diagram on page 59 (Orange Square).

When life gives you lemons... turn to crochet to find peace and make the cutest Lemon Granny Square.

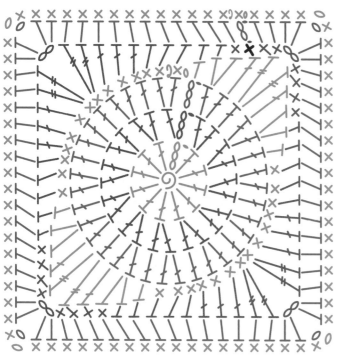

ORANGE SQUARE `80 stitch square`

Irene Strange — United Kingdom

@irenestrange · www.irenestrange.co.uk

Skill level: Beginner
Colors: Yarn A: Papaya / Yarn B: Cold Green / Yarn C: Amazon

INSTRUCTIONS

Rnd 1: {start with yarn A} start a magic ring with ch 3 (count as dc), 11 dc, slst in 3rd ch of initial ch 3 [12]

Rnd 2: ch 3 (count as dc), dc in same st, 2 dc in next 11 st, slst in 3rd ch of initial ch 3 [24]

Rnd 3: ch 3 (count as dc), 2 dc in next st, (dc in next st, 2 dc in next st) repeat 11 times, slst in 3rd ch of initial ch 3 [36]

Rnd 4: ch 1, (sc in next 2 st, 2 sc in next st) repeat 12 times, fasten off with an invisible join to 2nd sc [48]

Rnd 5: {join yarn B in any st, make your first stitch a standing stitch} (sc in next 4 st, hdc in next 3 st, 2 dc in next st, ch 2, 2 dc in next st, hdc in next 3 st) repeat 4 times, slst in initial sc [56 + 8 ch]

Rnd 6: ch 2 (count as hdc), hdc in next 8 st, 2 hdc + ch 1 + 2 hdc in ch-space, (hdc in next 14 st, 2 hdc + ch 1 + 2 hdc in next ch-space) repeat 3 times, hdc in next 5 st, slst in 2nd ch of initial ch 2 [72 + 4 ch]

Rnd 7: ch 1, sc in same st, sc in next 10 st, sc + ch 1 in ch-space, (sc in next 18 st, sc + ch 1 in ch-space) repeat 3 times, sc in next 7 st, fasten off with an invisible join to 2nd sc [76 + 4 ch]

LEAF

Rnd 1: {start with yarn C} ch 8, sc in 2nd ch from hook, hdc in next 2 ch, 2 dc in next ch, hdc in next 2 ch, 3 sc in next ch, continue on the other side of the starting ch, hdc in next 2 ch, 2 dc in next ch, hdc in next 2 ch, sc in next ch, slst below first st, ch 5 [23] Fasten off, leaving a tail for sewing. Sew the leaf to the square using the yarn tail.

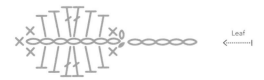

Leaf
<----------|

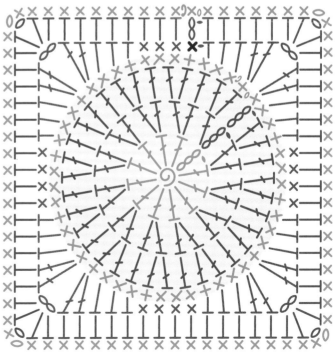

NECTARINE SQUARE `80 stitch square`

Irene Strange — United Kingdom

@irenestrange ⊕ www.irenestrange.co.uk

Skill level: Beginner
Colors: Yarn A: Sunflower / Yarn B: Salmon / Yarn C: Cold Green /
Yarn D: Peridot / Yarn E: Brownie

INSTRUCTIONS

Rnd 1: *{start with yarn A}* start a magic ring with ch 3 (count as dc), 11 dc, slst in 3rd ch of initial ch 3 [12]

Rnd 2: ch 3 (count as dc), dc in same st, 2 dc in in next 11 st, fasten off with an invisible join to first true dc [24]

Rnd 3: *{join yarn B in any st, make your first stitch a standing stitch}* hdc in this st, (2 sc in next st, sc in next st) repeat 3 times, 2 sc in next st, hdc in next st, 2 hdc in next st, hdc in next st, hdc + dc in next st, (dc in next st, 2 dc in next st) repeat 5 times, dc in next st, dc + hdc in next st, slst in initial hdc [36]

Rnd 4: ch 1, (sc in next 2 st, 2 sc in next st) repeat 3 times, hdc in next 2 st, 2 hdc in next st, dc in next 2 st, 2 tr in next st, (dc in next 2 st, 2 dc in next st) repeat 4 times, dc in next 2 st, sc in next st, slst in next st, (2 sc in next st, sc in next st) repeat 2 times, 2 sc in next st, fasten off with an invisible join to 2nd stitch [48]

Rnd 5: *{join yarn C in first st of last 2 sc in same st, make your first stitch a standing stitch}* sc in next 6 st, dc in next 2 st, 2 dc in next st, ch 2, 2 dc in next st, dc in next st, hdc in next st, sc in next 8 st, 2 sc in next st, ch 2, 2 sc in next st, sc in next 9 st, hdc in next st, 2 dc in next st, ch 2, 2 dc in next st, hdc in next st, sc in next 4 st, hdc in next st, dc in next 4 st, 2 dc in next st, ch 2, 2 dc in next st, sc in next 2 st, slst in initial sc [64]

Rnd 6: ch 2 (count as hdc), hdc in next 9 st, 2 hdc + ch 1 + 2 hdc in next ch-space, (hdc in next 14 st, 2 hdc + ch 1 + 2 hdc in next ch-space) repeat 3 times, hdc in next 4 st, slst in 2nd ch of initial ch 2 [72 + 4 ch]

Rnd 7: ch 1, sc in same st, sc in next 11 st, (sc + ch 1 in next ch-space, sc in next 18 st) repeat 3 times, sc in next 6 st, fasten off with an invisible join to 2nd stitch [76 + 4 ch]

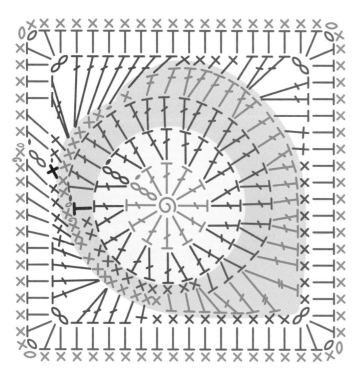

LEAF

Row 1: {*start with yarn D*} ch 6, hdc in 2nd ch from hook, 3 dc in next ch, hdc in next 2 ch, 3 sc in next ch, continue on the other side of the starting chain, hdc in next 2 ch, 3 dc in next ch, hdc in next ch, turn [15]

Row 2: ch 1, sc in next st, 2 sc in next 3 st, sc in next 3 st, 3 sc in next st, sc in next 3 st, 2 sc in next 3 st, sc in next st, slst in initial ch, ch 2 [26] Fasten off, leaving a tail for sewing. Sew the leaf to the square using the yarn tail. Using yarn E, embroider a small brown stalk in the heart-shaped dip.

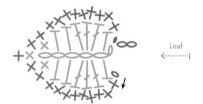

Leaf

HEARTFELT SQUARE 80 stitch square

RedAgape (Mandy O'Sullivan) — Australia
@crochethyredagape ⊛ www.redagapeblog.com f redagapeblog

Skill level: Beginner / Intermediate
Colors: Yarn A: Peony Pink / Yarn B: Golden Glow
Special stitches: Changing color mid-round

INSTRUCTIONS

Rnd 1: *{start with yarn A}* start a magic ring with ch 3 (count as dc), 2 dc, ch 1, (3 dc, ch 1) repeat 3 times, slst in 3rd ch of initial ch 3 [12 + 4 ch]

Rnd 2: slst in next 2 st, slst in corner-space, ch 3 (count as dc), 2 dc + ch 1 + 3 dc in same ch-space, (3 dc + ch 1 + 3 dc in next ch-space) repeat 3 times, slst in 3rd ch of initial ch 3 [24 + 4 ch]

Rnd 3: slst in next 2 st, slst in next ch-space, ch 3 (count as dc), 2 dc + ch 1 + 3 dc in same ch-space, *{switch to yarn B}* 3 dc in the gap between the 2 dc-groups, *{switch to yarn A}* 3 dc + ch 1 + 3 dc in corner-space, 3 dc in next gap between 2 dc-groups, (*{switch to yarn B}* 3 dc + ch 1 + 3 dc in corner-space, *{switch to yarn A}* 3 dc in next gap between 2 dc-groups) repeat 2 times, slst in 3rd ch of initial ch 3 [36 + 4 ch]

Rnd 4: slst in next 2 st, slst in next ch-space, ch 3 (count as dc), 2 dc + ch 1 + 3 dc in same ch-space, *{switch to yarn B}* 3 dc in next 2 gaps between dc-groups, *{switch to yarn A}* 3 dc + ch 1 + 3 dc in corner-space, 3 dc in next gap between the dc-groups, *{switch to yarn B}* 3 dc in next gap between dc-groups, 3 dc + ch 1 + 3 dc in corner-space, 3 dc in next 2 gaps between dc-groups, 3 dc + ch 1 + 3 dc in corner-space, 3 dc in next gap between the dc-groups, *{switch to yarn A}* 3 dc in last gap between dc-groups, fasten off with an invisible join to first true dc [48 + 4 ch]

Rnd 5: *{join yarn B in any corner-space, make your first stitch a standing stitch}* (3 dc + ch 1 + 3 dc in next corner-space, 3 dc in next 3 gaps between dc-groups) repeat 4 times, slst in initial dc [60 + 4 ch]

Rnd 6: slst in next 2 st, slst in next corner-space, ch 6 (count as dc + ch 3) + dc in same corner-space, dc in next 15 st, (dc + ch 3 + dc in next corner-space, dc in next 15 st) repeat 3 times, fasten off with an invisible join to 4th ch of initial ch 6 [68 + 12 ch]

KISSES SQUARE   80 stitch square

Crafty CC (Celine Semaan) — Australia
@crafty_cc   www.craftycc.com

Skill level: Beginner / Intermediate
Colors: Yarn A: Pastel Pink / Yarn B: Girly Pink

INSTRUCTIONS

CENTER OF 'X'

Row 1: *{start with yarn A}* ch 6, start in 2nd ch from hook, sc in next 5 ch [5]

Row 2 - 15: turn, ch 1, sc in next 5 st [5]
Fasten off. Turn your strip 90 degrees clockwise at the end of Row 15.

POINTS OF 'X'

Row 1: *{join yarn A in the 6th row-end on one side, make your first stitch a standing stitch}* sc in next 5 row-ends [5] You should have 5 row-ends remaining on either side.

Row 2 - 5: turn, ch 1, sc in next 5 st [5] Fasten off at the end of Row 5.
Repeat rows 1-5 on the other side of the center piece. Fasten off.

FILLING IN THE SQUARE

Rnd 1: *{join yarn B in the 2nd sc to the right in the top right corner of the motif, make your first stitch a standing stitch}* (tr in next st, dc in next st, hdc in next st, sc in next st, *{continue working into the row-ends}* 2 hdc, dc, tr, tr3tog across next st, into the space between and into the following st, tr, dc, 2 hdc, *{continue working in the top}* dc in next st) repeat 4 times, slst in initial tr [56]

  Note: In the next round the sequence (2 hdc + ch 2 + 2 hdc) will always be made in the dc to the left of a tr stitch.

Rnd 2: slst in next st, ch 1, 2 hdc + ch 2 + 2 hdc in same st as slst, hdc in next 13 st, (2 hdc + ch 2 + 2 hdc in next st, hdc in next 13 st) repeat 3 times, slst in initial hdc [60 + 8 ch]

Rnd 3: slst in next st, slst in next ch-space, ch 1, (hdc + ch 1 + hdc in ch-space, hdc in next 17 st) repeat 4 times, fasten off with an invisible join to first ch after initial hdc [76 + 4 ch]

Use the pattern for Orange Square on page 59 as a base to make an O-shaped square for a tic-tac-toe blanket. Work Rnd 3 and 4 in Pastel Pink, work all other rounds in Girly Pink.

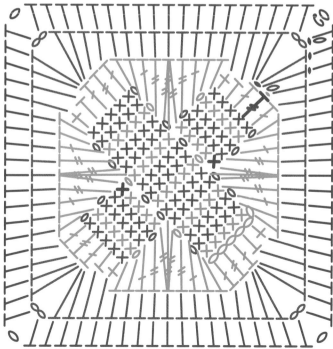

MESH STRAINER SQUARE `112 stitch square`

Madelenón (Soledad Iglesias Silva) — Argentina
🌐 www.madelenon.com 📷 @handmadelenon 🅕 madelenonface

Skill level: Intermediate
Colors: Yarn A: Sunflower / Yarn B: Cantaloupe / Yarn C: Peony Pink / Yarn D: Lettuce
Special stitches: 3-dc-bobble (3 double crochet bobble stitch)

INSTRUCTIONS

Rnd 1: {start with yarn A} start a magic ring with ch 4 (count as dc + ch 1), (dc + ch 1) repeat 11 times, fasten off with an invisible join to 4th ch of initial ch 4 [12 + 12 ch]

Rnd 2: {join yarn B in any ch-space, make your first stitch a standing stitch} (sc in ch-space, ch 2) repeat 12 times, fasten off with an invisible join to first ch after initial sc [12 + 24 ch]

Rnd 1-5 |·············⟩

Rnd 6-12 |·············⟩

Rnd 3: *{join yarn C in any ch-space, make your first stitch a standing stitch}* (3-dc-bobble in next ch-space, ch 3) repeat 12 times, fasten off with an invisible join to first ch after initial 3-dc-bobble [12 + 36 ch]

Rnd 4: *{join yarn B in any 3-dc-bobble, make your first stitch a standing stitch}* (sc in 3-dc-bobble, ch 3) repeat 12 times, slst in initial sc [12 + 36 ch] Fasten off.

Rnd 5: *{join yarn A in any ch-space, make your first stitch a standing stitch}* (sc + hdc + dc + hdc + sc in ch-space) repeat 12 times, slst in initial sc [60] Put a stitch marker in the last loop of yarn C to keep it from unraveling.

Rnd 6: *{Join yarn D in any unworked ch-space of Rnd 4, make your first stitch a standing stitch}* (sc in unworked ch-space of Rnd 4, ch 5) repeat 12 times, slst in initial sc [12 + 60 ch]

Rnd 7: (sc + hdc + 3 dc + hdc + sc in next ch-space) repeat 12 times, fasten off with an invisible join to 2nd stitch [84]

Rnd 8: *{continue working with yarn C, take the last loop in Rnd 5 back on your hook. Work in both Rnd 5 and 7}* slst in next 3 st to position the loop in the central dc of Rnd 5, ch 1, sc in same st, (ch 4, sc in the central dc of Rnd 7, ch 4, sc in the central dc of Rnd 5) repeat 11 times, ch 4, sc in the central dc of Rnd 7, ch 4, slst in initial sc [24 + 96 ch]

Rnd 9: 3 sc in all 24 ch-spaces, fasten off with an invisible join to 2nd stitch [72]

Rnd 10: *{join yarn D in any st, make your first stitch a standing stitch}* (sc in next 3 st, hdc in next 3 st, dc in next 3 st, ch 2, dc in next 3 st, hdc in next 3 st, sc in next 3 st) repeat 4 times, fasten off with an invisible join to 2nd stitch [72 + 8 ch]

Rnd 11: *{join yarn B in any ch-space, make your first stitch a standing stitch}* (2 hdc + ch 2 + 2 hdc in ch-space, hdc in next 18 st) repeat 4 times, fasten off with an invisible join in 2nd stitch [88 + 8 ch]

Rnd 12: *{join yarn C in any ch-space, make your first stitch a standing stitch}* (2 hdc + ch 2 + 2 hdc in ch-space, hdc in next 22 st) repeat 4 times, fasten off with an invisible join in 2nd stitch [104 + 8 ch]

 Mesh Strainer Square can be combined with Ponding Lily Square on page 150 when working with matching colors.

BARAHIR SQUARE 80 stitch square

Arteeni (Sari Åström) — Finland
⊕ www.arteeni.fi 📷 @arteeni **f** arteenidesign

Skill level: Beginner / Intermediate
Colors: Yarn A: Jade Gravel / Yarn B: Glass / Yarn C: Riverside / Yarn D: Cream / Yarn E: Pink Sand / Yarn F: Shark Gray
Special stitches: Work in the ring / 3-dc-bobble (3 double crochet bobble) / BPdc (Back post double crochet) / Changing color mid-round

INSTRUCTIONS

Rnd 1: *{start with yarn A}* ch 4, form a ring with slst in initial ch [4]

Rnd 2: ch 3 (count as dc), 11 dc in the ring, fasten off with an invisible join to first true dc [12]

Rnd 3: *{join yarn B in any st, make your first stitch a standing stitch}* 2 dc in all 12 st, fasten off with an invisible join to 2nd stitch [24]

Rnd 4: *{join yarn C in any st, make your first stitch a standing stitch}* [2 hdc in next st, ch 1, skip 1 st, (2 hdc in next st, hdc in next st) repeat 2 times] repeat 4 times, fasten off with an invisible join to 2nd stitch [32 + 4 ch]

Note: Rnd 5 can be worked in a single color or in 2 colors. In this sample we make Rnd 5 with 2 colors.

Rnd 5: *{join yarn D in any ch-space, make your first stitch a standing stitch}* (tr + ch 1 + tr + ch 1 + tr + ch 2 + tr + ch 1 + tr + ch 1 + tr + ch 1 in ch-space, skip 4 st, *{change to yarn E}* 3-dc-bobble between next 2 hdc stitches, *{change to yarn D}* ch 1, skip 4 st) repeat 4 times, fasten off with an invisible join to first ch after initial tr [28 + 32 ch]

Note: Work the sc stitches loosely in Rnd 6.

Rnd 6: *{join yarn F in any corner-space, make your first stitch a standing stitch}* (2 sc + ch 2 + 2 sc in corner-space, 2 sc in next 6 ch-spaces) repeat 4 times, fasten off with an invisible join to 2nd stitch [64 + 8 ch]

Rnd 7: *{join yarn D in any corner-space, make your first stitch a standing stitch}* (4 dc in corner-space, BPdc around next 16 st) repeat 4 times, fasten off with an invisible join to 2nd stitch [80]

Barahir and Gilwen are elf names, inspired by Tolkien's books. You find Gilwen Square on page 67. It matches beautifully with Barahir Square.

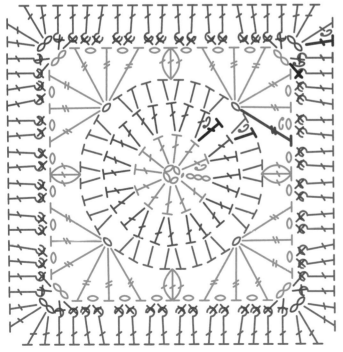

GILWEN SQUARE `80 stitch square`

Arteeni (Sari Åström) — Finland
🌐 www.arteeni.fi 📷 @arteeni 📘 arteenidesign

Skill level: Intermediate
Colors: yarn A: Golden Glow / yarn B: Glass / yarn C: Peridot /
yarn D: Graphite / yarn E: Shark Gray
Special stitches: Changing color mid-round / 4-tr-bobble (4 treble
crochet bobble) / BPdc (back post double crochet) / work into the ring

INSTRUCTIONS

*Note: If the center part of the square does not set well, you may want
to (1) replace the dc stitches in Rnd 2 with hdc stitches or (2) replace
the 4-tr-bobbles in Rnd 3 with 4-dc-bobbles.*

Rnd 1: *{start with yarn A}* ch 4, slst in initial ch to form a ring [4]

Rnd 2: ch 5 (count as dc + ch 2), (dc + ch 2) repeat 7 times into the ring,
fasten off with an invisible join to 4th ch [8 + 16 ch]

Rnd 3: *{join yarn B in any ch-space, make your first stitch a standing
stitch}* (4-tr-bobble in ch-space, ch 4 loosely) repeat 8 times, fasten off with
an invisible join to first ch after initial 4-tr-bobble [8 petals + 32 ch]

*Note: In Rnd 4, you change color by making the ch after the color-
change instructions with the new color. The next round of stitches will
cover the chain stitch, so it won't be visible.*

Rnd 4: *{join yarn C in any ch-space, make your first stitch a standing
stitch, Carry yarn A when not in use}* [5-dc-bobble + slst in ch-space,
{change to yarn D} ch 1, tr + ch 1 + tr + ch 1 + tr + ch 2 + tr + ch 1 + tr +
ch 1 + tr in next ch-space, *{change to yarn C}* ch 1] repeat 4 times, fasten
off with an invisible join to slst after initial 5-dc-bobble [28 + 32 ch]

Note: Work the sc stitches loosely in Rnd 5.

Rnd 5: *{join yarn E in any corner-space, make your first stitch a standing
stitch}* (2 sc + ch 2 + 2 sc in corner-space, 2 sc in next 6 ch-spaces) repeat
4 times, fasten off with an invisible join to 2nd stitch [64 + 8 ch]

Rnd 6: *{join yarn D in any corner-space, make your first stitch a standing
stitch}* (4 dc in corner-space, BPdc around next 16 st) repeat 4 times,
fasten off with an invisible join to 2nd stitch [80]

SUNROSE SQUARE 80 stitch square

Zipzipdreams (Edina Tekten) — Hungary / Turkey
@Zipzipdreams f Zipzipdreams

Skill level: Intermediate
Colors: Yarn A: Pearl / Yarn B: Peach / Yarn C: Sunflower /
Yarn D: Fuchsia / Yarn E: Cream / Yarn F: Nordic Blue
Special stitches: BPtr4tog (Back post treble crochet 4 stitches together)

INSTRUCTIONS

Rnd 1: *{start with yarn A}* start a magic ring with ch 3 (count as dc),
15 dc, fasten off with an invisible join to first true dc [16]

Rnd 2: *{join yarn B in any st, make your first stitch a standing stitch}*
(hdc in next st, 2 hdc in next st) repeat 8 times, fasten off with an invisible
join to 2nd stitch [24]

Rnd 3: *{join yarn C in top of any first hdc of an increase, make your first
stitch a standing stitch}* (sc in next 2 st, 2 sc in next st) repeat 8 times,
slst in initial sc [32]

Rnd 4: ch 2 + dc3tog (count as dc4tog), (ch 6, dc4tog over next 4 st)
repeat 7 times, ch 6, slst in top of initial dc4tog [8 clusters] Fasten off.

Rnd 5: *{join yarn D at the back around any first st of a sc increase in
Rnd 3, make your first stitch a standing stitch. Hold the ch 6 of Rnd 4
at the front of your work while crocheting the BPtr4tog clusters, work
over the stitches of Rnd 3}* (BPtr4tog over next 4 st, take the hook out of
the loop and bring the loop in front of the ch 6 of Rnd 4, ch 1 including
the ch of Rnd 4, ch 6) repeat 8 times, slst in top of initial BPtr4tog
[8 clusters] Fasten off.

Rnd 6: *{join yarn E in any ch-space of Rnd 5, make your first stitch
a standing stitch}* (hdc + 8 dc + hdc in next ch-space) repeat 8 times,
fasten off with an invisible join to 2nd stitch [80]

Rnd 7: *{join yarn F in the 6th st of any petal, make your first stitch a
standing stitch}* 2 tr + ch 1 + 2 tr in this st, tr in next 3 st, skip 2 st,
dc in next st, hdc in next st, sc in next 4 st, hdc in next st, dc in next st,
skip 2 st, tr in next 4 st, (2 tr + ch 1 + 2 tr in next st, tr in next 3 st,
skip 2 st, dc in next st, hdc in next st, sc in next 4 st, hdc in next st,
dc in next st, skip 2 st, tr in next 4 st) repeat 3 times, fasten off with an
invisible join to 2nd stitch [76 + 4 ch]

Rnd 1-4

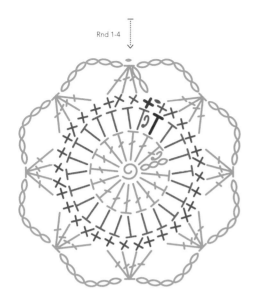

Rnd 5-7

BERRIES SQUARE `80 stitch square`

Ms.Eni (Simone Conrad) — Germany
@ms.eni f ms.eni.handmade

Skill level: Intermediate
Colors: Yarn A: Cream / Yarn B: Cardinal / Yarn C: Amazon
Special stitches: sc4tog (single crochet 4 stitches together)

INSTRUCTIONS

Rnd 1: {start with yarn A} start a magic ring with ch 3 (count as dc), 15 dc, slst in 3rd ch of initial ch 3 [16]

Rnd 2: ch 3 (count as dc), (skip 1 st, dc + ch 1 + dc in next st) repeat 7 times, skip 1 st, dc in next st, ch 1, fasten off with an invisible join to first true dc [16 + 8 ch]

Rnd 3: {join Yarn B in any ch-space between 2 dc, make your first stitch a standing stitch} (4 dc in ch-space, ch 3) repeat 8 times, fasten off with an invisible join to 2nd stitch [32 + 24 ch]

Note: In Rnd 4 we will use alternating colors, working with yarns A and C. Start each sc4tog with yarn C, finish it with yarn A. When you have 4 loops on your hook, yarn over with yarn A and pull through all 4 loops on your hook. Carry yarn C along when not in use.

Rnd 4: {join yarn C in any first dc, make your first stitch a standing stitch} sc4tog {finish and continue with yarn A} 6 sc in next ch-space, ({change to yarn C} sc4tog {finish and continue with yarn A}, 6 sc in next ch-space) repeat 7 times, slst in 2nd stitch [8 berries]

Rnd 5: ch 1 (count as sc), sc in next 4 st, (hdc in next st, 2 dc in next st, ch 1, 2 dc in next st, hdc in next st, sc in next 10 st) repeat 3 times, hdc in next st, 2 dc in next st, ch 1, 2 dc in next st, hdc in next st, sc in next 5 st, close with slst in initial ch 1 [64 + 4 ch]

Rnd 6: ch 1 (count as sc), sc in next 7 st, (hdc + ch 1 + hdc in next ch-space, sc in next 16 st) repeat 3 times, hdc + ch 1 + hdc in next ch-space, sc in next 8 st, close with slst in initial ch 1 [72 + 4 ch]

Rnd 7: ch 3 (count as dc), dc in next 8 st, (2 dc in next ch-space, dc in next 18 st) repeat 3 times, 2 dc in next ch-space, dc in next 9 st, fasten off with an invisible join to first true dc [80]

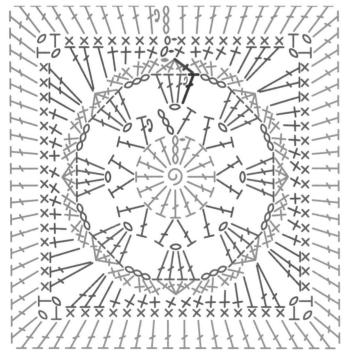

APRIL SQUARE `80 stitch square`

Zipzipdreams (Edina Tekten) — Hungary / Turkey
 @Zipzipdreams f Zipzipdreams

Skill level: Intermediate
Colors: Yarn A: Golden Glow / Yarn B: Pastel Pink / Yarn C: Peony
Pink / Yarn D: Peridot / Yarn E: Raspberry / Yarn F: Cream
Special stitches: 2-tr-bobble (2 treble crochet bobble stitch) /
2-dc-bobble (2 double crochet bobble stitch) / FPdc (Front post
double crochet)

INSTRUCTIONS

Rnd 1: {start with yarn A} start a magic ring with ch 2 (count as hdc),
11 hdc, fasten off with an invisible join to first true hdc [12]

Rnd 2: {join yarn B in any st, make your first stitch a standing stitch}
(2-dc-bobble in next st, ch 2) repeat 12 times, fasten off with an invisible join
to first ch after initial 2-dc-bobble [12 petals]

Rnd 3: {join yarn C in any ch-space, make your first stitch a standing
stitch} (4-dc-bobble in ch-space, ch 3) repeat 12 times, fasten off with an
invisible join to first ch after initial 4-dc-bobble [12 petals]

Rnd 4: {join yarn D from the front around the top of any petal of Rnd 3,
make your first stitch a standing stitch} (FPsc around bobble of Rnd 3,
ch 2, FPdc around next bobble of Rnd 2, ch 2) repeat 12 times, fasten off
with an invisible join to first ch after initial FPsc [24 + 48 ch]

Rnd 5: {join yarn E in any FPdc, make your first stitch a standing stitch}
(2-tr-bobble + ch 2 + 2-tr-bobble + ch 2 + 2-tr-bobble in FPdc, 2-dc-bobble
+ ch 2 + 2-dc-bobble + ch 2 + 2-dc-bobble in next 2 FPdc) repeat 4 times,
fasten off, invisible join to first ch after initial 2-tr-bobble [12 tulips]

Rnd 6: {join yarn F in any middle 2-tr-bobble, make your first stitch a
standing stitch} [tr + ch 1 + tr in top of 2-tr-bobble, 3 tr in next ch-space,
(tr in the space between 2 flowers, 2 dc in next 2 ch-spaces) repeat 2 times,
tr in the space between 2 flowers, 3 tr in next ch-space] repeat 4 times,
fasten off with an invisible join to first ch after initial tr [72 + 8 ch]

CARNATIONS GARDEN SQUARE `80 stitch square`

Zipzipdreams (Edina Tekten) — Hungary / Turkey
📷 @Zipzipdreams **f** Zipzipdreams

Skill level: Intermediate
Colors: Yarn A: Sunflower / Yarn B: Jade Gravel / Yarn C: Peridot /
Yarn D: Blue Lake / Yarn E: Cream
Special stitches: 5-dc-bobble (5 double crochet bobble stitch)

INSTRUCTIONS

Rnd 1: *{start with yarn A}* start a magic ring with ch 3 (count as dc), 2 dc, ch 1, (3 dc, ch 1) repeat 3 times, fasten off with an invisible join to first true dc [12 + 4 ch]

Rnd 2: *{join yarn B in any ch-space, make your first stitch a standing stitch}* [slst in ch-space, (ch 7, starting in 2nd ch from hook, sc in next ch, hdc in next ch, dc in next 3 ch, hdc in next ch, slst in initial ch-space) repeat 2 times, ch 3] repeat 4 times, fasten off with an invisible join in first ch after initial slst [8 leaves]

Rnd 3: *{join yarn C in any ch-space, make your first stitch a standing stitch. Keep the leaves created in Rnd 2 at the front of the work while crocheting}* (2 hdc in ch-space, ch 5, tr in next ch-space of Rnd 1 between the 2 leaves, ch 5) repeat 4 times, fasten off with an invisible join to 2nd stitch [12 + 40 ch]

Rnd 4: *{join yarn D in any tr, make your first stitch a standing stitch}* (4 tr + ch 1 + 4 tr in top of tr, sc in top of next leaf, ch 3, 5-dc-bobble in 2nd hdc, ch 3, sc in top of next leaf) repeat 4 times, fasten off with an invisible join to 2nd stitch [4 flowers and 4 bobbles]

Rnd 5: *{join yarn E in any corner-space, make your first stitch a standing stitch}* (2 tr + ch 2 + 2 tr in ch-space, 4 FPtr around next 4 tr, tr in next sc, 4 tr in top of 5-dc-bobble, tr in next sc, 4 FPtr around next 4 tr) repeat 4 times, fasten off with an invisible join to 2nd stitch [72 + 8 ch]

{ *Carnations Garden Square works beautifully when combined with April Square on page 71.* }

ROSE SQUARE `80 stitch square`

Madelenón (Soledad Iglesias Silva) — Argentina
🌐 www.madelenon.com 📷 @handmadelenon f madelenonface

Skill level: Intermediate
Colors: Yarn A: Peony Pink / Yarn B: Jade / Yarn C: Peach
Special stitches: 3-tr-bobble (3 treble crochet bobble stitch) /
BPsc (Back post single crochet)

INSTRUCTIONS

Rnd 1: {start with Yarn A} start a magic ring with 6 sc, slst in initial sc [6]

Rnd 2: ch 1, sc in next st, (ch 3, skip 1 st, sc in next st) repeat 2 times, ch 3, slst in initial sc [12]

Rnd 3: slst in next ch-space, sc + hdc + 3 dc + hdc + sc in same ch-space, (sc + hdc + 3 dc + hdc + sc in next ch-space) repeat 2 times, slst in initial sc [21]

Rnd 4: {work behind the petals of Rnd 3} ch 1, (BPsc around hdc of Rnd 3, ch 3) repeat 6 times, slst in initial BPsc [6 + 18 ch]

Rnd 5: slst in next ch-space, sc + hdc + 3 dc + hdc + sc in same ch-space, (sc + hdc + 3 dc + hdc + sc in next ch-space) repeat 5 times, slst in initial sc [42]

Rnd 6: {work behind the petals of Rnd 5} ch 2, (BPsc around the middle dc of Rnd 5, ch 5) repeat 6 times, slst in initial BPsc [6 + 30 ch]

Rnd 7: slst in next ch-space, sc + hdc + 5 dc + hdc + sc in same ch-space, (sc + hdc + 5 dc + hdc + sc in next ch-space) repeat 5 times, fasten off with an invisible join to first hdc [54]

Rnd 8: {join yarn B in the middle dc of a petal, make your first stitch a standing stitch} (sc in the middle dc of a petal, ch 5, 3-tr-bobble between hdc and first dc of next petal, ch 5, 3-tr-bobble in the same space, ch 2, sc between last dc and hdc of same petal, ch 5, sc between hdc and first dc of next petal, ch 2, 3-tr-bobble between last dc and hdc of same petal, ch 5, 3-tr-bobble in the same space, ch 5) repeat 2 times, fasten off with an invisible join to first ch after initial sc [14 + 58 ch]

Rnd 9: {join yarn C in a ch-space between 3-tr-bobble after a ch-2-space, make your first stitch a standing stitch} ch 2 (count as hdc) + 2 hdc in ch- space, 5 hdc in next 2 ch-spaces, 3 hdc + ch 3 + 3 hdc in next ch-space, 3 hdc in next ch-space, 4 hdc in next ch-space, 3 hdc in next ch-space, 3 hdc + ch 3 + 3 hdc in next ch-space, 5 hdc in next

2 ch-spaces, 3 hdc + ch 3 + 3 hdc in next ch-space, 3 hdc in next ch-space, 4 hdc in next ch-space, 3 hdc in next ch-space, ch 3, slst in 2nd ch of initial ch 2 [64 + 12 ch]

Rnd 10: ch 2 (count as hdc), hdc in next 15 st, (hdc + ch 2 + hdc in next ch-space, hdc in next 16 st) repeat 3 times, hdc + ch 2 + hdc in next ch-space, fasten off with an invisible join to first true hdc [72 + 8 ch]

Roses are red... but they're beautiful in yellow, blue and purple too! Look for inspiration in your yarn stash!

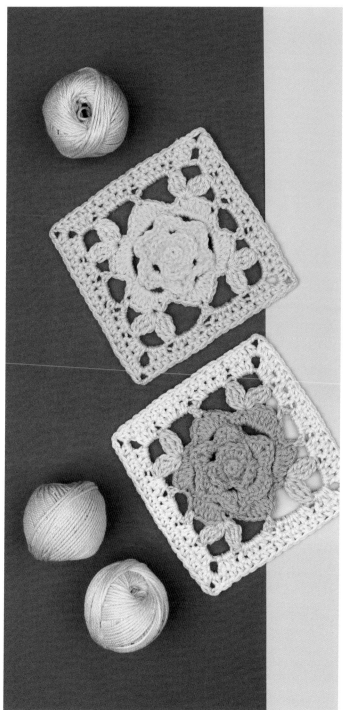

MARINE SQUARE `80 stitch square`

Conmismanoss (Susana Villalobos) — Argentina
📷 @conmismanoss f hilandosuenoss

Skill level: Intermediate
Colors: Yarn A: Sunflower / **Yarn B:** Ice Blue / **Yarn C:** Larimar /
Yarn D: Navy Blue

INSTRUCTIONS

Rnd 1: *{start with yarn A}* start a magic ring with (ch 6, slst in 2nd ch from hook, sc in next ch, hdc in next 2 ch, dc in next ch, slst in magic ring) repeat 5 times, fasten off with an invisible join to 2nd ch of initial ch 6 [5-pointed star]

Rnd 2: *{join yarn B in one of the tips of the star, make your first stitch a standing stitch. Work this round in BLO}* (sc in the first st of the star, sc in next st, hdc in next st, dc in next st, tr in next st, join the next point of the star with a slst, catching the top loop of Rnd 1 chains from back to front) repeat 5 times, slst in first sc [30]

Rnd 3: sc in same st, sc in next 4 st, 2 sc in next st, (sc in next 5 st, 2 sc in next st) repeat 4 times, slst in initial sc [35]

Rnd 4: sc in same st, sc in next 2 st, 2 sc in next st, (sc in next 6 st, 2 sc in next st) repeat 4 times, sc in next 3 st, fasten off with an invisible join to 2nd stitch [40]

Rnd 5: *{Join yarn C in any sc, make your first stitch a standing stitch}* (3 dc + ch 2 + 3 dc in next st, dc in next 9 st) repeat 4 times, fasten off with an invisible join to 2nd stitch [68]

Rnd 6: *{Join yarn D in any corner-space, make your first stitch a standing stitch}* (2 dc + ch 2 + 2 dc in corner-space, skip 1st st, dc in next 14 st) repeat 4 times, fasten off with an invisible join to 2nd stitch [72 + 8 ch]

{ *Marine Square is the perfect square to try out all of the beautiful shades of blue you have in your yarn stash!* }

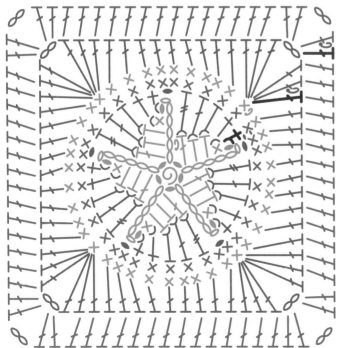

3D 8-PETAL SQUARE 112 stitch square

Ukaracraft (Nurul A. Putri) — Indonesia

Skill level: Intermediate / advanced
Colors: Yarn A: Burgundy / **Yarn B:** Peach / **Yarn C:** Salmon
Special stitches: FPdc (Front post double crochet) / FPtr (Front post treble crochet)

INSTRUCTIONS

Rnd 1: *{start with yarn A}* start a magic ring with 8 sc, fasten off with an invisible join to 2nd stitch [8]

Rnd 2: *{join yarn B in any st, make your first stitch a standing stitch. Work this round in BLO}* 2 hdc in all 8 st, fasten off with an invisible join to 2nd stitch [16]

Rnd 3: *{join yarn A in the 2nd hdc of any hdc increase, make your first stitch a standing stitch}* (BLO sc in next st, FLO tr in next sc of Rnd 1, skip 1 st) repeat 8 times, fasten off with an invisible join to 2nd stitch [16]

Rnd 1-9
|·············>

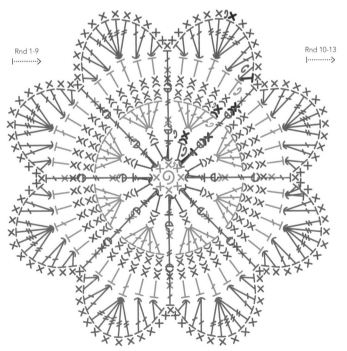

Rnd 10-13
|·············>

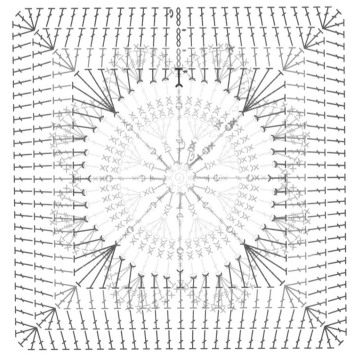

Rnd 4: *{join yarn C in any tr, make your first stitch a standing stitch. Work this round in BLO}* (sc in next st, 5 dc in next st) repeat 8 times, fasten off with an invisible join to 2nd stitch [48]

Rnd 5: *{join yarn A in any first dc of a 5-dc-group, make your first stitch a standing stitch. Work this round in BLO, except for FP stitches}* (sc in next 5 st, FPtr around tr of Rnd 3, skip 1 st) repeat 8 times, fasten off with an invisible join to 2nd stitch [48]

Rnd 6: *{join yarn B in any FPTR of Rnd 5, make your first stitch a standing stitch. Work this round in BLO}* sc in all 48 st, slst in initial sc [48]

Rnd 7: sc in same st, hdc in next 2 st, dc in next st, hdc in next 2 st, (sc in next st, hdc in next 2 st, dc in next st, hdc in next 2 st) repeat 7 times, fasten off with an invisible join to 2nd stitch [48]

Rnd 8: *{join yarn A in any hdc after a sc, make your first stitch a standing stitch. Work this round in FLO, except for FP stitches}* (2 hdc in next st, 2 dc in next st, 2 tr + dtr + 2 tr in next st, 2 dc in next st, 2 hdc in next st, FPdc around FPtr of Rnd 5, skip next st) repeat 8 times, fasten off with an invisible join to 2nd stitch [112]

Rnd 9: *{join yarn C in any st, make your first stitch a standing stitch}* sc in all 112 st, fasten off with an invisible join to 2nd stitch [112]

Rnd 10: *{join yarn A in a sc of Rnd 7 which is skipped in Rnd 8, exactly behind FPdc of Rnd 8. Make your first stitch a standing stitch. Work this round in the BLO of Rnd 7}* hdc in this sc, hdc in next 5 st, 5 hdc in next st, (hdc in next 11 st, 5 hdc in next st) repeat 3 times, hdc in next 5 st, slst in initial hdc [64]

Rnd 11: ch 3 (count as dc), dc in next 7 st, 5 dc in next st, (dc in next 15 st, 5 dc in next st) repeat 3 times, dc in next 7 st, slst in 3rd ch of initial ch 3 [80]

Rnd 12: ch 3 (count as dc), dc in next 9 st, 5 dc in next st, (dc in next 19 st, 5 dc in next st) repeat 3 times, dc in next 9 st, slst in 3rd ch of initial ch 3 [96]

Rnd 13: ch 3 (count as dc), dc in next 11 st, 5 dc in next st, (dc in next 23 st, 5 dc in next st) repeat 3 times, dc in next 11 st, fasten off with an invisible join to first true dc [112]

> *3D 8-Petal Square can be combined with Peacock Feather Puff Square on page 130 or Fairy Wheel Square on page 92 as the flowers have roughly the same size.*

MOSAIC SQUARE 80 stitch square

Madelenón (Soledad Iglesias Silva) — Argentina
🌐 www.madelenon.com 📷 @handmadelenon f madelenonface

Skill level: Intermediate
Color variation 1: Yarn A: Sunflower / Yarn B: Peach / Yarn C: Cantaloupe / Yarn D: Salmon / Yarn E: Pink Sand / Yarn F: Peony Pink / Yarn G: Girly Pink
Color variation 2: Yarn A: Sunflower / Yarn B: Cantaloupe / Yarn C: Girly Pink / Yarn D: Girly Pink / Yarn E: Sunflower / Yarn F: Canteloupe / Yarn G: Sunflower
Special stitches: 3-dc-bobble (3 double crochet bobble stitch)

This square generally turns out bigger than other 80-stitch squares in this book. You might want to use a smaller hook to make sizes match if you're planning to combine squares in a project.

INSTRUCTIONS

Rnd 1: *{start with yarn A}* start a magic ring with ch 3 (count as dc), 2 dc, ch 3, (3 dc, ch 3) repeat 3 times, fasten off with an invisible join to first true dc [12 + 12 ch]

Rnd 2: *{join yarn B in any ch-space, make your first stitch a standing stitch}* sc in ch-space, ch 1, skip 1 dc, 3-dc-bobble + ch 2 + 3-dc-bobble + ch 2 + 3-dc-bobble in next dc, skip 1 dc, (ch 1, sc in ch-space, ch 1, skip 1 dc, 3-dc-bobble + ch 2 + 3-dc-bobble + ch 2 + 3-dc-bobble in next dc, skip 1 dc) repeat 3 times, ch 1, fasten off with an invisible join to first ch after initial sc [16 + 24 ch]

Rnd 3: *{join yarn C in any ch-1-space before a sc, make your first stitch a standing stitch}* (3 hdc in ch-1-space, ch 3, skip next sc, 3 hdc in next ch-1-space, ch 2, skip next 3-dc-bobble, sc in next 3-dc-bobble, ch 2, skip next 3-dc-bobble) repeat 4 times, slst in initial hdc [28 + 28 ch]

Rnd 4: *{join yarn D in a center hdc of any first 3-hdc-group, make your first stitch a standing stitch}* 3-dc-bobble + ch 2 + 3-dc-bobble + ch 2 + 3-dc-bobble in same st, ch 1, skip next hdc, sc in next ch-space, ch 1, skip next hdc, 3-dc-bobble + ch 2 + 3-dc-bobble + ch 2 + 3-dc-bobble in next hdc, skip next hdc, sc in next sc, [skip next hdc, 3-dc-bobble + ch 2 + 3-dc-bobble + ch 2 + 3-dc-bobble in next hdc, ch 1, skip next hdc, sc in next ch-space, ch 1, skip next hdc, 3-dc-bobble + ch 2 + 3-dc-bobble + ch 2 + 3-dc-bobble in next hdc, skip next hdc, sc in next sc] repeat 3 times, fasten off with an invisible join to first ch after initial 3-dc-bobble [32 + 40 ch]

Rnd 5: *{join yarn E in a center 3-dc-bobble to the right of the Rnd 4 sc worked in a ch-space, make your first stitch a standing stitch}* (sc in center 3-dc-bobble, ch 2, skip 3-dc-bobble, 3 hdc in next ch-1-space, ch 3, skip next sc, 3 hdc in next ch-1-space, ch 2, skip next 3-dc-bobble, sc in center 3-dc-bobble, ch 2, skip next 3-dc-bobble, 3 hdc in next sc, ch 2, skip next 3-dc-bobble) repeat 4 times, fasten off with an invisible join to first ch after initial sc [44 + 44 ch]

Rnd 6: *{join yarn F in the center hdc of a 3-hdc-group before a ch-3-space, make your first stitch a standing stitch}* [3-dc-bobble + ch 2 + 3-dc-bobble + ch 2 + 3-dc-bobble in center hdc, ch 1, skip next hdc, sc in next ch-space, ch 1, skip next hdc, (3-dc-bobble + ch 2 + 3-dc-bobble + ch 2 + 3-dc-bobble in center hdc, ch 1, skip next hdc, sc in next sc, ch 1, skip next hdc) repeat 2 times] repeat 4 times, fasten off with an invisible join to first ch after initial 3-dc-bobble [48 + 72 ch]

Rnd 7: *{join yarn G in the center 3-dc-bobble before a corner, make your first stitch a standing stitch}* [2 sc in center 3-dc-bobble, skip next 3-dc-bobble, 3 dc in next ch-1-space, ch 2, skip next sc, 3 dc in next ch-1-space, (skip next 3-dc-bobble, 2 sc in the center 3-dc-bobble, skip next 3-dc-bobble, 3 dc in next sc) repeat 2 times] repeat 4 times, fasten off with an invisible join to 2nd stitch [72 + 8 ch]

AMBER SQUARE 112 stitch square

Madelenón (Soledad Iglesias Silva) — Argentina
⊕ www.madelenon.com ◎ @handmadelenon f madelenonface

Skill level: Intermediate
Colors: Yarn A: Pink Sand / Yarn B: Salmon / Yarn C: Peach
Special stitches: 4-puff (Puff stitch with 4 loops) / FPtr (Front post treble crochet)

INSTRUCTIONS

Rnd 1: *{start with yarn A}* start a magic ring with ch 2, (4-puff, ch 3) repeat 8 times, fasten off with an invisible join to first ch after puff [8 + 24 ch]

Rnd 2: *{join yarn C in any ch-space, make your first stitch a standing stitch}* (2 sc + ch 2 + 2 sc in ch-space) repeat 8 times, fasten off with an invisible join to 2nd stitch [32 + 16 ch]

Rnd 3: *{join yarn B in any ch-space, make your first stitch a standing stitch}* (3 dc + ch 1 + 3 dc in ch-space) repeat 8 times, slst in initial dc [48 + 8 ch]

Rnd 1-7
|············>

Rnd 8-10
|············>

Rnd 4: {Work 3 slst to position the loop in the ch-space of Rnd 3} ch 3 (count as hdc), 6 dc + ch 2 in same ch-space, (7 dc + ch 2 in next ch-space) repeat 7 times, fasten off with an invisible join to first true dc [56 + 16 ch]

Rnd 5: {join yarn C in any dc after a ch-space, make your first stitch a standing stitch} (sc in next 3 st, sc + ch 1 + sc in next st, sc in next 3 st, 4-puff in between sc of Rnd 2) repeat 8 times, fasten off with an invisible join to 2nd stitch [72 + 8 ch]

Rnd 6: {join yarn A in any ch-space, make your first stitch a standing stitch} (4-puff + ch 2 + 4-puff + ch 2 + 4-puff + ch 2 + 4-puff + ch 3 in ch-space) repeat 8 times, fasten off with an invisible join to first ch after initial puff [32 + 72 ch]

Rnd 7: {join yarn C in any first ch-2-space, make your first stitch a standing stitch} (3 sc in next ch-2-space, 2 sc + ch 2 + 2 sc in next ch-2-space, 3 sc in next ch-2-space, sc in next ch-3-space + FPtr around the puff of Rnd 5 + sc in the same ch-3-space) repeat 8 times, slst in initial sc [112 + 8 ch]

Rnd 8: {In this round we're going to work only 4 tips and leave the other 4 unworked} sc in same st, sc in next 4 st, sc + ch 2 + sc in next ch-2 space, sc in next 6 st, ch 9, skip FPtr and 1 tip, (sc in next sc after FPtr, sc in next 5 st, sc + ch 2 + sc in ch-2-space, sc in next 6 st, ch 9, skip FPtr and 1 tip) repeat 3 times, fasten off with an invisible join to 2nd stitch [56 + 44 ch]

Rnd 9: {join yarn B in any ch-2-space, make your first stitch a standing stitch} (sc + ch 2 + sc in ch-space, sc in next 7 st, 8 sc in next ch-9-space, sc in next 7 st) repeat 4 times, fasten off with an invisible join to first ch after initial sc [96 + 8 ch]

Rnd 10: {join yarn C in any ch-space, make your first stitch a standing stitch} (sc + ch 2 + sc in ch-space, sc in next 12 st, sc through ch-space of the unworked tip of Rnd 8 and through the next sc of Rnd 9 at the same time, sc in next 11 st) repeat 4 times, fasten off with an invisible join to first ch after initial sc [104 + 8 ch]

> *Amber is fossilized tree resin, which is appreciated for its warm yellow and red color and natural beauty. Amber is much valued from antiquity to the present as a gemstone, and the colors work up beautifully in a granny square too!*

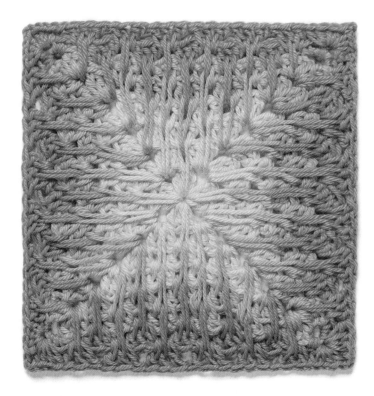

SPIKE SQUARE 112 stitch square

Madelenón (Soledad Iglesias Silva) — Argentina
🌐 www.madelenon.com 📷 @handmadelenon **f** madelenonface

Skill level: Intermediate
Color variation 1: Yarn A: Sunflower / Yarn B: Cantaloupe /
Yarn C: Pink Sand
Color variation 2: Yarn A: Lavender / Yarn B: Plum /
Yarn C: Fuchsia
Special stitches: Spike-dc (spike double crochet)

INSTRUCTIONS

Rnd 1: *{start with yarn A}* start a magic ring with ch 3 (count as dc), 2 dc, ch 2, (3 dc, ch 2) repeat 3 times, slst in 3rd ch of initial ch 3 [12 + 8 ch]

Rnd 2: *{work 3 slst more to position the loop in the next ch-space}* ch 3 (count as dc) + 2 dc + ch 2 + 3 dc in ch-space, (3 dc + ch 2 + 3 dc in next ch-space) repeat 3 times, slst in 3rd ch of initial ch 3 [24 + 8 ch]

Rnd 3: *{work 3 slst more to position the loop in next ch-space. Work the spike-dc in the center of the magic ring}* ch 3 (count as dc) + 2 dc + ch 2 + 3 dc in ch-space, (dc + spike-dc + dc in the gap between 3-dc-groups, 3 dc + ch 2 + 3 dc in next ch-space) repeat 3 times, dc + spike-dc + dc in the gap between 3-dc-groups, slst in 3rd ch of initial ch 3 [36 + 8 ch]

> *Note: In Rnd 4 to 8 we continue working the dc + spike-dc + dc in the gap between 2 groups of 3 dc. To shorten instructions, we mention "in next gap".*

Rnd 4: *{work 3 slst more to position the loop in the next ch-space. Work the spike-dc in Rnd 1}* ch 3 (count as dc) + 2 dc + ch 2 + 3 dc in same ch-space, [(dc + spike-dc + dc in next gap) repeat 2 times, 3 dc + ch 2 + 3 dc in next ch-space] repeat 3 times, (dc + spike-dc + dc in next gap) repeat 2 times, fasten off with an invisible join to first true dc [48 + 8 ch]

Rnd 5: *{join yarn B in any ch-space, make your first stitch a standing stitch. Work the spike-dc in Rnd 2}* [3 dc + ch 2 + 3 dc in ch-space (dc + spike-dc + dc in next gap) repeat 3 times] repeat 4 times, slst in initial dc [60 + 8 ch]

Rnd 6: *{work 3 slst more to position the loop in the next ch-space. Work the spike-dc in Rnd 3}* ch 3 (count as dc) + 2 dc + ch 2 + 3 dc in ch-space, [(dc + spike-dc + dc in next gap) repeat 4 times, 3 dc + ch 2 + 3 dc in next ch-space] repeat 3 times, (dc + spike-dc + dc in next gap) repeat 4 times, fasten off with an invisible join to first true dc [72 + 8 ch]

Rnd 7: {join yarn C in any ch-space, make your first stitch a standing stitch. Work the spike-dc in Rnd 4} [2 sc + ch 1 + 2 sc in ch-space, (dc + spike-dc + dc in next gap) repeat 5 times] repeat 4 times, slst in initial sc [76 + 4 ch]

Rnd 8: {work 2 slst more to position the loop in the next ch-space. Work the spike-dc in Rnd 5} ch 2 (count as hdc) + 3 hdc + ch 2 + 4 hdc in ch-space, [(dc + spike-dc + dc in next gap) repeat 6 times, 4 hdc + ch 2 + 4 hdc in next ch-space] repeat 3 times, (dc + spike-dc + dc in next gap) repeat 6 times, fasten off with an invisible join to first true hdc [104 + 8 ch]

{ *The Spike square works beautifully in an ombré color palette, moving tints and shades from light to dark or one color to the other.* }

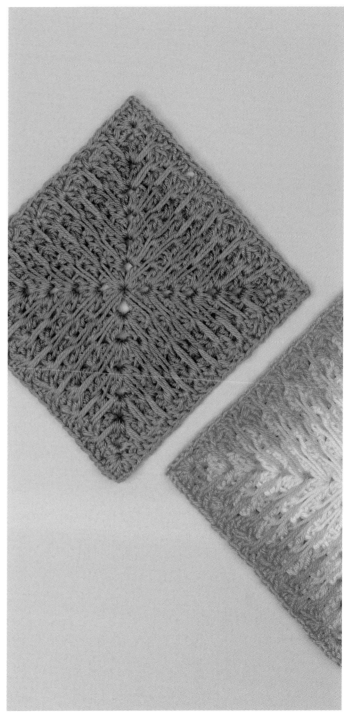

SWIRL SQUARE 80 stitch square

Madelenón (Soledad Iglesias Silva) — Argentina
🌐 www.madelenon.com 📷 @handmadelenon f madelenonface

Skill level: Intermediate
Colors: Yarn A: Cream / Yarn B: Vanilla / Yarn C: Pearl / Yarn D: Blossom / Yarn E: Old Pink / Yarn F: Peony Pink / Yarn G: Pink Sand
Special stitches: BPhdc (Back post half double crochet) / BPdc (Back post double crochet) / BPtr (Back post treble crochet)

INSTRUCTIONS

Rnd 1: {*start with yarn A*} start a magic ring with ch 3 (count as dc), 15 dc, fasten off with an invisible join to first true dc [16]

Rnd 2: {*join yarn B in any st, make your first stitch a standing stitch*} (BPsc around next st, BPhdc around next st, BPdc around next st, BPtr around next st, ch 4) repeat 4 times, fasten off with an invisible join to 2nd stitch [16 + 16 ch]

Rnd 3: {*join yarn C in any ch-space, make your first stitch a standing stitch*} (2 sc + 2 hdc in ch-space, BPdc around next 2 st, BPtr around next 2 st, ch 4) repeat 4 times, fasten off with an invisible join to 2nd stitch [32 + 16 ch]

Rnd 4: {*join yarn D in any ch-space, make your first stitch a standing stitch*} (3 sc + hdc in ch-space, BPhdc around next 2 st, BPdc around next 3 st, BPtr around next 3 st, ch 4) repeat 4 times, fasten off with an invisible join to 2nd stitch [48 + 16 ch]

Rnd 5: {*join yarn E in any ch-space, make your first stitch a standing stitch*} (4 sc in ch-space, BPhdc around next 4 st, BPdc around next 4 st, BPtr around next 4 st, ch 4) repeat 4 times, fasten off with an invisible join to 2nd stitch [64 + 16 ch]

Rnd 6: {*join yarn F in any ch-space, make your first stitch a standing stitch*} (sc in ch-space, ch 2, BPhdc around next 6 st, BPdc around next 5 st, BPtr around next 5 st, ch 2) repeat 4 times, fasten off with an invisible join to first ch after initial sc [68 + 16 ch]

Rnd 7: {*join yarn G in any first ch-space, make your first stitch a standing stitch*} (hdc in ch-space, ch 2, hdc in next ch-space, BPdc around next 16 st) repeat 4 times, fasten off with an invisible join to first ch after initial hdc [72 + 8 ch]

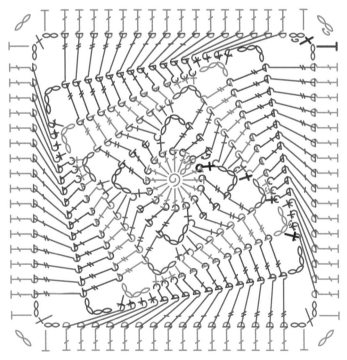

CLUSTER FLOWER SQUARE `80 stitch square`

RedAgape (Mandy O'Sullivan) — Australia
@crochetbyredagape www.redagapeblog.com redagapeblog

Skill level: Intermediate
Colors: Yarn A: Sunflower / Yarn B: Cantaloupe / Yarn C: Cream /
Yarn D: Green ice / Yarn E: Peony Pink
Special stitches: 3-dc-bobble (3 double crochet bobble stitch) /
6-tr-bobble (6 treble crochet bobble stitch) / **spike hdc** (spike half
double crochet) / dc2tog (double crochet 2 stitches together /
Changing color mid-round

INSTRUCTIONS

Rnd 1: *{start with yarn A}* ch 4, slst in initial ch to form a ring [4]

Rnd 2: ch 2 + 2-dc-bobble in the ring (count as 3-dc-bobble), ch 1,
(3-dc-bobble in the ring, ch 1) repeat 7 times, fasten off with an invisible
join to first ch after initial 2-dc-bobble [8 bobbles + 8 ch]

Rnd 3: *{join yarn B in any ch-space, make your first stitch a standing
stitch}* (3-dc-bobble + ch 1 + 3-dc-bobble + ch 1 in ch-space) repeat
8 times, fasten off with an invisible join to first ch after initial 3-dc-bobble
[16 bobbles + 16 ch]

Rnd 4: *{join yarn C in any ch-space after a 3-dc-bobble pair, make your
first stitch a standing stitch}* (slst in ch-space, ch 5, 6-tr-bobble in next
ch-space, ch 5) repeat 8 times, fasten off with an invisible join to first ch
after initial slst [8 petals]

Rnd 5: *{join yarn D in a ch-5-space after a 6-tr-bobble, make your first
stitch a standing stitch}* (hdc + dc + tr in ch-5-space, ch 3, tr + dc + hdc
in next ch-5-space, *{switch to yarn E}* ch 3, dc2tog over next 2 ch-5-spaces,
ch 3, *{switch to yarn D}*) repeat 3 times, hdc + dc + tr in ch-5-space, ch
3, tr + dc + hdc in next ch-5-space, *{switch to yarn E}* ch 3, dc2tog over
next 2 ch-5-spaces, ch 3, slst in initial hdc [28 + 36 ch] Fasten off yarn D.

Rnd 6: ch 2 (count as hdc), hdc in next 2 st, 2 dc + ch 3 + 2 dc in corner-
space (hdc in next 3 st, 3 hdc in next ch-space, spike hdc over dc2tog
from Rnd 5, 3 hdc in next ch-space, hdc in next 3 st, 2 dc + ch 3 + 2 dc
in corner space) repeat 3 times, hdc in next 3 st, 3 hdc in next ch-space,
spike hdc over dc2tog from Rnd 5, 3 hdc in next ch-space, fasten off with
an invisible join to first true hdc [68 + 12 ch]

DAISY WHEEL SQUARE `112 stitch square`

RedAgape (Mandy O'Sullivan) — Australia
@crochetbyredagape · www.redagapeblog.com **f** redagapeblog

Skill level: Intermediate
Colors: Yarn A: Golden Glow / **Yarn B:** Cream / **Yarn C:** Opaline Glass / **Yarn D:** Pastel Pink / **Yarn E:** Peony Pink
Special stitches: 5-dc-pc (5 double crochet popcorn stitch) / FPtr (Front post treble crochet) / dc2tog (double crochet 2 stitches together)

INSTRUCTIONS

Rnd 1: *{start with yarn A}* start a magic ring with 8 sc, fasten off with an invisible join to 2nd stitch [8]

Rnd 2: *{join yarn B in any st, make your first stitch a standing stitch}* (5-dc-pc + ch 1 in next st) repeat 8 times, fasten off with an invisible join to first ch after initial pc [16]

Rnd 3: *{join yarn C in any ch-space, make your first stitch a standing stitch}* 4 dc in all 8 ch-spaces, fasten off with an invisible join to 2nd stitch [32]

Rnd 4: *{join yarn D in any st, make your first stitch a standing stitch}* (dc in next st, 2 dc in next st) repeat 16 times, fasten off with an invisible join to 2nd stitch [48]

Rnd 5: *{join yarn E in any st, make your first stitch a standing stitch}* (dc + ch 1 + dc + ch 1 in next st, skip 1 st, 5-dc-pc in next st, ch 1, skip 1 st) repeat 12 times, fasten off with an invisible join to first ch after initial dc [36 + 36 ch]

Rnd 6: *{join yarn C in the ch-space between any 2 dc, make your first stitch a standing stitch}* (5-dc-pc in ch-space, ch 2, dc2tog over ch-spaces on either side of the pc from Rnd 5, ch 2) repeat 12 times, fasten off with an invisible join to first ch after initial pc [24 + 48 ch]

Rnd 7: *{join yarn B in any ch-space before a pc, make your first stitch a standing stitch}* (2 sc in ch-space + FPtr around the dc below in Rnd 5 + 2 sc in same ch-space) repeat 24 times, fasten off with an invisible join to 2nd stitch [120]

Rnd 8: *{join yarn D in any FPtr from Rnd 7, make your first stitch a standing stitch}* (slst in the top of next FPtr, ch 2, slst in between the pairs of 2 sc, ch 2) repeat 24 times, fasten off with an invisible join to first ch after initial slst [96]

Rnd 9: *{join yarn B in any ch-2-space from Rnd 8 to the right of a pc from Rnd 6, make your first stitch a standing stitch}* (2 tr + ch 2 in ch-space, 2 tr in next ch-space, 3 dc in next ch-space, 2 hdc in next ch-space, 2 sc in next 6 ch-spaces, 2 hdc in next ch-space, 3 dc in next ch-space) repeat 4 times, fasten off with an invisible join to 2nd stitch [112]

LEVANTINE SQUARE 80 stitch square

Spincushions (Shelley Husband) — Australia
⊕ www.spincushions.com ⓘ @spincushions f Spincushions

Skill level: Intermediate
Colors: Yarn A: Blue Lake / Yarn B: Turquoise / Yarn C: Opaline Glass / Yarn D: Cream
Special stitches: Crochet into the third loop

INSTRUCTIONS

Rnd 1: *{start with yarn A}* start a magic ring with ch 3 (count as dc), 15 dc, slst in 3rd ch of initial ch 3 [16]

Rnd 2: ch 3 (count as dc), 3 dc in same st, (skip 1 st, sc in third loop of next st, skip 1 st, 7 dc in next st) repeat 3 times, skip 1 st, sc in third loop of next st, skip 1 st, 3 dc in same st as first st, fasten off with an invisible join to first true dc [32]

Rnd 3: *{join yarn B to the middle dc of a 7-dc corner, make your first stitch a standing stitch}* sc in this st, (sc in third loop of next 3 st, skip 1 st, sc in third loop of next 3 st, sc + ch 2 + sc in next st) repeat 3 times, sc in third loop of next 3 st, skip 1 st, sc in third loop of next 3 st, sc in same st as initial sc, ch 1, sc in initial sc [32 + 8 ch]

Note: You start Rnd 4 and 6 by working over the joining sc. Treat the joining stitch as a chain loop and work over it, covering it entirely.

Rnd 4: ch 3 (count as dc) + dc over joining sc, (dc in next 8 st, 3 dc in ch-space) repeat 3 times, dc in next 8 st, dc in same ch-space as first 2 st, fasten off with an invisible join to first true dc [44]

Rnd 5: *{join yarn C in the middle dc of a 3-dc corner, make your first stitch a standing stitch}* sc in this st, (sc in third loop of next 10 st, sc + ch 2 + sc in next st) repeat 3 times, sc in third loop of next 10 st, sc in same st as initial sc, ch 1, sc in initial sc [48 + 8 ch]

Rnd 6: ch 3 (count as dc) + dc over joining sc, (dc in next 12 st, 3 dc in ch-space) repeat 3 times, dc in next 12 st, dc in same ch-space as first 2 st, fasten off with an invisible join to first true dc [60]

Rnd 7: *{join yarn D to the middle dc of a 3-dc corner, make your first stitch a standing stitch}* sc in this st, (sc in third loop of next 14 st, sc + ch 2 + sc in next st) repeat 3 times, sc in third loop of next 14 st, sc in same st as first st, ch 1, sc in initial sc [64 + 8 ch]

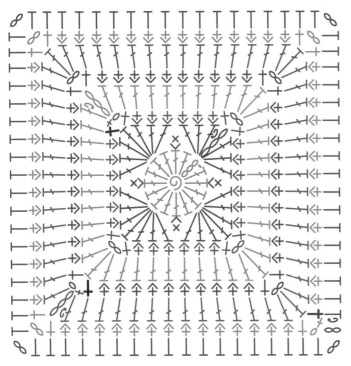

Rnd 8: ch 2 (count as hdc), (hdc in next 16 st, hdc + ch 2 + hdc in ch-space) repeat 3 times, hdc in next 16 st, hdc in same st as initial ch 2, ch 2, fasten off with an invisible join to first true hdc [72 + 8 ch]

Designer Spincushions named several of her square designs after seas and oceans of the world. The dreamy calm blues of the sea are her main color inspiration. The Levantine (eastern-most part of the Mediterranean Sea) Square looks gorgeous in her favorite turquoise-blue color scheme, but of course you can use any color combination you like.

FAIRY WHEEL SQUARE `112 stitch square`

Zipzipdreams (Edina Tekten) — Hungary / Turkey
@Zipzipdreams Zipzipdreams

Skill level: Intermediate
Colors: Yarn A: Pastel Pink / Yarn B: Girly Pink / Yarn C: Sunflower /
Yarn D: Green Ice / Yarn E: Cream / Yarn F: Plum
Special stitches: FPdc (Front post double crochet) / BPsc (Back post
single crochet) / BPhdc (Back post half double crochet)

INSTRUCTIONS

Rnd 1: *{start with yarn A}* start a magic ring with ch 3 (count as dc),
11 dc, fasten off with an invisible join to first true dc [12]

Rnd 2: *{join yarn B in any st, make your first stitch a standing stitch}*
(sc in next st, ch 5, sc in 2nd ch from hook, hdc in next 2 ch, sc in next ch,
slst in same st where you have started the ch, ch 2, skip 1 st) repeat
6 times, fasten off with an invisible join to first ch after initial sc [6 petals]

Rnd 3: *{join yarn C in any skipped st of Rnd 1, make your first stitch a
standing stitch. Keep the chains of Rnd 2 at the back side of the work}*
(sc in next st, ch 8, sc in 2nd ch from hook, hdc in next ch, dc in next 4 ch,
hdc in next ch, slst in same st where you have started the ch, ch 3 behind
the petal of Rnd 2, skip 1 st of Rnd 1) repeat 6 times, fasten off with an
invisible join to first ch after initial sc [6 petals]

Rnd 4: *{join yarn D in the top sc of any petal of round 3, make your first
stitch a standing stitch}* (sc in top sc of petal of Rnd 3, ch 4, 3 dc in top sc
of next petal of Rnd 2, ch 4) repeat 6 times, slst in initial sc [24 + 48 ch]

Rnd 5: slst in next ch-space, ch 3 (count as dc), 4 dc in same ch-space, (FPdc
around next 3 st, 5 dc in next ch-space, FPdc around next st, 5 dc in next
ch-space) repeat 5 times, 3 FPdc around next 3 st, 5 dc in next ch-space,
FPdc around next st, fasten off with an invisible join to first true dc [84]

Rnd 6: *{join yarn E from the back side around the middle FPdc of any
3 FPdc-cluster, make your first stitch a standing stitch}* (BPhdc around
next st, ch 1, skip 1 st, sc in next st, hdc in next st, dc in next 2 st, tr in
next st, 3 tr in top of the FPdc, tr in next st, dc in next 2 st, hdc in next st,
sc in next st, ch 1, skip 1 st) repeat 6 times, fasten off with an invisible join
in first ch after initial BPhdc [84 + 12 ch]

Rnd 7: *{join yarn F from the back side around a FPdc in the middle of
any petal of Rnd 5, make your first stitch a standing stitch}* (BPsc around

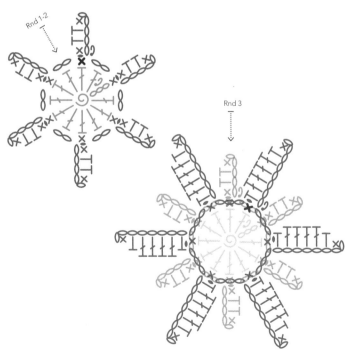

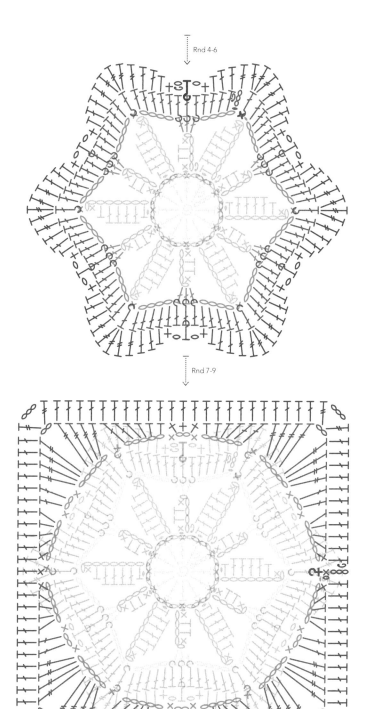

FPdc of Rnd 5, ch 5, sc in next ch-space, ch 2, sc in next ch-space, ch 5) repeat 6 times, slst in initial BPsc [18 + 72 ch]

Rnd 8: ch 1, sc in same st, sc + 4 hdc in next ch space, 2 dc in next ch-space, 4 tr + ch 2 + 4 tr in next ch-space, 2 dc + 4 hdc in next ch space, 3 sc in next ch-space, 4 hdc + 2 dc in next ch-space, 4 tr + ch 2 + 4 tr in next ch-space, 2 dc in next ch space, 4 hdc + sc in next ch-space, sc in the top of the Bpsc, sc + 4 hdc in next ch space, 2 dc in next ch-space, 4 tr + ch 2 + 4 tr in next ch-space, 2 dc + 4 hdc in next ch space, 3 sc in next ch-space, 4 hdc + 2 dc in next ch-space, 4 tr + ch 2 + 4 tr in next ch-space, 2 dc in next ch space, 4 hdc + sc in next ch-space, slst in initial sc [92 + 8 ch]

Rnd 9: ch 3 (count as dc), dc in next 11 st, tr + ch 3 + tr in next ch-space, (dc in next 23 st, tr + ch 3 + tr in next ch-space) repeat 3 times, dc in next 11 st, fasten off with an invisible join to first true dc [100 + 12 ch]

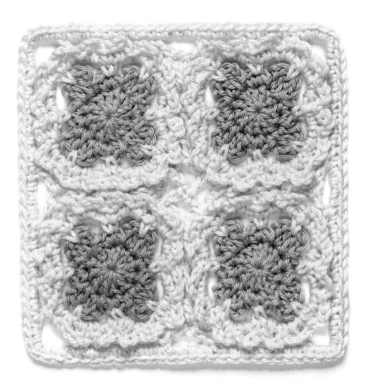

FOUR SQUARE 112 stitch square

TurtleBunny Creations (Chrissy Callahan) — United States
🏀 www.turtlebunnycreations.com 📷 @turtlebunnycreations
f TurtleBunnyCreations

Skill level: Intermediate
Colors: Yarn A: Old Pink / Yarn B: Mustard / Yarn C: Limestone /
Yarn D: Peridot / Yarn E: Cream
Special stitches: dc2tog (double crochet 2 stitches together)

INSTRUCTIONS

MOTIF (MAKE 4)

Rnd 1: *{with yarn A/B/C/D}* start a magic ring with ch 3 (count as dc),
11 dc, slst in 3rd ch of initial ch 3 [12]

Rnd 2: (ch 2, dc in same st, dc + ch 2 + slst in next st, 3 sc in next st, slst in
next st) repeat 4 times, fasten off with an invisible join to 2nd ch [20]

Rnd 3: *{join yarn E between any 2 corner dc stitches, make your first
stitch a standing stitch}* (sc between 2 corner dc stitches, ch 4, sc in 2nd sc
of 3-sc-group, ch 4) repeat 4 times, slst in initial sc [8 + 32 ch]

Rnd 4: sc in same st, ch 4, sc in ch-space, ch 4, (sc in next st, ch 4, sc in
ch-space, ch 4) repeat 7 times, fasten off with an invisible join to first ch
after initial sc [16 + 64 ch / 16 ruffles]

CENTER BRAID JOIN

*Note: All stitches are worked in Rnd 3 spaces, under and behind the
ruffles of Rnd 4. Each ch-4-space from Rnd 3 is divided into two spaces
by the sc stitches from Rnd 4, for a total of 4 spaces on each side of
each motif. Each of these divisions will be referred to as "space."*

With right sides facing up, arrange the motifs in a square. Directions (right,
left, bottom, top) will be based on this arrangement regardless of how you
turn the motifs to work. You will work Rnd 5 in a continuous cross-shaped
round, but I have divided the instructions as follows (see diagram):

Rnd 5a - right to left across top edge of motif 1 (lower left)
Rnd 5b - join left to right with bottom edge of motif 2 (top left)
Rnd 5c - bottom to top on right edge of motif 2
Rnd 5d – join top to bottom with left edge of motif 3 (top right)
Rnd 5e – left to right on bottom edge of motif 3
Rnd 5f – join right to left with top edge of motif 4 (bottom right)
Rnd 5g – top to bottom on left edge of motif 4

Rnd 5h – join bottom to top with right edge of motif 1
Rnd 5i – join center corners

Rnd 5a: {join yarn E in the farthest right space on the top edge of motif 1, make your first stitch a standing stitch} dc in this space, (ch 4, sc in next space) repeat 2 times, ch 4, dc in next space, ch 2.

Rnd 5b: dc in farthest left space on the bottom edge of motif 2, (ch 2, remove hook and pull loop through ch-4-space on motif 1, ch 2, sc in next space of motif 2) repeat 2 times, ch 2, pull loop through last ch-4-space on motif 1, ch 2, dc in last space of motif 2 [1st joined braid]

Rnd 5c: dc in next (right edge) space of motif 2, (ch 4, sc in next space) repeat 2 times, ch 4, dc in next space, ch 2.

Rnd 5d: dc in top space on left edge of motif 3, (ch 2, remove hook and pull loop through ch-4-space on motif 2, ch 2, sc in next space of motif 3) repeat 2 times, ch 2, pull loop through last ch-4-space on motif 2, ch 2, dc in last space of motif 3 [2nd joined braid]

Rnd 5e: dc in next (bottom edge) space of motif 3, (ch 4, sc in next space) repeat 2 times, ch 4, dc in next space, ch 2.

Rnd 5f: dc in right space on top edge of motif 4, (ch 2, remove hook and pull loop through ch-4-space on motif 3, ch 2, sc in next space of motif 4) repeat 2 times, ch 2, pull loop through last ch-4-space on motif 3, ch 2, dc in last space of motif 4 [3rd joined braid]

Rnd 5g: dc in next (left edge) space of motif 4, (ch 4, sc in next space) repeat 2 times, ch 4, dc in next space, ch 2.

Rnd 5h: dc in bottom space on right edge of motif 1, (ch 2, remove hook and pull loop through ch-4-space on motif 4, ch 2, sc in next space of motif 1) repeat 2 times, ch 2, pull loop through last ch-4-space on motif 4, ch 2, dc in last space of motif 1, slst in initial dc of Rnd 5a [4th joined braid]

Rnd 5i: ch 3 (count as dc), dc between corner dc stitches of motif 2 (last dc of Rnd 5b and first dc of Rnd 5c), dc between corner dc stitches of motif 3 (last dc of Rnd 5d and first dc of Rnd 5e), dc between corner dc stitches of motif 4 (last dc of Rnd 5f and first dc of Rnd 5g), fasten off with an invisible join to first true dc.

BORDER

Rnd 6: {join yarn E in the far right space of any edge, make your first stitch a standing stitch. Work in leftover spaces of Rnd 3} (dc in ch-space, ch 3, dc2tog next 2 spaces, ch 3, dc2tog next space of motif and ch-2-space of center braid, ch 4, dc2tog same ch-space of center braid and first ch-space of next motif, ch 3, dc2tog next 2 spaces, ch 3, dc in next space, ch 4) repeat 4 times, slst in initial dc [24 + 80 ch]

Rnd 7: sc in same st, (3 sc in next ch-space, sc in next st, 3 sc in next ch-space, sc in next st, 4 sc in next ch-space, sc in next st, 3 sc in next ch-space, sc in next st, 3 sc in next ch-space, sc in next st, 6 sc in next ch-space, sc in next st) repeat 3 times, 3 sc in next ch-space, sc in next st, 3 sc in next ch-space, sc in next st, 4 sc in next ch-space, sc in next st, 3 sc in next ch-space, sc in next st, 3 sc in next ch-space, sc in next st, 6 sc in next ch-space, fasten off with an invisible join to 2nd stitch [112]

Motif

Center braid join + border

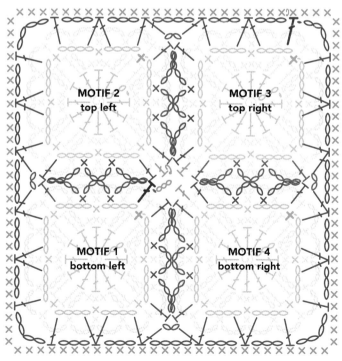

MOTIF 2
top left

MOTIF 3
top right

MOTIF 1
bottom left

MOTIF 4
bottom right

X MARKS THE SPOT SQUARE `112 stitch square`

TurtleBunny Creations (Chrissy Callahan) — United States
🌐 www.turtlebunnycreations.com 📷 @turtlebunnycreations
f TurtleBunnyCreations

Skill level: Intermediate
Colors: Yarn A: Mustard
Special stitches: FPsc (Front post single crochet) / FPdc (Front post double crochet) / FPhdc (Front post half double crochet)

INSTRUCTIONS

Rnd 1: {start with yarn A} start a magic ring with 8 sc, slst in initial sc [8]

Rnd 2: ch 5 (count as dc + ch 2) + dc in same st, 3 dc in next st, (dc + ch 2 + dc in next st, 3 dc in next st) repeat 3 times, slst in 3rd ch of initial ch 5 [20 + 8 ch]

Rnd 3: slst in next ch-space, ch 5 (count as dc + ch 2) + dc in same ch-space, skip 2 st, 5 dc in next st, skip 2 st, (dc + ch 2 + dc in next ch-space, skip 2 st, 5 dc in next st, skip 2 st) repeat 3 times, slst in 3rd ch of initial ch 5 [28 + 8 ch]

Rnd 4: slst in next ch-space, ch 5 (count as dc + ch 2) + dc in same ch-space, ch 1, FPdc around next st, ch 1, skip 2 st, 5 dc in next st, (ch 1, skip 2 st, FPdc around next st, ch 1, dc + ch 2 + dc in ch-space, ch 1, FPdc around next st, ch 1, skip 2 st, 5 dc in next st) repeat 3 times, ch 1, skip 2 st, FPdc around next st, ch 1, slst in 3rd ch of initial ch 5 [36 + 24 ch]

Rnd 5: slst in next ch-2-space, ch 5 (count as dc + ch 2) + dc in same ch-2-space, ch 1, FPdc + ch 1 around next 2 st, skip 2 st, 5 dc in next st, (ch 1, skip 2 st, FPdc + ch 1 around next 2 st, dc + ch 2 + dc in ch-2-space, ch 1, FPdc + ch 1 around next 2 st, skip 2 st, 5 dc in next) repeat 3 times, ch 1, skip 2 st, FPdc + ch 1 around next 2 st, slst in 3rd ch of initial ch 5 [44 + 32 ch]

Rnd 6: slst in next ch-2-space, ch 5 (count as dc + ch 2) + dc in same ch-2-space, ch 1, FPdc + ch 1 in next 3 st, skip 2 st, 5 dc in next st, (ch 1, skip 2 st, FPdc + ch 1 in next 3 st, dc + ch 2 + dc in ch-2-space, ch 1, FPdc + ch 1 in next 3 st, skip 2 st, 5 dc in next) repeat 3 times, ch 1, skip 2 st, FPdc + ch 1 in next 3 st, slst in 3rd ch of initial ch 5 [52 + 40 ch]

Rnd 7: (2 sc in ch-2-space, FPsc around next st, ch 1, FPhdc around next st, ch 1, FPdc around next st, ch 1, FPtr around next st, ch 1, skip 2 st, 5 dc in next st, ch 1, skip 2 st, FPtr around next st, ch 1, FPdc

around next st, ch 1, FPhdc around next st, ch 1, FPsc around next st) repeat 4 times, slst in initial sc [60 + 32 ch]

Rnd 8: sc in same st, sc in next st, FPsc around next st, sc in ch-space, FPhdc around next st, sc in ch-space, FPdc around next st, hdc in next ch-space, FPdc around next st, ch 2, skip 2 st, 5 dc in next st, ch 2, skip 2 st, FPdc around next st, hdc in next ch-space, FPdc around next st, sc in next ch-space, FPhdc around next st, sc in next ch-space, FPsc around next st, (sc in next 2 st, FPsc around next st, sc in ch-space, FPhdc around next st, sc in ch-space, FPdc around next st, hdc in next ch-space, FPdc around next st, ch 2, skip 2 st, 5 dc in next st, ch 2, skip 2 st, FPdc around next st, hdc in next ch-space, FPdc around next st, sc in next ch-space, FPhdc around next st, sc in next ch-space, FPsc around next st) repeat 3 times, slst in initial sc [84 + 16 ch]

Rnd 9: sc in same st, sc in next 8 st, (2 sc in ch-2-space, sc in next st, 2 sc in next 3 st, sc in next st, 2 sc in next ch-2-space, sc in next 16 st) repeat 3 times, 2 sc in next ch-2-space, sc in next st, 2 sc in next 3 st, sc in next st, 2 sc in next ch-2-space, sc in next 7 st, fasten off with an invisible join to 2nd stitch [112]

> *X Marks The Spot Square* makes a fun combination with *Rainbow Puff Square* on page 52, as both have the x-shape. Or try combining it with *Daisy Wheel Square* on page 88.

LAUREN ROSE SQUARE `112 stitch square`

A Yarn of Serendipity (Pam Knighton-Haener) — USA
Ⓟ PKnightonHaener ⊕ www.pknightonhaener.wordpress.com
f A Yarn of Serendipity

Skill level: Intermediate
Colors: Yarn A: Raspberry / Yarn B: Ecru / Yarn C: Antique Pink /
Yarn D: Graphite / Yarn E: Olive / Yarn F: Cream / Yarn G: Old Pink
Special stitches: BPsc (Back post single crochet) / FPsc2tog (Front post
single crochet 2 together) / FPdc (Front post double crochet)

INSTRUCTIONS

Rnd 1: *{start with yarn A}* start a magic ring with ch 4 (count as dc + ch 1),
dc, ch 2, (dc, ch 1, dc, ch 2) repeat 3 times, fasten off with an invisible join
to 4th ch of initial ch 4 [8 + 12 ch]

Rnd 2: *{join yarn B in any ch-2-space, make your first stitch a standing
stitch}* (2 dc + ch 3 + 2 dc in ch-2-space, skip 1 dc, 2 dc in next ch-1-space,
skip 1 dc) repeat 4 times, fasten off with an invisible join to 2nd stitch
[24 + 12 ch]

Rnd 3: *{join yarn C in any ch-3-space, make your first stitch a standing
stitch}* (6 dc + ch 2 + 6 dc in ch-3-space, skip 2 dc, FPsc2tog around the
top of next 2 dc, skip 2 dc) repeat 4 times, fasten off with an invisible join
to 2nd stitch [52 + 8 ch]
Use a surface slst to embellish the petals in Rnd 3. On the wrong side
of your work, use Yarn B and work around the dc stitches, skipping the
FPsc2tog.

Rnd 4: *{join yarn D around the top of any FPsc2tog. Make your first
stitch a standing stitch. Work the stitches around the petal in BLO}*
(FPdc around top of FPsc2tog, dc in next st, hdc in next 2 st, sc in next
3 st, ch 2, skip corner-space, sc in next 3 st, hdc in next 2 st, dc in next st)
repeat 4 times, fasten off with an invisible join to 2nd stitch [52 + 8 ch]

Rnd 5: *{join yarn E in any corner-space, make your first stitch a standing
stitch}* [2 dc + ch 2 + 2 dc + ch 1 in corner-space, skip 2 st, (dc + ch 1 +
dc + ch 1 in next st, skip 3 st) repeat 2 times, dc + ch 1 + dc + ch 1 in
next st, skip 2 st] repeat 4 times, fasten off with an invisible join to 2nd
stitch [40 + 36 ch]

Rnd 6: *{join yarn F in any corner-space, make your first stitch a standing
stitch}* (sc + ch 2 + sc in corner-space, sc in next 2 st, hdc in next ch-1-
space, skip 1 st, 2 dc in next ch-1-space, skip 1 st, 2 tr in next ch-1-space,

Rnd 1-7
|··········>

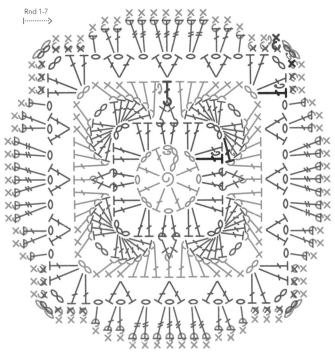

skip 1 st, 3 tr in next ch-1-space, skip 1 st, 2 tr in next ch-1-space, skip 1 st, 2 dc in next ch-1-space, skip 1 st, hdc in next ch-1-space, sc in next 2 st) repeat 4 times, fasten off with an invisible join to first ch after initial sc [76 + 8 ch]

Rnd 7: *{join yarn G in the first sc after ch-2-space, make your first stitch a standing stitch}* (BPsc around next 19 st, ch 2 behind ch 2 corner space from Rnd 6) repeat 4 times, ch 2, fasten off with an invisible join to 2nd stitch [76 + 8 ch]

Rnd 8: *{join yarn A in the second BPsc of any side, make your first stitch a standing stitch}* (BPsc around next 18 BPsc, ch 1, 5 dc in corner-space, ch 1, BPsc around next BPsc) repeat 4 times, fasten off with an invisible join to 2nd stitch [96 + 8 ch]

Rnd 9: *{join yarn F in the first BPsc of any side, make your first stitch a standing stitch}* (dc in next 4 st, hdc in next 3 st, sc in next 5 st, hdc in next 3 st, dc in next 4 st, skip next ch-space, BLO hdc in next 2 st, BLO dc + ch 1 + BLO dc + ch 1 + BLO dc in next st, BLO hdc in next 2 st, skip next ch-1-space) repeat 4 times, fasten off with an invisible join to 2nd stitch [104 + 8 ch]

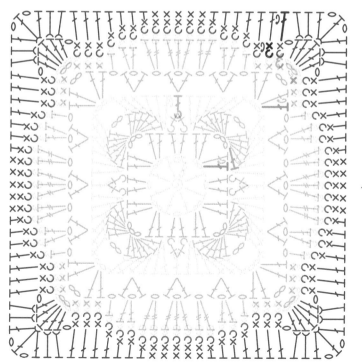

Rnd 8-9
<-------------|

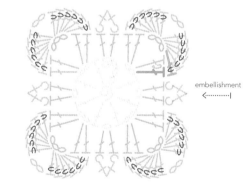

embellishment
<-------------|

ANTIQUITY SQUARE 112 stitch square

TurtleBunny Creations (Chrissy Callahan) — United States
🔗 www.turtlebunnycreations.com 📷 @turtlebunnycreations
f TurtleBunnyCreations

Skill level: Intermediate
Colors: Yarn A: Old Pink / Yarn B: Limestone / Yarn C: Cream
Special stitches: 2-dc-bobble (2 double crochet bobble stitch) /
3-dc-bobble (3 double crochet bobble stitch) / Work in third loop /
Surface slst (surface slip stitch)

This square generally turns out bigger than other 112-stitch squares
in this book. You might want to change the hook size to make sizes
match if you're planning to combine squares in a project.

INSTRUCTIONS

*Note: To maintain the proper look of the rounds worked in the third
loop, we use an invisible join on the previous round and re-attach the
yarn for the third loop only round, even if not changing colors.*

Rnd 1: {start with yarn A} start a magic ring with 8 sc, slst in initial sc [8]

Rnd 2: ch 3 + 2-dc-bobble in same st (count as 3-dc-bobble), 3-dc-bobble
in next st, ch 2, (3-dc-bobble in next 2 st, ch 2) repeat 3 times, slst in initial
3-dc-bobble [8 bobbles + 8 ch]

Rnd 3: ch 3 + 2-dc-bobble in same st (count as 3-dc-bobble), ch 1,
(3-dc-bobble in next st, ch 1, 3-dc-bobble + ch 2 + 3-dc-bobble in
corner-space, ch 1, 3-dc-bobble in next st, ch 1) repeat 3 times,
3-dc-bobble in next st, ch 1, 3-dc-bobble + ch 2 + 3-dc-bobble in
corner-space, ch 1, slst in initial 3-dc-bobble [16 bobbles + 20 ch]

Rnd 4: (3 sc in next ch-space, 2 sc in next ch-space, 3 sc in corner-space,
2 sc in next ch-space) repeat 4 times, fasten off with an invisible join to 2nd
stitch [40]

Rnd 5: {join yarn B in the third loop of the first st of a 3-sc-corner, make
your first stitch a standing stitch. Work all stitches in this round in the
third loop} (2 sc in next st, sc + ch 2 + sc in next st, 2 sc in next st, sc in
next 7 st) repeat 4 times, slst in initial sc [52 + 8 ch]

Rnd 6: slst in next st, ch 3 + 2-dc-bobble in same st (count as 3-dc-bobble),
[ch 1, skip 1 st, 3-dc-bobble + ch 2 + 3-dc-bobble in corner-space,
(ch 1, skip 1 st, 3-dc-bobble in next st) repeat 6 times] repeat 3 times,
ch 1, skip 1 st, 3-dc-bobble + ch 2 + 3-dc-bobble in corner-space,
(ch 1, skip 1 st, 3-dc-bobble in next st) repeat 5 times, ch 1, skip 1 st,

slst in initial 3-dc-bobble [32 bobbles + 36 ch]

Rnd 7: (2 sc in next ch-space, 3 sc in corner-space, 2 sc in next 3 ch-spaces, 3 sc in next ch-space, 2 sc in next 2 ch-spaces) repeat 4 times, fasten off with an invisible join to 2nd stitch [72]

Rnd 8: {*join yarn C in the third loop of the first st of a 3-sc-corner, make your first stitch a standing stitch. Work all stitches in this round in the third loop*} (2 sc in next st, sc + ch 2 + sc in next st, 2 sc in next st, sc in next 15 st) repeat 4 times, slst in initial sc [84 + 8 ch]

Rnd 9: slst in next st, ch 3 + 2-dc-bobble in same st (count as 3-dc-bobble), [ch 1, skip 1 st, 3-dc-bobble + ch 2 + 3-dc-bobble in corner-space, (ch 1 + skip 1 st + 3-dc-bobble in next st) repeat 10 times] repeat 3 times, ch 1, skip 1 st, 3-dc-bobble + ch 2 + 3-dc-bobble in corner-space, (ch 1 + skip 1 st + 3-dc-bobble in next st) repeat 9 times, ch 1, skip 1 st, slst in initial 3-dc-bobble [48 bobbles + 52 ch]

Rnd 10: (2 sc in next ch-space, 3 sc in corner-space, 2 sc in next 10 ch-spaces) repeat 4 times, fasten off with an invisible join to 2nd stitch [100]

Rnd 11: {*join yarn C in the third loop of the first st of a 3-sc-corner, make your first stitch a standing stitch. Work all stitches in this round in the third loop*} (2 hdc in next 3 st, hdc in next 22 st) repeat 4 times, fasten off with an invisible join to 2nd stitch [112]

OVERLAY CROCHET (not shown in diagram)

Rnd 5a: {*with yarn C*} work 48 surface slst over Rnd 5 above Rnd 4 [48]
Rnd 8a: {*with yarn A*} work 80 surface slst over Rnd 8 above Rnd 7 [80]
Rnd 11a: {*with yarn B*} work 108 surface slst over Rnd 11 above Rnd 10 [108]

EMBROIDERY

Embroider a flower detail in the center of your square, using the Woven Wheel Stitch and Detached Chain Stitch, as described below. When working your embroidery, pay attention to the back of your square. Consider hiding the yarn by weaving it into the crochet fabric, work the stitches as neatly and close together as possible.

Woven Wheel Stitch: Stitch 5 straight "spokes" to form a star shape where you would like to place your rose. Bring your needle through the fabric from back to front near the center of your star, and weave the yarn around the circle alternating over and under the spokes until the circle is filled in. Weave over the final spoke and insert needle from front to back just past the spoke. Fasten off and weave in the yarn end.

Detached Chain Stitch: Bring your needle through the fabric from back to front at the point of your first leaf. Insert the needle from front to back through the same hole and pull through until there is a small loop on front

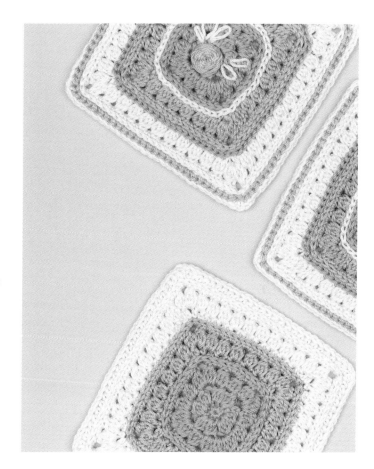

of the fabric. Bring the needle up from the back where you would like the center of the round part of your leaf, bringing it up through the loop as you draw it through the fabric. Insert the needle back down through the same hole to tack the loop in place. Repeat for as many leaves as desired.

Try different colors for the embroidered elements... or combine elements with embroidery with basic unembroidered squares as seen in the picture on this page!

SUNLOVER SQUARE `112 stitch square`

RedAgape (Mandy O'Sullivan) — Australia
@crochetbyredagape ⊛ www.redagapeblog.com f redagapeblog

Skill level: Intermediate
Colors: Yarn A: Sunflower / Yarn B: Peach / Yarn C: Peony Pink
Special stitches: 5-dc-pc (5 double crochet popcorn stitch)

INSTRUCTIONS

Rnd 1: {start with yarn A} start a magic ring with ch 3 (count as dc) + 4 dc, form first pc, ch 1, (5-dc-pc + ch 1) repeat 5 times, slst in initial pc [12]

Rnd 2: slst in next ch-space, 5-dc-pc + ch 2 + 5-dc-pc + ch 2 in same ch-space, (5-dc-pc + ch 2 + 5-dc-pc + ch 2 in next ch-space) repeat 5 times, slst in initial pc [36]

Rnd 3: 3 sc in all 12 ch-spaces, fasten off with an invisible join to 2nd stitch [36]

Rnd 4: {join yarn B in any first sc, make your first stitch a standing stitch} (slst in next st, ch 5, skip 2 st) repeat 12 times, slst in initial slst [36]

Rnd 5: {work in front of the ch in Rnd 4} (slst + ch 4 + 2 tr + ch 2 in next empty sc of Rnd 3, 2 tr + ch 4 + slst in next empty sc of Rnd 3) repeat 12 times, slst in initial slst [12 Petals]

Rnd 6: {work in the stitches of Rnd 4} (slst in ch-space at rear of square, ch 4 + 4 tr + ch 2 + 4 tr + ch 4 in same ch-space) repeat 12 times, slst in initial slst [12 petals]

Rnd 7: (ch 5, slst in space between petals) repeat 12 times [12 + 60 ch]

Rnd 8: slst in next ch-space, ch 4 (count as tr) + 2 tr + ch 3 + 3 tr in same ch-space, 3 tr in next 2 ch-spaces, (3 tr + ch 3 + 3 tr in next ch-space, 3 tr in next 2 ch-spaces) repeat 3 times, fasten off with an invisible join to first true tr [60]

Rnd 9: {join yarn C in any corner-space, make your first stitch a standing stitch} (2 dc + ch 3 + 2 dc in corner-space, dc in next 12 st) repeat 4 times, slst in initial dc [76]

Rnd 10: slst in next st, slst in next ch-space, ch 3 (count as dc) + dc + ch 3 + 2 dc in same ch-space, dc in next 16 st, (2 dc + ch 3 + 2 dc in next ch-space, dc in next 16 st) repeat 3 times, fasten off with an invisible join to first true dc [92]

Rnd 11: {join yarn A in any corner-space, make your first stitch a standing stitch} (3 sc + ch 2 + 3 sc in corner-space, sc in next 20 st) repeat 4 times, fasten off with an invisible join to 2nd stitch [112]

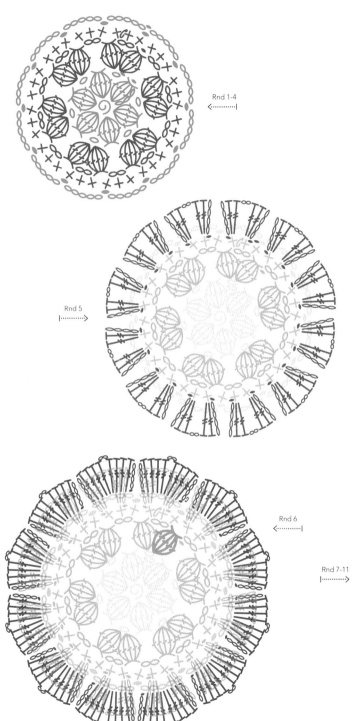

Rnd 1-4

Rnd 5

Rnd 6

Rnd 7-11

ROMANCE SQUARE `112 stitch square`

TurtleBunny Creations (Chrissy Callahan) — United States
🌐 www.turtlebunnycreations.com 📷 @turtlebunnycreations
f TurtleBunnyCreations

Skill level: Intermediate
Colors: Yarn A: Cream / Yarn B: Graphite
Special stitches: FPhdc2tog (Front post half double crochet 2 stitches together) / FPsc (Front post single crochet) / FPdc (Front post double crochet)

INSTRUCTIONS

Note: Do not work chain spaces too tight as this may cause the square to curl.

Rnd 1: *{start with yarn A}* start a magic ring with 9 sc, slst in initial sc [9]

Rnd 2: ch 3 (count as dc), FPdc around same stitch, (dc in next st, FPdc around same stitch) repeat 8 times, slst in 3rd ch of initial ch 3 [18]

Rnd 3: (2 sc in next FPdc, FPhdc2tog over same FPdc and next dc) repeat 9 times, slst in initial sc [27]

Rnd 4: sc in same st, sc in next st, (2 sc in FPhdc2tog, sc in next 2 st) repeat 8 times, 2 sc in next st, slst in initial sc [36]

Rnd 5: ch 5 (count as dc + ch 2) + dc in same st, ch 1, skip 2 st, (dc + ch 2 + dc in next st, ch 1, skip 2 st) repeat 11 times, slst in 3rd ch of initial ch 5 [24 + 36 ch]

Rnd 6: (3 sc in next ch-2-space, FPsc around next 2 dc) repeat 12 times, fasten off with an invisible join to 2nd stitch [60]

Rnd 7: *{Working behind Rnd 6, join yarn B in any skipped ch-1-space of Rnd 5. Make your first stitch a standing stitch. Work all stitches in skipped ch-1-spaces of Rnd 5}* (3 sc in ch-1-space, ch 1) repeat 12 times, slst in initial sc [36 + 12 ch]

Rnd 8: ch 4 (count as dc + ch 1), (dc + ch 2 + dc + ch 1 in next ch-space) repeat 11 times, dc in next ch-space, ch 2, slst in 3rd ch of initial ch 4 [24 + 36 ch]

Rnd 9: FPsc around starting ch-3 of Rnd 8, FPsc around next dc, 4 sc in ch-2-space, (FPsc around next 2 dc, 4 sc in ch-2-space) repeat 11 times, fasten off with an invisible join to 2nd stitch [72]

Rnd 1-6

Rnd 10: {Working behind Rnd 9, join yarn A in any skipped ch-1-space of Rnd 8. Make your first stitch a standing stitch. Working all stitches in skipped ch-1-spaces of Rnd 8} (5 dc in ch-1-space, ch 2, 5 dc + ch 1 in next 2 ch-1-spaces) repeat 4 times, slst in initial dc [60 + 16 ch]

Rnd 11: ch 4 (count as dc + ch 1), dc + ch 2 + dc + ch 2 + dc + ch 2 + dc in ch-2-corner-space, ch 1, (dc + ch 2 + dc + ch 1 in next 2 ch-spaces, dc + ch 2 + dc + ch 2 + dc + ch 2 + dc in corner-space, ch 1) repeat 3 times, dc + ch 2 + dc + ch 1 in next ch-space, dc in next ch-space, ch 2, slst in 3rd ch of initial ch 4 [32 + 36 ch]

Rnd 12: FPhdc around starting ch-3 from Rnd 11, FPhdc around next dc, 5 sc in ch-2-space, FPsc around next dc, 2 sc in ch-2-corner-space, FPsc around next dc, 5 sc in ch-2-space, FPhdc around next 2 dc, 5 sc in ch-2-space, FPhdc around next 2 dc, 5 sc in next ch-2-space (FPhdc around next 2 dc, 5 sc in ch-space, FPsc around next dc, 2 sc in ch-2-corner-space, FPsc around next dc, 5 sc in ch-2-space, FPhdc around next 2 dc, 5 sc in ch-2-space, FPhdc around next 2 dc, 5 sc in next ch-2-space) repeat 3 times, fasten off with an invisible join to 2nd FPhdc [120]

Rnd 13: {Working behind Rnd 12, join yarn B in any farthest right skipped ch-1-space of Rnd 11. Make your first stitch a standing stitch. Work all stitches in skipped ch-1-spaces of Rnd 11} (2 sc + ch 4 in next 3 ch-1-spaces, sc + ch 4 + sc in ch-2-corner space (beside stitches of Rnd 12), ch 4) repeat 4 times, slst in initial sc [32 + 80 ch]

Rnd 14: sc in same st, sc in next st, (4 sc in next ch-4-space, sc in next 2 st) repeat 2 times, (4 sc in next ch-4-space, sc in next st) repeat 2-times [(4 sc in next ch-4-space, sc in next 2 st) repeat 3 times, (4 sc in next ch-4-space, sc in next st) repeat 2 times] repeat 3 times, 4 sc in next ch-4 space, fasten off with an invisible join to 2nd stitch [112]

{ *Romance squares works up beautifully in two colors, but it can be made with up to five colors for a totally different effect!* }

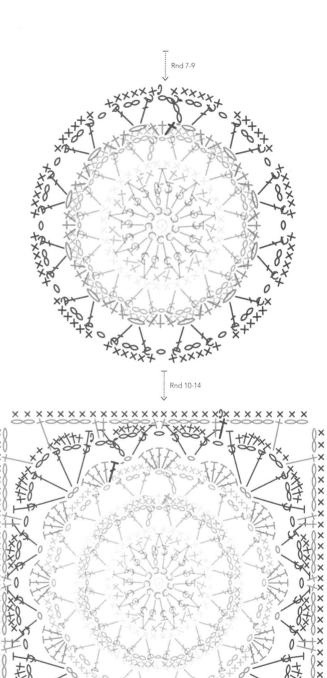

Rnd 7-9

Rnd 10-14

LEMONS AND LIMES SQUARE `112 stitch square`

A Yarn of Serendipity (Pam Knighton-Haener) — USA
PKnightonHaener ⊕ www.pknightonhaener.wordpress.com
f A Yarn of Serendipity

Skill level: Beginner to Intermediate
Colors: Yarn A: Golden Glow / Yarn B: Peridot
Special stitches: FPsc (Front post single crochet) / FPsc2tog (Front post single crochet 2 together) / Dc5tog (Double crochet 5 together)

INSTRUCTIONS

Rnd 1: *{start with yarn A}* start a magic ring with ch 5 (count as dc + ch 2), (dc, ch 2) repeat 3 times, invisible join to 4th ch of initial ch 5 [4 + 8 ch]

Rnd 2: *{join yarn A in any ch-2-space, make your first stitch a standing stitch}* (2 dc + ch 2 + 2 dc in ch-2-space, dc in next st) repeat 4 times, fasten off with an invisible join to 2nd stitch [20 + 8 ch]

Rnd 3: *{join yarn B in any ch-2-corner-space, make your first stitch a standing stitch}* (2 tr + ch 2 + 2 tr in ch-2- corner-space, dc in next 5 st) repeat 4 times, slst in initial tr [36 + 8 ch]

Rnd 4: slst in next tr, slst in corner-space, ch 3 (count as dc) + dc + ch 2 + 2 dc in ch-2-corner-space, ch 3, skip 2 st, dc in next 5 st, ch 3, skip 2 st, (2 dc + ch 2 + 2 dc in corner-space, ch 3, skip 2 st, dc in next 5 st, ch 3, skip 2 st) repeat 3 times, fasten off with an invisible join to first true dc [36 + 20 ch]

Rnd 5: *{join yarn A in any ch-2-corner-space, make your first stitch a standing stitch}* (sc + ch 2 + sc in ch-2-corner-space, sc in next 2 dc, 3 hdc in next ch-3-space, ch 1, FPsc2tog around next 2 dc, FPsc around next dc, FPsc2tog around next 2 dc, ch 1, 3 hdc in next ch-3-space, sc in next 2 st) repeat 4 times, fasten off with an invisible join to first ch after initial sc [60 + 16 ch]

Rnd 6: *{join yarn B in any ch-2-corner-space, make your first stitch a standing stitch}* (2 dc + ch 2 + 2 dc in ch-2-corner-space, BLO dc in next 6 st, ch 2, dc5tog next 5 dc stitches from Rnd 4, ch 2, BLO dc in next 6 st) repeat 4 times, fasten off with an invisible join to 2nd stitch [68 + 24 ch]

Rnd 7: *{join yarn A in any ch-2-corner-space, make your first stitch a standing stitch}* (2 dc + ch 2 + 2 dc in ch-2-corner-space, hdc in next 8 st, 2 hdc in next ch-space, dc in next st, 2 hdc in next ch-space, hdc in next 8 st) repeat 4 times, slst in initial dc [100 + 8 ch]

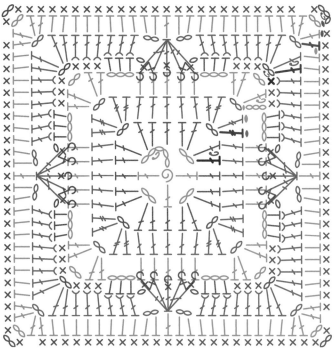

Rnd 8: slst in next dc, slst in corner-space, ch 3 (count as sc + ch 2) + sc in ch-2-corner-space, skip next st, sc in next 24 st, (sc + ch 2 + sc in ch-2-corner-space, skip next st, sc in next 24 st) repeat 3 times, fasten off with an invisible join to 2nd ch [104 + 8 ch]

Don't let this square's name withhold you from trying different colors. It's beautiful in any two colors combined!

RAINBOW BLOSSOM SQUARE `112 stitch square`

Crafty CC (Celine Semaan) — Australia
@crafty_cc ⊛ www.craftycc.com

Skill level: Intermediate
Colors: Yarn A: Plum / Yarn B: Cream / Yarn C: Opaline Glass /
Yarn D: Pistachio / Yarn E: Sunflower / Yarn F: Papaya /
Yarn G: Girly Pink
Special stitches: 5-dc-bobble (5 double crochet bobble), **work in
third loop**

INSTRUCTIONS

Rnd 1: *{start with yarn A}* start a magic ring with ch 3 (count as dc),
11 dc, fasten off with an invisible join [12] Turn to WS.

Rnd 2: *{join yarn B in any st, make your first stitch a standing stitch}*
(5-dc-bobble, ch 3, skip 1 st) repeat 6 times, fasten off with an invisible
join [6 bobbles + 18 ch] Turn to RS.

Rnd 3: *{join yarn C in any skipped st from Rnd 2, make your first stitch
a standing stitch}* (3 hdc in skipped st, sc in 5-dc-bobble) repeat 6 times,
slst in initial hdc [24]

Rnd 4: (slst in next st, skip 1 st, 7 hdc in next st, skip 1 st) repeat 6 times,
fasten off with an invisible join to first hdc [42]

Rnd 5: *{join yarn D in any slst from Rnd 4, make your first stitch a standing stitch}* (7 hdc in slst, ch 4) repeat 6 times, fasten off with an invisible
join to 2nd hdc [42 + 24 ch]

Rnd 6: *{join yarn E in third loop of 4th hdc in any 7-hdc-group from Rnd 4,
make your first stitch a standing stitch. Work in stitches from Rnd 4. Work
over chains from Rnd 5}* (7 hdc in third loop of 4th hdc of 7-hdc-group, ch
5) repeat 6 times, fasten off with an invisible join to 2nd hdc [42 + 30 ch]

Rnd 7: *{join yarn F in third loop of 4th hdc in any 7-hdc-group from Rnd 5,
make your first stitch a standing stitch. Work in stitches from Rnd 5. Work
over chains from Rnd 6}* (7 hdc in third loop of 4th hdc of 7-hdc-group,
ch 5) repeat 6 times, fasten off with an invisible join to 2nd hdc [42 + 30 ch]

Rnd 8: *{join yarn G in third loop of 4th hdc in any 7-hdc-group from Rnd 6,
make your first stitch a standing stitch. Work in stitches from Rnd 6. Work
over chains from Rnd 7}* (7 hdc in third loop of 4th hdc of 7-hdc-group, ch 5)
repeat 6 times, fasten off with an invisible join to 2nd hdc [42 + 30 ch]

Rnd 1-9
|··········>

Rnd 9: *{Join yarn B in the third loop of 4th hdc in any 7-hdc-group from Rnd 8, make your first stitch a standing stitch. Work over chains from Rnd 8}* (slst in third loop of 4th hdc of next 7-hdc-group from Rnd 8, ch 6, slst in third loop of 4th hdc of next 7-hdc-group from Rnd 7, ch 6) repeat 6 times, slst in initial slst [12 + 72 ch]

Rnd 10: slst in next ch-space, ch 4 (count as tr), 3 tr + ch 2 + 4 tr in same ch-space, 5 dc in next ch-space, ch 1, 5 dc in next ch space, (4 tr + ch 2 + 4 tr in next ch-space, 5 dc in next ch-space, ch 1, 5 dc in next ch-space) repeat 3 times, slst in 4th ch of initial ch 4 [72 + 12 ch]

Rnd 11: slst in next 3 st, slst in next ch-space, ch 2 (count as hdc), hdc + ch 2 + 2 hdc in same ch-space, hdc in next 9 hdc, hdc in next ch-space, hdc in next 9 hdc, (2 hdc + ch 2 + 2 hdc in next ch-space, hdc in next 9 hdc, hdc in next ch-space, hdc in next 9 hdc) repeat 3 times, slst in 2nd ch of initial ch 2 [92+ 8 ch]

Rnd 12: slst in next st, slst in next ch-space, ch 2 (count as hdc), hdc + ch 1 + 2 hdc in same ch-space, hdc in next 23 st, (2 hdc + ch 1 + 2 hdc in next ch-space, hdc in next 23 st) repeat 3 times, fasten off with an invisible join to first true hdc [108 + 4 ch]

Rnd 10-12

RING AROUND THE ROSY SQUARE `112 stitch square`

TurtleBunny Creations (Chrissy Callahan) — United States

🏀 www.turtlebunnycreations.com 📷 @turtlebunnycreations
ƒ TurtleBunnyCreations

<u>Skill level:</u> Intermediate
<u>Colors:</u> Yarn A: Graphite / Yarn B: Cream /Yarn C: Silver
<u>Special stitches:</u> **Spike-dc** (Spike double crochet) / **Spike-sc** (Spike single crochet)
<u>Pattern-specific special stitch:</u> Standing-spike-dc: working over the st in the previous round, with your slip knot on the hook, yarn over and insert into designated stitch or space, (holding the tail tight against the hook to avoid twisting and loosening) yarn over and draw through, pull up to the height of the current round, yarn over and draw through two loops, yarn over and draw through remaining two loops on the hook to complete the dc.

INSTRUCTIONS

Rnd 1: *{start with yarn A}* start a magic ring with ch 3 (count as dc), 2 dc, ch 2, (3 dc + ch 2) repeat 3 times, slst in 3rd ch of initial ch 3 [12 + 8 ch]

Rnd 2: sc in same st, sc in next 2 st, 4 sc in ch-space, (sc in next 3 st, 4 sc in ch-space) repeat 3 times, fasten off with an invisible join to 2nd stitch [28]

Rnd 3: *{join yarn B, working over Rnd 2, in any ch-space below a 4-sc-corner. Make your first stitch a standing stitch. Work all stitches over the sc from Rnd 2, into the spaces created in Rnd 1}* (3 spike-dc + ch 2 + 3 spike-dc in ch-space below a 4-sc-corner, ch 1) repeat 4 times, slst in initial spike-dc [24 + 12 ch]

Rnd 4: sc in same st, sc in next 2 st, 4 sc in next ch-space, sc in next 3 st, sc in next ch-space, (sc in next 3 st, 4 sc in next ch-space, sc in next 3 st, sc in next ch-space) repeat 3 times, fasten off with an invisible join to 2nd stitch [44]

Rnd 5: *{join yarn A, working over Rnd 4, in any ch-space below a 4-sc-corner. Make your first stitch a standing stitch. Work all stitches over the sc from Rnd 4, into the spaces created in Rnd 3}* (3 spike-dc + ch 2 + 3 spike-dc in ch-space below a 4-sc-corner, ch 1, 3 spike-dc in next ch-space, ch 1) repeat 4 times, slst in initial spike-dc [36 + 16 ch]

Rnd 6: sc in same st, sc in next 2 st, 4 sc in next ch-space, sc in next 3 st, sc in next ch-space, sc in next 3 st, sc in next ch-space, (sc in next 3 st, 4 sc in next ch-space, sc in next 3 st, sc in next ch-space, sc in next 3 st, sc in next ch-space) repeat 3 times, fasten off with an invisible join to 2nd stitch [60]

Rnd 7: *{join yarn C, working over Rnd 6, in any ch-space below a 4-sc-corner. Make your first stitch a standing stitch. Work all stitches over the sc from Rnd 6, into the spaces created in Rnd 5}* (3 spike-dc + ch 2 + 3 spike-dc in ch-space below a 4-sc-corner, ch 1, spike-dc in next ch-space, ch 5, spike-dc in next ch-space, ch 1) repeat 4 times, slst in initial spike-dc [32 + 36 ch]

Rnd 8: sc in same st, sc in next 2 st, 4 sc in next ch-space, sc in next 3 st, sc in next ch-space, sc in next st, 2 sc in next ch-space + spike-sc into center st of 3-dc-group in Rnd 5 + 2 sc in same ch-space, sc in next st, sc in next ch-space, (sc in next 3 st, 4 sc in next ch-space, sc in next 3 st, sc in next ch-space, sc in next st, 2 sc in next ch-space + spike-sc into center st of Rnd 5 + 2 sc in same ch-space, sc in next st, sc in next ch-space) repeat 3 times, fasten off with an invisible join to 2nd stitch [76]

Rnd 9: *{join yarn B, working over Rnd 8, in any ch-space below a 4-sc-corner. Make your first stitch a standing stitch. Work all stitches over the sc from Rnd 8, into the ch-spaces created in Rnd 7}* (3 spike-dc + ch 2 + 3 spike-dc in next ch-space below a 4-sc-corner, ch 1, spike-dc in next ch-space, ch 1, 3 spike-dc in next ch-space, ch 1, 3 spike-dc in next ch-space, ch 1, spike-dc in next ch-space, ch 1) repeat 4 times, slst in initial spike-dc [56 + 28 ch]

Rnd 10: sc in same st, sc in next 2 st, 4 sc in ch-2-space, sc in next 3 st, sc in next ch-space, sc in next st, sc in next ch-space, sc in next 3 st, sc in next ch-space, sc in next 3 st, sc in next ch-space, sc in next st, sc in next ch-space (sc in next 3 st, 4 sc in ch-2-space, sc in next 3 st, sc in next ch-space, sc in next st, sc in next ch-space, sc in next 3 st, sc in next ch-space, sc in next 3 st, sc in next ch-space, sc in next st, sc in next ch-space) repeat 3 times, fasten off with an invisible join to 2nd stitch [92]

Rnd 11: *{join yarn A, working over Rnd 10, in any ch-space below a 4-sc-corner. Make your first stitch a standing stitch. Work all stitches over the sc from Rnd 10, into the spaces created in Rnd 9}* (3 spike-sc + ch 3 + 3 spike-sc in ch-space below a 4-sc-corner, ch 2, spike-sc in next ch-space, ch 1, spike-sc in next ch-space, ch 2, 3 spike-sc in next ch-space, ch 2, spike-sc in next ch-space, ch 1, spike-sc in next ch-space, ch 2) repeat 4 times, slst in initial spike-sc [52 + 52 ch]

Rnd 12: sc in same st, sc in next 2 st, 5 sc in ch-3-space, sc in next 3 st, 2 sc in next ch-2-space, sc in next st, sc in next ch-space, sc in next st, 2 sc in next ch-2-space, sc in next 3 st, 2 sc in next ch-2-space, sc in next st, sc in next ch-space, sc in next st, 2 sc in next ch-2-space, (sc in next 3 st, 5 sc in ch-3-space, sc in next 3 st, 2 sc in next ch-2-space, sc in next st, sc in next ch-space, sc in next st, 2 sc in next ch-2-space, sc in next 3 st, 2 sc in next ch-2-space, sc in next st, sc in next ch-space, sc in next st, 2 sc in next ch-2-space) repeat 3 times, fasten off with an invisible join to 2nd stitch [112]

 Use high contrast colors in this square for the best result.

BUSTY BLOOM SQUARE

RedAgape (Mandy O'Sullivan) — Australia

@crochetbyredagape ⊕ www.redagapeblog.com f redagapeblog

Skill level: Intermediate
Colors: Yarn A: Sunflower / Yarn B: Peach / Yarn C: Pastel Pink / Yarn D: Lettuce / Yarn E: Cream
Special stitches: 5-dc-pc (5 double crochet popcorn stitch) / FPtr (Front post treble crochet)

INSTRUCTIONS

Rnd 1: {start with yarn A} start a magic ring with ch 3 (count as dc) + 4 dc (form first pc), ch 1, (5-dc-pc + ch 1) repeat 5 times, fasten off with an invisible join to first ch after initial pc [6 + 6 ch]

Rnd 2: {join yarn B in any ch-space, make your first stitch a standing stitch} (5-dc-pc + ch 2 + 5-dc-pc + ch 2 in ch-space) repeat 6 times, slst in initial pc [12 + 24 ch]

Rnd 1-5 ⊢·········➔

Rnd 6-11 ⊢·········➔

Rnd 3: 3 sc in all 12 ch-2-spaces, fasten off with an invisible join to 2nd stitch [36]

Rnd 4: *{join yarn C in any first sc, make your first stitch a standing stitch}* (slst in next st, ch 5, skip 2 st) repeat 12 times, slst in initial slst [12 + 60 ch]

Rnd 5: *{keep ch-5-spaces at the back}* slst in first leftover sc of Rnd 3, (ch 4 + 2 tr + ch 2 in same st, 2 tr + ch 4 + slst in next st, slst in next leftover st) repeat 12 times [12 Petals]

Rnd 6: slst in first ch-space of Rnd 4, (ch 4 + 4 tr + ch 2 + 4 tr + ch 4 + slst in same ch-space, slst in next ch-space) repeat 12 times, fasten off with an invisible join to first ch after initial slst [12 petals]

Rnd 7: *{join yarn D in between any pair of petals, make your first stitch a standing stitch}* (slst in between pair of petals, ch 5) repeat 12 times, slst in initial slst [12 + 60 ch]

Rnd 8: slst in next ch-space, ch 4 (count as tr), 3 tr in same ch-space, (4 tr in next ch space) repeat 11 times, slst in 4th ch of initial ch 4 [48]

Rnd 9: slst in next 3 st, slst in next gap between two pairs of 4-tr-groups, ch 3 (count as dc), 2 dc + ch 3 + 3 dc in same gap, (ch 4 + slst in the gaps between next 4-tr-groups) repeat 2 times, ch 4, [3 dc + ch 3 + 3 dc + ch 4 in next gap, (slst + ch 4 in the gap between next 4-tr-groups) repeat 2 times] repeat 3 times, fasten off with an invisible join in first true dc [32 + 60 ch]

Rnd 10: *{join yarn E in any corner-space, make your first stitch a standing stitch}* (3 dc + ch 3 + 3 dc + ch 1 in corner-space, 4 dc + ch 1 in next 3 ch-spaces) repeat 4 times, fasten off with an invisible join to 2nd stitch [72 + 28 ch]

Rnd 11: *{join yarn C in any corner-space, make your first stitch a standing stitch}* (2 hdc + ch 2 + 2 hdc in ch-space, hdc in next 3 st, dc in ch-space, hdc in next 4 st, FPtr around the slst from Rnd 9, hdc in next 4 st, FPtr around the slst from Rnd 9, hdc in next 4 st, dc in ch-space, hdc in next 3 st) repeat 4 times, fasten off with an invisible join to 2nd stitch [104 + 8 ch]

Busty Bloom Square is a beautiful 3D square. It can be combined with Twisted Lily Square on page 196 as both flowers have the same size and density.

SWEET PEACH SQUARE `80 stitch square`

Yarn Blossom Boutique (Melissa Bradley) — USA
🅾 @yarnblossomboutique f yarnblossomboutique

Skill level: Intermediate
Colors: Yarn A: Vanilla / Yarn B: Peony Pink / Yarn C: Cream
Special stitches: FPsc (Front post single crochet) / FPdc (Front post double crochet)

INSTRUCTIONS

Rnd 1: {start with yarn A} start a magic ring with ch 4 (count as dc + ch 1), (dc, ch 1) repeat 7 times, slst in 3rd ch of initial ch 4 [8 + 8 ch]

Rnd 2: slst in next ch-space, ch 3 (count as dc) + dc in same ch-space, FPdc around next st, (2 dc in next ch-space, FPdc around next st) repeat 7 times, fasten off with an invisible join to first true dc [24]

Rnd 3: {Join yarn B in any Fpdc, make your first stitch a standing stitch} (FPsc around FPdc, ch 4) repeat 8 times, slst in initial FPsc [8 + 32 ch]

Rnd 4: slst in next ch-space, ch 3 (count as dc) + dc + ch 2 + 2 dc in same ch-space, FPdc around next FPsc, (2 dc + ch 2 + 2 dc in next ch-space, FPdc around next FPsc) repeat 7 times, slst in 3rd ch of initial ch 3 [40 + 16 ch]

Rnd 5: (7 dc in next ch-space, FPsc around next FPdc) repeat 8 times, fasten off with an invisible join in 2nd dc [64]

Rnd 6: {Join yarn C in any FPsc, make your first stitch a standing stitch} (hdc in FPsc, ch 4, sc in 4th dc in next 7-dc-group, ch 4) repeat 8 times, slst in initial hdc [16 + 64 ch]

Rnd 7: slst in next ch-space, ch 2 (count as hdc) + hdc + 2 sc in same ch-space, 2 sc + 2 hdc in next ch-space, 3 dc + 2 tr in next ch-space, ch 2, 2 tr + 3 dc in next ch-space, (2 hdc + 2 sc in next ch-space, 2 sc + 2 hdc in next ch-space, 3 dc + 2 tr in next ch-space ch 2, 2 tr + 3 dc in next ch-space) repeat 3 times, fasten off with an invisible join in first true hdc [72 + 8 ch]

Sweet Peach Square allows for endless play with colors, or you could combine it with Sugarplum Square on page 40 for variation.

RASHEEDA SQUARE 80 stitch square

inas.craft (Inas Fadil Basymeleh) — Indonesia
@inas.craft ⊗ www.inascraft.com

Skill level: Intermediate
Colors: Yarn A: Cream / Yarn B: Fuchsia / Yarn C: Grape /
Yarn D: Pastel Pink / Yarn E: Plum
Special stitches: 4-dc-pc (4 double crochet popcorn stitch) /
3-dc-bobble (3 double crochet bobble stitch) / FPtr (Front post treble
crochet) / sc2tog (single crochet 2 stitches together)

INSTRUCTIONS

Rnd 1: *{start with yarn A}* start a magic ring with 8 sc, slst in initial sc [8]

Rnd 2: sc + ch 1 in all 8 st, fasten off with an invisible join to first ch after
initial sc [8 + 8 ch]

Rnd 3: *{join yarn B in any ch-space, make your first stitch a standing
stitch}* (4-dc-pc in next ch-space, ch 2) repeat 8 times, fasten off with an
invisible join to first ch after initial pc [8 + 16 ch]

Rnd 4: *{join yarn C in top of any pc, make your first stitch a standing
stitch}* (hdc + ch 2 + hdc in pc, ch 1, FPtr around sc in Rnd 2, ch 1) repeat
8 times, fasten off with an invisible join to first ch after initial hdc [24 + 32 ch]

Rnd 5: *{join yarn D in any FPtr, make your first stitch a standing stitch}*
(3-dc-bobble + ch 3 + 3-dc-bobble in FPtr, ch 2) repeat 8 times, fasten off
with an invisible join to first ch after initial 3-dc-bobble [16 + 40 ch]

Rnd 6: *{join yarn C in any ch-3-space, make your first stitch a standing
stitch}* (5 sc in ch-3-space, ch 1, tr in ch-2-space of Rnd 4, ch 1) repeat
8 times, slst in initial sc [48 + 16 ch]

Rnd 7: sc in same st, sc in next 2 st, skip 2 st, 3 hdc in next ch-space,
ch 2, skip 1 st, 3 hdc in next ch-space, skip 2 st, sc in next 3 st, sc in next
ch-space, sc2tog {over next st and ch-space} (sc in next 3 st, skip 2 st,
3 hdc in next ch-space, ch 2, skip 1 st, 3 hdc in next ch-space, skip 2 st,
sc in next 3 st, sc in next ch-space, sc2tog over next st and ch-space)
repeat 3 times, fasten off with an invisible join to 2nd stitch [56 + 8 ch]

Rnd 8: *{join yarn E in any sc2tog, make your first stitch a standing stitch}*
(sc in next 5 st, hdc in next 2 st, hdc + dc + ch 2 + dc + hdc in next
ch-2-space, hdc in next 2 st, sc in next 5 st) repeat 4 times, fasten off with
an invisible join to 2nd stitch [72 + 8 ch]

EMBRACE SQUARE `112 stitch square`

Vivid Kreations (Mikaela Bates) — Australia
🏀 www.vividkreations.com.au   📷 @vividkreations   f VK.VividKreations

Skill level: Intermediate
Colors: Yarn A: Mint / Yarn B: Green Ice / Yarn C: Opaline Glass /
Yarn D: Turquoise / Yarn E: Blue Lake
Special stitches: FPdc (Front post double crochet) / FPhdc (Front post
half double crochet) / hdc2tog (half double crochet 2 stitches together)

INSTRUCTIONS

Rnd 1: *{start with yarn A}* start a magic ring with ch 4 (count as dc + ch 1), dc, ch 2, (dc, ch 1, dc, ch 2) repeat 3 times, slst in 3rd ch of initial ch 4 [8 + 12 ch]

Rnd 2: slst in ch-1-space, ch 4 (count as dc + ch 1) + dc in same ch-1-space, FPdc around dc, (dc + ch 2 + dc in ch-2-space, FPdc around dc, dc + ch 1 + dc in ch-1-space, FPdc around dc) repeat 3 times, dc + ch 2 + dc in ch-2-space, FPdc around dc, fasten off with an invisible join to 4th ch [24 + 12 ch]

Rnd 3: *{join yarn B in any ch-1-space, make your first stitch a standing stitch}* (dc + ch 1 + dc in ch-1-space, FPdc around Fpdc, 2 dc + ch 1 + 2 dc in ch-2-space, FPdc around FPdc) repeat 4 times, slst in initial dc [32 + 8 ch]

Rnd 4: slst in ch-1-space, ch 5 (count as dc + ch 2) + dc in same ch-1-space, FPdc around FPdc, (3 dc + ch 1 + 3 dc in ch-1-space, FPdc around FPdc, dc + ch 2 + dc in ch-1-space, FPdc around FPdc) repeat 3 times, 3 dc + ch 1 + 3 dc in ch-1-space, FPdc around FPdc, fasten off with an invisible join to 4th ch of initial ch 5 [40 + 12 ch]

Rnd 5: *{join yarn C in any ch-2-space, make your first stitch a standing stitch}* (dc + ch 3 + dc in ch-2-space, FPdc around FPdc, 4 dc + ch 1 + 4 dc in ch-1-space, FPdc around FPdc) repeat 4 times, fasten off with an invisible join to first ch after initial dc [48 + 16 ch]

Rnd 6: *{join yarn D in any ch-3-space, make your first stitch a standing stitch}* (4 hdc in ch-3-space, ch 2, FPdc around FPdc, ch 4, hdc + ch 2 + hdc in ch-1-space, ch 4, FPdc around FPdc, ch 1) repeat 4 times, slst in initial hdc [32 + 52 ch]

Rnd 7: slst in next st, ch 3 (count as dc), dc in same st, 2 dc in next 2 st, ch 1, FPdc around FPdc, (6 hdc in next ch-4-space, 2 dc + ch 2 + 2 dc in next ch-2-space, 6 hdc in next ch-4-space, FPdc around FPdc, ch 1, skip first st, 2 dc in next 3 st, ch 1, FPdc around FPdc) repeat 3 times,

6 hdc in next ch-4-space, 2 dc + ch 2 + 2 dc in next ch-2-space, 6 hdc in next ch-4-space, FPdc around FPdc, ch 1, fasten off with an invisible join to first true dc [96 + 16 ch]

Rnd 8: *{join yarn E in any first ch-1-space, make your first stitch a standing stitch}* (2 hdc in ch-1-space, skip 1 st, hdc in next 5 st, 2 hdc in next ch-1-space, FPhdc around FPdc, skip 2 st, hdc in next 3 st, hdc2tog, hdc in next st, 2 hdc + ch 2 + 2 hdc in next ch-2-space, skip 1 st, hdc in next st, hdc2tog, hdc in next 3 st, skip 1 st, FPhdc around FPdc) repeat 4 times, slst in initial hdc [100 + 8 ch]

Rnd 9: sc in same st, sc in next 16 st, sc + ch 2 + sc in next ch-2-space, (skip 1 st, sc in next 24 st, sc + ch 2 + sc in next ch-2-space) repeat 3 times, skip 1 st, sc in next 7 st, fasten off with an invisible join to 2nd stitch [104 + 8 ch]

This square was named Embrace Square as designer Vivid Kreations really embraced what the yarn wanted to do, how it behaved, without knowing what would happen next. She added round after round to arrive at this beautiful result.

BLUEBERRY FIELDS SQUARE `112 stitch square`

Vivid Kreations (Mikaela Bates) — Australia
🌐 www.vividkreations.com.au 📷 @vividkreations 𝐟 VK.VividKreations

Skill level: Intermediate
Colors: Yarn A: Silver / Yarn B: Mustard
Special stitches: HBdc (herringbone double crochet)

INSTRUCTIONS

Note: the corners may seem a little tight but they stretch to fit the stitches.
Note: Turn your crochet work at the end of each round.

Rnd 1: {start with yarn A} start a magic ring with ch 3 (count as dc), 2 dc, ch 1, (3 dc, ch 1) repeat 3 times, slst in 3rd ch of initial ch 3 [12 + 4 ch] Turn to WS.

Rnd 2: slst in ch-space, ch 3 (count as dc) + HBdc in same ch-space, (HBdc in next 3 st, HBdc + ch 1 + dc + HBdc in next ch-space) repeat 3 times, HBdc in next 3 st, HBdc in next ch-space, ch 1, slst in 3rd ch of initial ch 3 [24 + 4 ch] Turn to RS.

Rnd 3: slst in ch-space, ch 3 (count as dc) + HBdc in same ch-space, (HBdc in next 6 st, HBdc + ch 1 + dc + HBdc in next ch-space) repeat 3 times, HBdc in next 6 st, HBdc in next ch-space, ch 1, slst in 3rd ch of initial ch 3 [36 + 4 ch] Turn to WS.

Rnd 4: slst in ch-space, ch 3 (count as dc) + HBdc in same ch-space, (HBdc in next 9 st, HBdc + ch 1 + dc + HBdc in next ch-space) repeat 3 times, HBdc in next 9 st, HBdc in next ch-space, ch 1, fasten off with an invisible join in first true HBdc [48 + 4 ch] Turn to RS.

Rnd 5: {join yarn B in any ch-1-space, make your first stitch a standing stitch} dc in ch-1-space, ch 1, [(HBdc in next st, ch 1, skip 1 st) repeat 6 times, HBdc + ch 1 + dc in next ch-space, ch 1] repeat 3 times, (HBdc in next st, ch 1, skip 1 st) repeat 6 times, HBdc + ch 1 in same ch-1-space as first stitch, slst in initial dc [32 + 32 ch] Turn to WS.

Rnd 6: {The only ch-spaces you will work into in this round are the corners, all other ch-spaces are skipped} slst in ch-space, ch 4 (count as dc + ch 1) in same ch-space, [(HBdc in next st, ch 1, skip 1 st) repeat 7 times, HBdc in next st, HBdc + ch 1 + dc in next ch-space, ch 1] repeat 3 times, (HBdc in next st, ch 1, skip 1 st) repeat 7 times, HBdc in next st, HBdc in next ch-space, ch 1, fasten off with an invisible join in 4th ch of

initial ch 4 [40 + 36 ch] Turn to RS.

Rnd 7: *{join yarn A in any ch-1-space, make your first stitch a standing stitch}* dc + HBdc in ch-space, (HBdc in next 18 st and ch-1-spaces, HBdc + ch 1 + dc + HBdc in next ch-space) repeat 3 times, HBdc in next 18 st and ch-1-spaces, HBdc in next ch-space, ch 1, slst in initial dc [84 + 4 ch] Turn to WS.

Rnd 8: slst in ch-space, ch 3 (count as dc) + HBdc in same ch-space, (HBdc in next 21 st, HBdc + ch 1 + dc + HBdc in next ch-space) repeat 3 times, HBdc in next 21 st, HBdc in next ch-space, ch 1, fasten off with an invisible join in first true HBdc [96 + 4 ch] Turn to RS.

Rnd 9: *{join yarn B in any ch-1-space, make your first stitch a standing stitch}* sc in ch-space, [(BLO sc in next st, FLO sc in next st) repeat 12 times, sc + ch 2 + sc in next ch-space) repeat 3 times, (BLO sc in next st, FLO sc in next st) repeat 12 times, sc in next ch-space, ch 2, fasten off with an invisible join to 2nd stitch [104 + 8 ch]

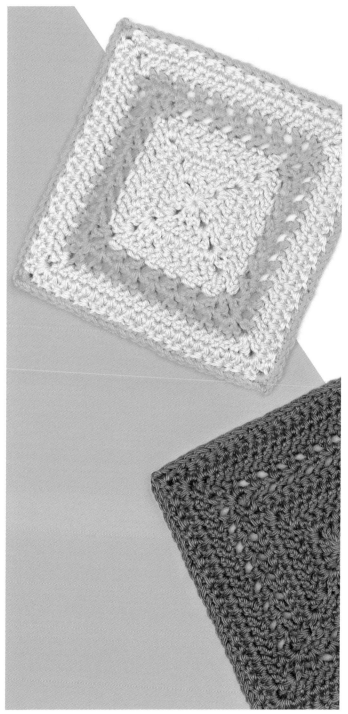

WATERMELON SQUARE `112 stitch square`

Emmi Hai — Germany
⊕ www.emmihai.net

Skill level: Intermediate
Colors: Yarn A: Pink Sand / Yarn B: Anthracite / Yarn C: Cream /
Yarn D: Lettuce / Yarn E: Aventurine
Special stitches: FPdc (Front post double crochet)
Pattern-specific special stitch: melon-seed: Complete previous stitch
in color A. Wrap color B over the hook and pull up a loop as if you would
make a puff stitch. Repeat three times so that you have six loops in color
B and one loop in color A on the hook. Then yarn over and pull through
six loops, yarn over again and pull through one loop. Change back to
color A by yarn over and pull through two loops.

INSTRUCTIONS

Rnd 1: *{start with yarn A}* start a magic ring with ch 3 (count as dc), 11
dc, slst in 3rd ch of initial ch 3 [12]

Rnd 2: *{work this round between stitches of Rnd 1}* ch 3 (count as dc),
dc in next 2 gaps, (2 dc in next gap, dc in next gap) repeat 5 times, slst in
3rd ch of initial ch 3 [18]

Rnd 3: *{work this round between stitches of Rnd 2}* ch 3 (count as dc),
(melon-seed in next gap, 2 dc in next 2 gaps) repeat 5 times, melon-seed
in next gap, 2 dc in next gap, dc in next gap, slst in 3rd ch of initial ch 3 [30]

Rnd 4: *{work this round between stitches of Rnd 3}* ch 3 (count as dc),
dc in next gap, 2 dc in next gap, dc in next gap, melon-seed in next gap,
dc in next gap, (2 dc in next 2 gaps, dc in next gap, melon-seed in next
gap, dc in next gap) repeat 5 times, slst in 3rd ch of initial ch 3 [42]

Rnd 5: *{work this round between stitches of Rnd 4}* ch 3 (count as dc),
dc in next 3 gaps, (2 dc in next gap, dc in next 2 gaps) repeat 13 times,
slst in 3rd ch of initial ch 3 [56]

Rnd 6: ch 2, 2 FPdc around initial ch 3 of Rnd 5, FPdc around next 6 st,
(2 FPdc around next st, FPdc around next 6 st) repeat 7 times, fasten off
with an invisible join to 2nd FPdc [64]

Rnd 7: *{join yarn C in first FPdc of Rnd 6, make your first stitch a standing
stitch}* (dc in next st, 2 dc in next st, 2 tr in next st, 3 tr in next st, 2 tr in
next st, 2 dc in next st, dc in next st, hdc in next 2 st, sc in next 5 st, hdc in
next 2 st) repeat 4 times, fasten off with an invisible join to 2nd stitch [88]

Rnd 8: *{join yarn D in first st of Rnd 7, make your first stitch a standing stitch}* (sc in next 5 st, 2 sc in next st, 3 sc in next st, 2 sc in next st, sc in next 14 st) repeat 4 times, fasten off with an invisible join to 2nd stitch [104]

Rnd 9: *{join yarn E in first st of Rnd 8, make your first stitch a standing stitch}* (hdc in next 8 st, 3 hdc in next st, hdc in next 17 st) repeat 4 times, fasten off with an invisible join in 2nd stitch [112]

A watermelon picnic blanket makes the perfect accessory for your summer outing!

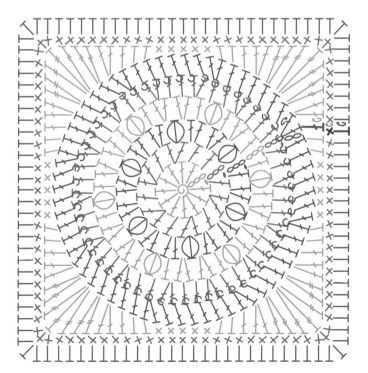

SUNNY SQUARE `112 stitch square`

Emmi Hai — Germany
⊕ www.emmihai.net

Skill level: Intermediate
Colors: Yarn A: Cream / Yarn B: Riverside / Yarn C: Mustard
Special stitches: FPdc (Front post double crochet) / dtr (Double treble crochet) / FPdtr (Front post double treble crochet) / **crossed FPdc** (crossed front post double crochet)

INSTRUCTIONS

Rnd 1: {start with yarn A} start a magic ring with ch 3 (count as dc), 11 dc, slst in 3rd ch of initial ch 3 [12]

Rnd 2: ch 1, sc in same st, ch 1, (sc in next st, ch 1) repeat 11 times, fasten off with an invisible join to first ch after initial sc [12 + 12 ch]

Rnd 3: {join yarn B in any ch-space, make your first stitch a standing stitch} (2 dc in ch-space, ch 1, skip next st) repeat 12 times, fasten off with an invisible join to 2nd stitch [24 + 12 ch]

Rnd 1-5
|··········>

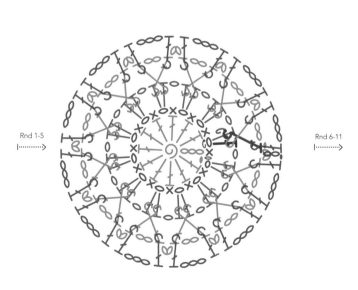

Rnd 6-11
|··········>

Rnd 4: *{skip first dc of Rnd 3, join yarn C in second dc, make your first stitch a standing stitch}* (FPdc around next dc, ch 2, crossed FPdc around skipped dc, ch 2, skip next dc) repeat 12 times, slst in initial FPdc [24 + 48 ch]

Rnd 5: ch 2, (FPdc around lower FPdc, ch 3, FPdc around upper FPdc) repeat 12 times, slst in initial FPdc [24 + 36 ch] Fasten off.

Rnd 6: *{join yarn A in first ch-2-space of Rnd 4, make your first stitch a standing stitch. Work over ch-3-spaces of Rnd 5}* (4 dc in ch-2-space of Rnd 4, ch 1) repeat 12 times, slst in initial dc [48 + 12 ch]

Note: Color change for FPdc in Rnd 7: Complete previous stitch in yarn A, then yarn over with yarn C and work stitch as normal until only the last two loops (one in yarn A and the other in yarn C) are left on the hook. Yarn over with yarn A and pull through both loops on the hook.

Rnd 7: *{in this round we switch from yarn A to yarn C for each FPdc}* ch 1, sc in same st, sc in next 3 st, *{change to yarn C}* FPdc around both FPdc of Rnd 5, (*{change to yarn A}* sc in next 4 st, *{change to yarn C}* FPdc around both FPdc) repeat 11 times, slst in initial sc [60]

Rnd 8: *{continue working in yarn A}* ch 1, sc in same stitch, sc in next 2 st, ch 4, skip 4 st, dc + tr + dtr + tr + dc in next st, ch 4, skip 4 st, sc in next 3 st, (sc in next 3 st, ch 4, skip 4 st, dc + tr + dtr + tr + dc in next st, ch 4, skip 4 st, sc in next 3 st) repeat 3 times, fasten off with an invisible join to 2nd stitch [44 + 32 ch]

Rnd 9: *{join yarn B in first sc of Rnd 8, make your first stitch a standing stitch}* (sc in next 3 st, 2 sc in next ch-space, 4-dc-bobble in FPdc of Rnd 7, 2 sc in same ch-space, sc in next 2 st, 3 sc in next dtr, sc in next 2 st, 2 sc in next ch-space, 4-dc- bobble in FPdc of Rnd 7, 2 sc in same ch-space, sc in next 3 st) repeat 4 times, fasten off with an invisible join to 2nd stitch [92]

Rnd 10: *{join yarn A in first sc of Rnd 9, make your first stitch a standing stitch}* (dc in next 11 st, 3 dc in next st, dc in next 11 st) repeat 4 times, slst in initial dc [100]

Note: Color change for FPdtr in Rnd 11: Complete previous stitch in yarn A, then yarn over three times with yarn C and work stitch as normal until only the last two loops (one in yarn A and the other in yarn C) are left on the hook. Yarn over with yarn A and pull through both loops on the hook.

Rnd 11: *{in this round we switch from yarn A to yarn C for each FPdtr, continue working in yarn A}* ch 1, sc in same st, sc in next 11 st, 3 sc in next st, sc in next 12 st, *{change to yarn C}* FPdtr around FPdc of Rnd 7, (*{change to yarn A}* sc in next 12 st, 3 sc in next st, sc in next 12 st, *{change to yarn C}* FPdtr around FPdc of Rnd 7) repeat 3 times, fasten off with an invisible join to 2nd stitch [112]

GARDEN IN BLOOM SQUARE `80 stitch square`

Yarn Blossom Boutique (Melissa Bradley) — USA

@yarnblossomboutique yarnblossomboutique

Skill level: Intermediate
Colors: Yarn A: Golden Glow / Yarn B: Girly Pink / Yarn C: Cream / Yarn D: Peridot
Special stitches: 4-puff (Puff stitch with 4 loops) / FPdc (Front post double crochet) / FPtr (Front post treble crochet) / BPsc (Back post single crochet)

INSTRUCTIONS

Rnd 1: *{start with yarn A}* start a magic ring with (sc, ch 2, 4-puff, ch 3) repeat 4 times, fasten off with an invisible join to first ch after initial sc [8 + 20 ch]

Rnd 2: *{join yarn B in any puff, make your first stitch a standing stitch}* (hdc in puff, ch 3, hdc in next sc, ch 3) repeat 4 times, slst in initial hdc [8 + 24 ch]

Rnd 3: slst in next ch-3-space, ch 2 (count as hdc), 2 hdc in same ch-3-space, ch 1, (3 hdc in next ch-3-space, ch 1) repeat 7 times, slst in 2nd ch of initial ch 2 [24 + 8 ch]

Rnd 4: ch 2, 4-puff in next st, ch 3, slst in next st, FPtr around hdc from Rnd 2, skip ch-space, (slst in next st, ch 2, 4-puff in next st, ch 3, slst in next st, FPtr around hdc from Rnd 2, skip ch-space) repeat 7 times, fasten off with an invisible join to 2nd ch [32 + 40 ch]

Rnd 5: *{join yarn C in any puff, make your first stitch a standing stitch}* (sc in puff, FPtr + ch 3 + FPtr around next FPtr) repeat 8 times, slst in initial sc [24 + 24 ch]

Rnd 6: slst in next st, slst in next ch-space, ch 3 (count as dc) + 2 dc + ch 1 + 3 dc in same ch-space, FPdc around both of next 2 FPtr to join them together (3 dc + ch 1 + 3 dc in next ch-space, FPdc around both of next 2 FPtr to join them together) repeat 7 times, fasten off with an invisible join to first true dc [56 + 8 ch]

Rnd 7: *{Join yarn D to first dc of any 6-dc-group, make your first stitch a standing stitch}* (BPsc around next 3 st, skip ch-space, BPsc around next 3 st, FPdc around next FPdc, BPsc around next 3 st, dc + ch 2 + dc in next ch-space, BPsc around next 3 st, FPdc around next FPdc) repeat 4 times, fasten off with an invisible join to 2nd stitch [64 + 8 ch]

Rnd 1-4
|⋯⋯⋯⋯>

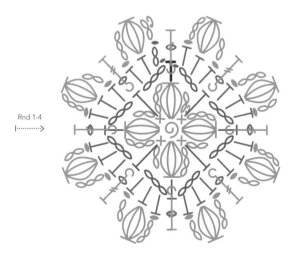

Rnd 8: {*Join yarn C in the first BPsc of any 6-Bpsc-group, make your first stitch a standing stitch*} (dc in next 6 st, FPtr around next FPdc, dc in next 4 st, dc + ch 2 + dc in next ch-space, dc in next 4 st, FPtr around next FPdc) repeat 4 times, fasten off with an invisible join to 2nd stitch [72 + 8 ch]

{ *Garden In Bloom Square could be combined with the 80-stitch variant of Alchemy Garden Square on page 164.* }

Rnd 5-8

LABYRINTH SQUARE 80 stitch square

inas.craft (Inas Fadil Basymeleh) — Indonesia
@inas.craft ⊗ www.inascraft.com

Skill level: Intermediate
Colors: Yarn A: Forest / Yarn B: Lettuce
Special stitches: BPdc (Back post double crochet) / FPdc (Front post double crochet) / FPtr (Front post treble crochet)

INSTRUCTIONS

Rnd 1: {start with yarn A} start a magic ring with ch 7 (count as tr + ch 3), (3 tr, ch 3) repeat 3 times, 2 tr, fasten off with an invisible join to 5th ch of initial ch 7 [12 + 12 ch]

Rnd 2: {join yarn B in any ch-space, make your first stitch a standing stitch} (dc + ch 2 + dc + ch 2 + dc in ch-space, BPdc around next 3 st) repeat 4 times, fasten off with an invisible join to first ch after initial dc [24 + 16 ch]

Rnd 3: {each corner has 2 ch-spaces (right and left), join yarn A in any ch-2 space to the right, make your first stitch a standing stitch} (2 dc in ch-space, 2 FPdc around next dc, 2 dc in next ch-space, BPdc around next 5 st) repeat 4 times, fasten off with an invisible join to 2nd stitch [44]

Rnd 4: {join yarn B in 3rd BPdc of a 5-BPdc-group, make your first stitch a standing stitch} (4 tr + ch 2 + 4 tr in next st, skip 2 st, hdc in next st, ch 4, skip 4 st, hdc in next st, skip 2 st) repeat 4 times, fasten off with an invisible join to 2nd stitch [40 + 24 ch]

Rnd 5: {join yarn A in any ch-2-space, make your first stitch a standing stitch} (2 dc + ch 2 + 2 dc in ch-2-space, BPdc around next 5 st, FPtr around next 4 skipped dc in Rnd 3 working in front of ch 4 in Rnd 4, BPdc around next 5 st) repeat 4 times, fasten off with an invisible join to 2nd stitch [72 + 8 ch]

{ *Make this square in high contrast colors to not get lost in your own crocheted labyrinth!* }

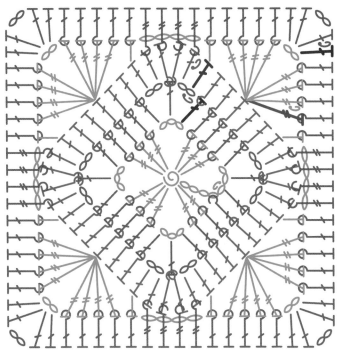

PASSIONATE PEONY SQUARE `112 stitch square`

Crochet Road (Joy Clements) — Australia
@crochetroad f Crochet Road © Crochet Road

Skill level: Intermediate
Colors: Yarn A: Golden glow / Yarn B: Jade Gravel / Yarn C: Pastel
Pink / Yarn D: Green Ice / Yarn E: Cream
Special stitches: Work in third loop / ch-3-picot (Picot stitch) / v-stitch:
dc + ch 2 + dc / BPsc (Back post single crochet) / BPhdc (Back post half
double crochet)

INSTRUCTIONS

Rnd 1: {start with yarn A, work Rnd 1 loosely} start a magic ring with 8 sc,
close the magic ring, leaving a small hole in the center, fasten off with an
invisible join to 2nd sc [8]

> Note: Weave in ends of Rnd 1 later, otherwise it can be difficult to
> work Rnd 2.

Rnd 2: {join yarn B in third loop of any stitch, make your first stitch a
standing stitch. Work this entire round in third loop} 3 dc in third loop of
all 8 st, fasten off with an invisible join to 2nd dc [24]

Rnd 3: {join yarn C in third loop of any stitch, make your first stitch a standing
stitch. Work this entire round in third loop} (v-stitch in next st, skip 1 st)
repeat 12 times, fasten off with an invisible join in first dc [24 + 24 ch]

Rnd 4: {join yarn A in any ch-space, make your first stitch a standing stitch}
(3 sc in ch-space, sc in the gap between 2 v-stitches) repeat 12 times, fasten
off with an invisible join to 2nd sc [48]

Rnd 5: {join yarn B in any sc between v-stitches, make your first stitch a
standing stitch} (sc in sc between v-stitches, ch 4, skip 3 st) repeat 12 times,
slst in initial sc [12 + 48 ch]

Rnd 6: (3 sc + ch 2 + 3 sc in next ch-space, slst in sc) repeat 12 times,
fasten off with an invisible join to first sc [12 petals]

Rnd 7: {join yarn C around any sc in Rnd 5, make your first stitch a
standing stitch. Work this round behind Rnd 6, with the right side of the
flower facing you. Crochet the BPhdc stitches loosely so you can easily
work into them in Rnd 8} (BPhdc around sc from Rnd 5, ch 3) repeat
12 times, slst in initial BPhdc [12 + 36 ch]

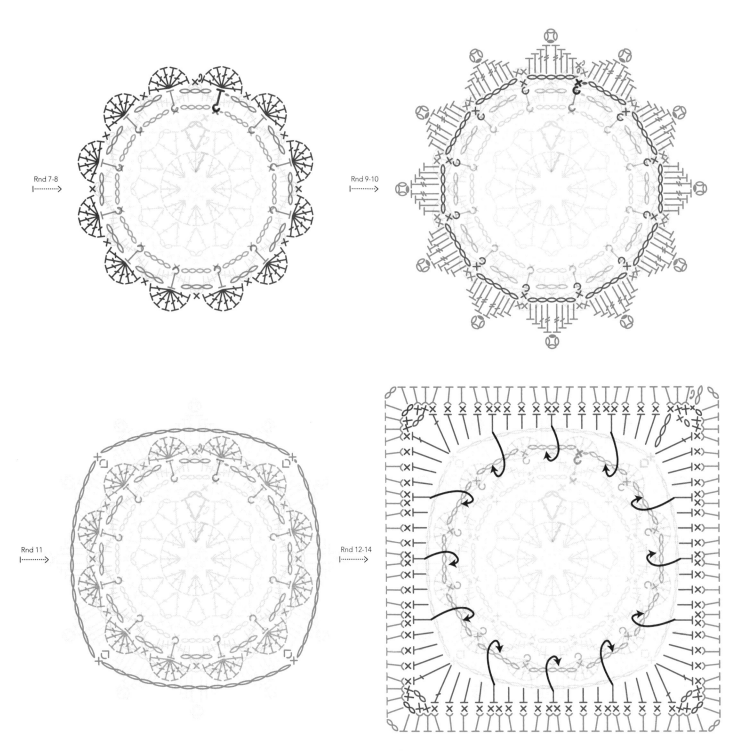

Rnd 7-8

Rnd 9-10

Rnd 11

Rnd 12-14

Rnd 8: (sc in ch-space, 7 dc in top of next BPhdc) repeat 12 times, fasten off with an invisible join in first sc [12 petals]

Rnd 9: *{join yarn D around any BPhdc in Rnd 7, make your first stitch a standing stitch. Work behind the flower petals}* (BPsc around BPhdc, ch 5) repeat 12 times, slst in initial BPsc [12 + 60 ch]

Rnd 10: slst in ch-space, ch 1, (sc + 2 hdc + dc + tr + ch-3-picot + tr + dc + 2 hdc + sc) repeat in all 12 ch-spaces, fasten off with an invisible join in first sc [12 leaves]

Rnd 11: *{join yarn E in back loop and third loop of 4th stitch of any shell in Rnd 8, make your first stitch a standing stitch. Work behind the leaves with the right side of the flower facing you}* (sc in back loop and third loop of 4th stitch of next 7-dc-group, ch 14, skip 2 7-dc-groups) repeat 4 times, slst in initial sc [4 ch-14-spaces]

Rnd 12: ch 3 (count as a dc), [(3 hdc in ch-space, hdc *{this hdc catches both the ch from this Rnd and the ch made in Rnd 9, between 2 tr stitches}*) repeat 3 times, 3 hdc in ch-space, dc + ch 2 + dc in next sc] repeat 3 times, (3 hdc in ch-space, hdc *{this hdc catches both the ch from this Rnd and the ch made in Rnd 9, between 2 tr stitches}*) repeat 3 times, 3 hdc in ch-space, dc + ch 1 + sc in 3rd ch of initial ch 3 [56 + 7 ch]

Note: You start Rnd 13 by working over the joining sc. Treat the joining stitch as a chain loop and work over it, covering it entirely.

Rnd 13: 2 sc over joining sc, [sc in next 4 st, 2 sc in next st, (sc in next 3 st, 2 sc in next st) repeat 2 times, sc in next 4 st, 2 sc + ch 2 + 2 sc in corner-space] repeat 3 times, sc in next 4 st, 2 sc in next st, (sc in next 3 st, 2 sc in next st) repeat 2 times, sc in next 4 st, 2 sc + ch 1 + sc in initial sc [96 + 7 ch]

Rnd 14: *{work this round in BLO}* ch 2 (count as a hdc), (hdc in next 24 st, hdc + ch 2 + hdc in corner-space) repeat 3 times, hdc in next 24 st, hdc + ch 2 in corner-space, fasten off with an invisible join to first true hdc [104 + 8 ch]

PEACOCK FEATHER PUFF SQUARE `112 stitch square`

Crochet Road (Joy Clements) — Australia

@crochetroad **f** Crochet Road © Crochet Road

Skill level: Intermediate
Colors: Yarn A: Denim / Yarn B: Larimar / Yarn C: Cream / Yarn D: Mustard
Special stitches: esc (Extended single crochet) / **standing esc** (Standing extended single crochet) / **4-puff** (Puff stitch with 4 loops) / **Work in third loop** / **spike-hdc** (spike half double crochet) / **htr** (half treble crochet)

INSTRUCTIONS

Note: When the pattern states to work in BLO, you can work through BLO + third loop at the same time. This avoids gaps in your work, and makes it look neater.

Rnd 1: *{start with yarn A}* Wrap yarn 7 times around a pencil. Slip all of these wraps together off the end of the pencil very carefully. Holding the yarn wraps together, make a slst in the center of the 7 wraps as if they were a magic ring. Insert your hook in this central hole and work 12 sc around the ring, fasten off with an invisible join in 2nd sc [12]

Rnd 2: *{join yarn B with a slst in BLO of any sc}* (BLO 4-puff, ch 1) repeat in all 12 st, fasten off with an invisible join in initial puff [12 puffs + 12 ch]

Rnd 3: *{join yarn C in top of any puff, make your first stitch a standing stitch. Don't work this round too tight}* (sc in top of puff, 2 sc in ch-space) repeat 12 times, fasten off with an invisible join in 2nd stitch [36]

Rnd 4: *{join yarn D in any st, make your first stitch a standing stitch}* (esc in next st, crossed hdc around post of the stitch just made, ch 1, skip 1 st) repeat 18 times, fasten off with an invisible join to 2nd stitch [18 clusters]

Rnd 5: *{join yarn B in any ch-space, make your first stitch a standing stitch}* (slst in ch-space, ch 3) repeat 18 times, slst in initial slst [18 + 54 ch]

Rnd 6: (sc in next ch-space, 9 dc in next ch-space) repeat 9 times, fasten off with an invisible join in initial dc [9 petals]

Rnd 7: *{Join yarn A, make your first stitch a standing spike stitch over sc in Rnd 6 and into ch-space of Rnd 5 below. Work all stitches in this round in BLO except for spike stitches}* (spike-hdc over top of sc into ch-space of Rnd 5 below, slst in first dc of petal, sc in next 3 st, sc + hdc + sc in next st,

Rnd 1-6

sc in next 3 st, slst in last st of petal) repeat 9 times, fasten off with an invisible join in initial slst [9 petals]

Note: In Rnd 8 we will be working a number of stitches around the bar of spike stitches in Rnd 7. In the diagram we have depicted these stitches as worked in third loop, as no specific symbol is available. Please take this into account when working this round.

Rnd 8: *{with the right side of the flower facing you, work behind the petals. Join yarn C under the bar of the spike hdc made in Rnd 7, make your first stitch a standing stitch. Work this round behind Rnd 6. It helps to fold adjacent petals right sides together while you work the sc. Work chains loosely in this round}* (sc around bar of spike hdc, ch 4) repeat 9 times, slst in initial sc [9 + 36 ch]

Rnd 9: *{fold the petals forward as you work this round}* ch 1, 7 hdc in each of next 8 ch-spaces, 8 hdc in last ch-space, slst in initial hdc [64]

Rnd 10: ch 4 (count as tr), (htr + dc in next st, dc in next st, hdc in next 3 st, sc in next 5 st, hdc in next 3 st, dc in next st, dc + htr in next st, tr + ch 1 + tr in next st) repeat 3 times, htr + dc in next st, dc in next st, hdc in next 3 st, sc in next 5 st, hdc in next 3 st, dc in next st, dc + htr in next st, tr + ch 1 in next st, sc in 4th ch of initial ch 4 [76 + 4 ch]

Note: You start Rnd 11 by working over the joining sc. Treat the joining stitch as a chain loop and work over it, covering it entirely.

Rnd 11: *{work this round in BLO}* ch 2 (count as a hdc) + hdc over joining sc, hdc in next 19 st, (2 hdc + ch 1 + 2 hdc in ch-1-space, hdc in next 19 st) repeat 3 times, 2 hdc + ch 1 in corner-space, fasten off with an invisible join to first true hdc [92 + 4 ch]

Rnd 12: *{join yarn B in first stitch after any corner-space, make your first stitch a standing stitch}* (sc in next 23 st, 2 sc + ch 1 + 2 sc in corner-space) repeat 4 times, fasten off with an invisible join to 2nd sc [108 + 4 ch]

Peacock Feather Puff Square can be combined with 3D 8-Petal Flower Square on page 78 or Fairy Wheel Square on page 92 as the flowers have roughly the same size.

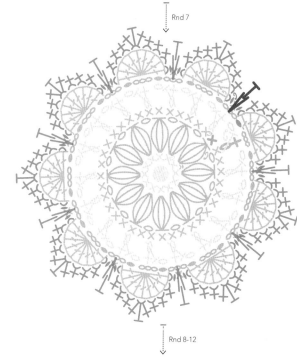

Rnd 7

Rnd 8-12

COTTAGE FLOWER SQUARE 112 stitch square

Crochet Road (Joy Clements) — Australia
@crochetroad Crochet Road Crochet Road

Skill level: Intermediate
Colors: yarn A: Golden Glow / Yarn B: Mint / Yarn C: Green ice /
Yarn D: Cream
Special stitches: Work in third loop / 4-dc-bobble (4 double crochet
bobble) / ch-3-picot (Picot stitch) / BPsc (Back post single crochet) /
BPdc (Back post double crochet)

This square can turn out bigger than other 112-stitch squares in this
book. You might want to change the hook size to make sizes match
if you're planning to combine squares in a project.

INSTRUCTIONS

Rnd 1: {start with yarn A} start a magic ring with 8 sc, close the magic
ring, leaving a small hole in the center, fasten off with an invisible join to
2nd stitch [8]

*Note: Weave in ends of Rnd 1 later, otherwise it can be difficult to
work Rnd 2.*

Rnd 2: {join yarn B in any st, make your first stitch a standing stitch.
Work the entire round in third loop only}* (4-dc-bobble in next st,
ch 2) repeat 8 times, fasten off with an invisible join to first ch after initial
4-dc-bobble [8 bobbles]

Rnd 3: {join yarn C in top of any bobble, make your first stitch a
standing stitch}* (sc in top of bobble, 3 sc in ch-space) repeat 8 times, slst
in first sc [32]

Rnd 4: (ch 4, skip 3 st, sc in next st) repeat 7 times, ch 4, skip 3 st, sc in
slst at end of Rnd 3 [8 + 32 ch]

Rnd 5: (2 hdc + 2 dc + ch-3-picot + 2 dc + 2 hdc in ch-space, slst in top
of sc) repeat 8 times [8 petals] Fasten off.

Rnd 6: {join yarn B around the post of any sc made in Rnd 4, make your
first stitch a standing stitch. Work behind the flower petals with the
right side facing you. It helps to pinch 2 adjacent petals together to
work the BPdc}* (BPdc around post of next st, ch 4) repeat 8 times, slst in
initial BPdc [8 + 32 ch]

Rnd 7: 7 hdc in all 8 ch-spaces, slst in initial hdc [56]

Rnd 1-5
|·········>

Rnd 8: (slst in between 7-hdc-groups, skip 3 st, 9 dc in 4th hdc of 7-hdc-group, skip 3 st) repeat 8 times, fasten off with an invisible join to first dc [8 petals]

Note: When working surface slst in Rnd 9, you place the hook under both front and back loops but not under the 'third loop' of each stitch, to give it a neater appearance.

Rnd 9: *{join yarn D with a slst around the post of the first dc of any petal from Rnd 8, work in the underside of the flower petals with the wrong side facing you}* (surface slst in next 9 st, at base of the petal, slst in space between 7-hdc-groups) repeat 8 times, fasten off [72 + 8 ch]

Rnd 10: *{join yarn D around the post of any BPdc from Rnd 6, make your first stitch a standing stitch}* (BPsc around BPdc from Rnd 6, ch 4) repeat 8 times, slst in initial BPsc [8 + 32 ch]

Rnd 11: slst in next 2 ch, sc in same ch-space, (ch 7, sc in next ch-space, ch 5, sc in next ch-space) repeat 3 times, ch 7, sc in next ch-space, ch 5, slst in initial sc [4 ch-7 spaces, 4 ch-5 spaces]

Note: The final 4 sc in Rnd 12 would be worked over the original 4 slst, covering them entirely.

Rnd 12: slst in next 4 ch, 6 sc in same ch-7-space, 5 sc in ch-5-space, (10 sc in next ch-7-space, 5 sc in next ch-5-space) repeat 3 times, 4 sc over initial 4 slst, slst in first sc [60]

Rnd 13: ch 3 (count as dc) + 2 dc in same st, [(skip 2 st, 3 dc in next st) repeat 4 times, skip 2 st, 3 dc + ch 2 + 3 dc in next st] repeat 3 times, (skip 2 st, 3 dc in next st) repeat 4 times, skip 2 st, 3 dc + ch 1 + sc in 3rd ch of initial ch 3 [72 + 8 ch]

Note: You start Rnd 14 by working over the joining sc. Treat the joining stitch as a chain loop and work over it, covering it entirely.

Rnd 14: ch 3 (count as dc) + 2 dc in corner-space, working over joining sc, [(skip 3 st, 3 dc between dc-groups from Rnd 13) repeat 5 times, skip 3 st, 3 dc + ch 2 + 3 dc in corner-space) repeat 3 times, (skip 3 st, 3 dc between 3-dc-groups from Rnd 13) repeat 5 times, skip 3 st, 3 dc + ch 2 in initial corner-space, fasten off with an invisible join to 2nd dc [84 + 8 ch]

Rnd 15: *{join yarn C in any corner-space, make your first stitch a standing stitch}* (3 sc in corner-space, sc in all 21 st) repeat 4 times, fasten off with an invisible join in 2nd sc [96]

Rnd 16: *{join yarn D in any middle sc in a corner, make your first stitch a standing stitch}* [3 dc + ch 1 + 3 dc in next st, (skip 2 st, 3 dc in next st) repeat 7 times, skip 2 st] repeat 4 times, fasten off with an invisible join to 2nd dc [108 + 4 ch]

Rnd 6-8

Rnd 9

Rnd 10-16

SATELLITE SQUARE `112 stitch square`

Emmi Hai — Germany ⊛ www.emmihai.net

Skill level: Intermediate
Colors: Yarn A: Graphite / Yarn B: Cantaloupe / Yarn C: Glass / Yarn D: Cream
Special stitches: ch-3-picot (picot stitch) / **FPtr** (Front post treble crochet) / **BPdc** (Back post double crochet)
Pattern-specific special stitch: 4-dc-bobble with extra loops: Begin a bobble-stitch by yarn over, insert hook into indicated stitch, yarn over and pull up a loop. Yarn over again and pull through two loops. Add an extra loop by yarn over and pull through one loop. Repeat this four times into the same stitch and complete by yarn over and pull through all loops.

INSTRUCTIONS

Rnd 1: {start with yarn A} start a magic ring with ch 4 (count as dc + ch 1), (dc, ch 1) repeat 5 times, fasten off with an invisible join to 4th ch [12]

Rnd 2: {join yarn B in any ch-space, make your first stitch a standing stitch} (dc + ch 2 + dc in ch-space) repeat 6 times, fasten off with an invisible join to first ch after initial dc [12 + 12 ch]

Rnd 3: {join yarn C in any ch-space, make your first stitch a standing stitch} (sc + hdc + dc + tr + ch-3-picot + tr + dc + hdc + sc in ch-space) repeat 6 times, fasten off with an invisible join to 2nd stitch [6 spikes]

Rnd 4: {join yarn B between first and last dc of Rnd 2, make your first stitch a standing stitch} (sc in gap between dc of Rnd 2, ch 4 behind petal) repeat 6 times, fasten off with an invisible join to first ch after initial sc [6 + 24 ch]

Rnd 5: {join yarn D in any ch-space, make your first stitch a standing stitch} 6 dc in next 6 ch-spaces, slst in initial dc [36]

Rnd 6: ch 3 (count as dc), dc in same st, dc in next 2 st, (2 dc in next st, dc in next 2 st) repeat 11 times, slst in 3rd ch of initial ch 3 [48] Do not fasten off. Put a stitch marker in the last loop to prevent it from unraveling.

Rnd 7: {join yarn A in any sc of Rnd 4, make your first stitch a standing stitch} (FPtr around sc of Rnd 4, ch 9) repeat 6 times, fasten off with an invisible join to first ch after initial FPtr [6 + 54 ch]

Rnd 8: {join yarn B in any FPtr, make your first stitch a standing stitch} (4-dc-bobble with extra loops in FPtr, ch 10) repeat 6 times, fasten off with an invisible join to first ch after initial 4-dc-bobble [6 + 60 ch]

Rnd 9: {put the yarn D loop at the end of Rnd 6 back on your hook, work

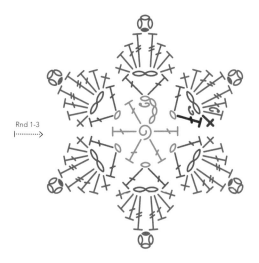

Rnd 1-3
|···········>

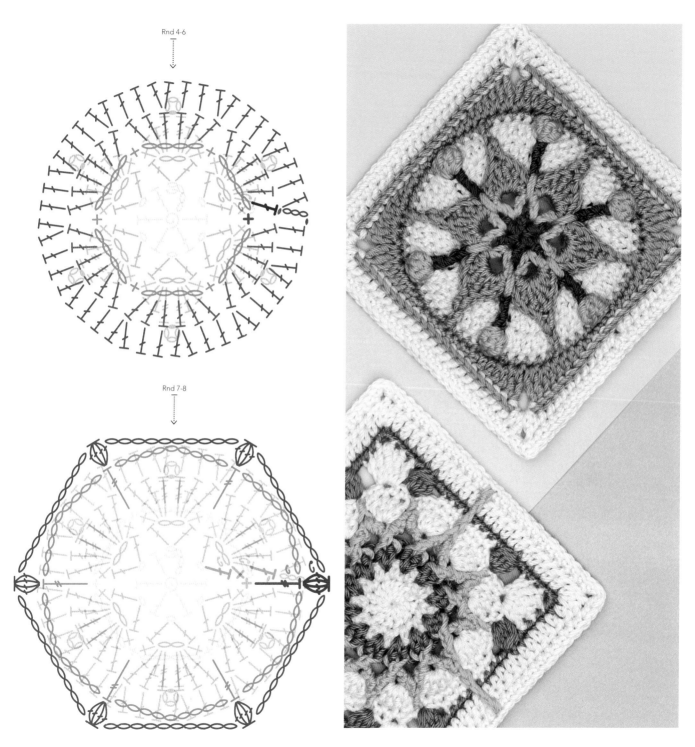

Rnd 4-6

Rnd 7-8

in Rnd 6} ch 3 (count as dc), dc in same st, dc in next 3 st, 2 dc in next st, dc in next 3 st, slst in 4-dc-bobble with extra loops of Rnd 8, [(2 dc in next st, dc in next 3 st) repeat 2 times, slst in 4-dc-bobble with extra loops of Rnd 8] repeat 5 times, fasten off with an invisible join to 2nd stitch [66]

Rnd 10: *{join yarn C in 3rd ch of ch-3-start of Rnd 9, make your first stitch a standing stitch}* (sc in next 5 st, FPtr in picot of petal, sc in next 6 st) repeat 6 times, slst in initial sc [72]

Rnd 11: ch 1, sc in same st, sc in next 2 st, hdc in next 2 st, dc in next 2 st, 2 dc in next st, 2 tr in next st, ch 2, 2 tr in next st, 2 dc in next st, dc in next 2 st, hdc in next 2 st, sc in next 3 st, (sc in next 3 st, hdc in next 2 st, dc in next 2 st, 2 dc in next st, 2 tr in next st, ch 2, 2 tr in next st, 2 dc in next st, dc in next 2 st, hdc in next 2 st, sc in next 3 st) repeat 3 times, fasten off with an invisible join to 2nd stitch [88 + 8 ch]

Rnd 12: *{join yarn D in first sc of Rnd 11, make your first stitch a standing stitch}* (BPdc around next 11 st, 2 dc + ch 2 + 2 dc in next ch-space, BPdc around next 11 st) repeat 4 times, slst in initial BPdc [104 + 8 ch]

Rnd 13: ch 1, sc in same st, sc in next 12 st, sc + ch 1 + sc in next ch-space, skip next dc, sc in next 12 st, (sc in next 13 st, sc + ch 1 + sc in next ch-space, skip next dc, sc in next 12 st) repeat 3 times, fasten off with an invisible join to 2nd stitch [108 + 4 ch]

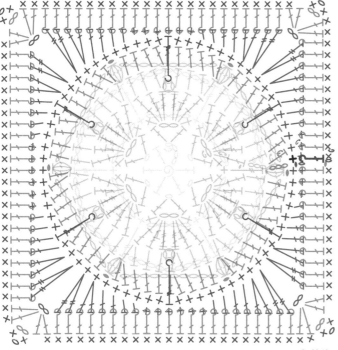

Rnd 9-13

LOTUS FLOWER SQUARE `80 stitch square`

Yarn Blossom Boutique (Melissa Bradley) — USA
@yarnblossomboutique yarnblossomboutique

Skill level: Intermediate
Colors: Yarn A: Vanilla / **Yarn B:** Cream / **Yarn C:** Pastel Pink /
Yarn D: Salmon
Special stitches: 2-tr-bobble (2 treble crochet bobble stitch) /
FPsc (Front post single crochet) / **BPsc** (Back post single crochet)

INSTRUCTIONS

Rnd 1: *{start with yarn A}* start a magic ring with ch 3 + tr (count as 2-tr-bobble), ch 2, (2-tr-bobble, ch 2) repeat 7 times, fasten off with an invisible join to first ch after first true tr [8 + 16 ch]

Rnd 2: *{Join yarn B in any ch-space, make your first stitch a standing stitch}* 4 sc in all 8 ch-spaces, slst in initial sc [32]

Rnd 3: slst in next st, ch 6 (count as dc + ch 3), dc in next st, skip next 2 st, (dc in next st, ch 3, dc in next st, skip next 2 st) repeat 7 times, fasten off with an invisible join to 4th ch of initial ch 6 [12 + 28 ch]

Rnd 4: *{join yarn C in any ch-space, make your first stitch a standing stitch}* 6 hdc in all 8 ch-spaces, slst in initial hdc [48]

Rnd 5: (skip next 2 st, 4 dc + ch 2 + 4 dc in next st, skip next 2 st, sc in next st) repeat 8 times, fasten off with an invisible join to 2nd stitch [72 + 16 ch]

Rnd 6: *{join yarn D in the first dc after a sc, make your first stitch a standing stitch}* (BPsc around next 4 st, sc + ch 2 + sc in next ch-space, BPsc around next 4 st, FPsc around next sc) repeat 8 times, fasten off with an invisible join to 2nd stitch [88 + 16 ch]

Rnd 7: *{join yarn B in the first BPsc after a sc + ch 2 + sc group, make your first stitch a standing stitch}* (dc in next 6 st, ch 2, skip next 4 st + ch-space + 4 st, dc in next 6 st, hdc in next st, hdc + ch 2 + hdc in next ch-space, hdc in next st) repeat 4 times, fasten off with an invisible join to 2nd stitch [64 + 16 ch]

SUNNY SIDE POP SQUARE `112 stitch square`

Crochetedbytess (Therese Eghult) — Sweden
⊕ www.sistersinstitch.com

Skill level: Intermediate
Colors: Yarn A: Cream / Yarn B: Ice Blue / Yarn C: Pea Green /
Yarn D: Pearl / Yarn E: Birch / Yarn F: Limestone
Special stitches: 5-dc-pc (5 double crochet popcorn stitch) / 3-dc-pc
(3 double crochet popcorn stitch) / BPhdc (Back post half double crochet)
/ FPdc (Front post double crochet) / FPtr (Front post treble crochet)
Pattern-specific special stitch: starting 3-dc-pc: Ch 3, Make 2 dc in the
same stitch. Take off the hook and put it through the 3rd ch of the initial
ch 3, catch the last eyelet again and pull through. Close with a ch (does
not count as a st).

INSTRUCTIONS

*Note: Please beware of mentioned hidden stitches as they easily
hide behind the one you just worked.*

Rnd 1: *{start with yarn A}* start a magic ring with 8 sc, slst in initial sc [8]

Rnd 2: starting 3-dc-pc + ch 1 + 3-dc-pc + ch 2 in next st, (3-dc-pc + ch 1
+ 3-dc-pc + ch 2 in next st) repeat 7 times, fasten off with an invisible join
to 2nd stitch [16 + 8 ch]

Rnd 3: *{join Yarn B in any ch-1-space between 2 groups of pc-stitches,
make your first stitch a standing stitch. Skip all pc-stitches and work
only in the ch-spaces and gaps between them}* (3 hdc in next ch-1-space,
skip 1 st, 2 hdc in the gap between 2 pc-stitches, skip 1 st) repeat 8 times,
slst in initial hdc [40]

Rnd 4: ch 1, BPhdc in next 40 st, fasten off with an invisible join to 2nd
BPhdc [40]

Rnd 5: *{join yarn C in any st, make your first stitch a standing stitch}*
(3-dc-bobble in next st, ch 3, 3-tr-bobble in next st, ch 3, 3-dc-bobble
in next st, ch 1, skip 2 st, 5-dc-pc + ch 2 in next 3 st, skip 2 st) repeat
4 times, fasten off with an invisible join to first ch after initial 3-dc-bobble
[24 + 32 ch]

Rnd 6: *{join yarn D in any first ch-3-space, make your first stitch a
standing stitch}* [4 hdc in ch-3-space, FPdc + ch 2 + FPdc around next st,
4 hdc in next ch-space, FPdc around next st, (2 hdc in next ch-space, skip
1 st) repeat 3 times, 2 hdc in next ch-space, FPdc around next st] repeat

4 times, fasten off with an invisible join to 2nd stitch [80 + 8 ch]

Rnd 7: *{join yarn A in any ch-space, make your first stitch a standing stitch}* (hdc + ch 2 + hdc in ch-space, FPdc around next FPdc, hdc in next 18 st, FPdc around next FPdc) repeat 4 times, fasten off with an invisible join to first ch after initial hdc [88 + 8 ch]

Rnd 8: *{Join yarn E in any ch-space, make your first stitch a standing stitch}* (dc + ch 2 + dc in ch-space, FPtr around next 2 st, dc in next 18 st, FPtr around next 2 st) repeat 4 times, fasten off with an invisible join to first ch after initial hdc [96 + 8 ch]

Rnd 9: *{Join Yarn F in any ch-space, make your first stitch a standing stitch}* (sc + ch 2 + sc in ch-space, sc in next 24 st) repeat 4 times, fasten off with an invisible join to first ch after initial sc [104 + 8 ch]

{ *Sunny Side Pop Square shines in her calm presence next to a bursting granny square like Cotton Candy Square on page 204.* }

YUMNA SQUARE `80 stitch square`

inas.craft (Inas Fadil Basymeleh) — Indonesia
🅾 @inas.craft ⊛ www.inascraft.com

Skill level: Intermediate
Colors: Yarn A: Cream / Yarn B: Peony Pink / Yarn C: Burgundy
Special stitches: ch-4-picot (Picot stitch) / FPtr (Front post treble crochet) / 3-dc-bobble (3 double crochet bobble stitch)

INSTRUCTIONS

Rnd 1: *{start with yarn A}* start a magic ring with 8 sc, slst in initial sc [8]

Rnd 2: (sc in next st, ch 3) repeat 8 times, fasten off with an invisible join to first ch after initial sc [8 + 24 ch]

Rnd 3: *{join yarn B in any ch-space, make your first stitch a standing stitch}* (slst + ch 5 + 3-dc-bobble + ch 5 + slst in next ch-space) repeat 8 times, fasten off with an invisible join to first ch after initial slst [24 + 80 ch]

Rnd 4: *{join yarn C in any ch-space before a 3-dc-bobble, make your first stitch a standing stitch}* (sc + hdc + dc in ch-space, ch-4-picot, skip bobble, dc + hdc + sc in next ch-space, FPtr around next sc in Rnd 2) repeat 8 times, fasten off with an invisible join to 2nd stitch [96]

Rnd 5: *{join yarn C in any 3-dc-bobble in Rnd 3 at the back of the flower, make your first stitch a standing stitch}* (slst in 3-dc-bobble, ch 3) repeat 8 times, fasten off with an invisible join to first ch after initial slst [8 + 24 ch]

Rnd 6: *{join yarn A in any ch-space, make your first stitch a standing stitch)* (4 hdc in ch-space, 3 dc + ch 2 + 3 dc in next ch-space) repeat 4 times, slst in initial hdc [40 + 8 ch]

Rnd 7: ch 3 (count as dc), dc in next 6 st, 2 dc + ch 2 + 2 dc in next ch-space, (dc in next 10 st, 2 dc + ch 2 + 2 dc in next ch-space) repeat 3 times, dc in next 3 st, slst in 3rd ch of initial ch 3 [56 + 8 ch]

Note: Make tr stitches in Rnd 8 through the back of the picot's loop in Rnd 4, into the ch-space between 2 dc at the bottom of the picot.

Rnd 8: ch 3 (count as dc), dc in next 4 st, tr in next petal, skip 1 st on Rnd 7, dc in next 3 st, 2 dc + ch 2 + 2 dc in next ch-space, (dc in next 3 st, tr in next petal, skip 1 st on Rnd 7, dc in next 6 st, tr in next petal, skip 1 st on Rnd 7, dc in next 3 st, 2 dc + ch 2 + 2 dc in next ch-space) repeat 3 times, dc in next 3 st, tr in next petal, skip 1 st on Rnd 7, dc in next st, fasten off with an invisible join to first true dc [72 + 8 ch]

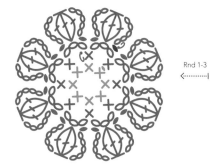

Rnd 1-3
⟵∙∙∙∙∙∙∙∙∙∙∙|

Rnd 4

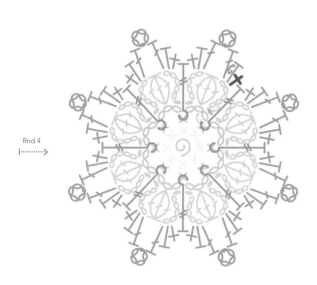

Rnd 5-8

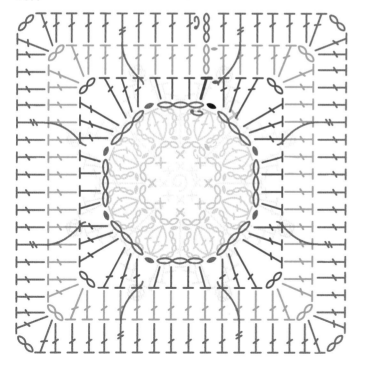

FLORAL PRINCESS SQUARE `112 stitch square`

Crochet Road (Joy Clements) — Australia
@crochetroad Crochet Road Crochet Road

Skill level: Intermediate
Colors: Yarn A: Peony Pink / Yarn B: Pastel Pink / Yarn C: Cream / Yarn D: Twilleys Goldfingering
Special stitches: Crossed stitch / 2-dc-bobble (2 double crochet bobble stitch) / FPdc (Front post double crochet) / BPdc (Back post double crochet) / htr (Half treble crochet)

INSTRUCTIONS

Rnd 1: *{start with yarn A}* start a magic ring with 8 sc, fasten off with an invisible join to 2nd stitch [8]

Rnd 2: *{join yarn B in any st, make your first stitch a standing stitch}* (2-dc-bobble in next st, ch 2) repeat 8 times, fasten off with an invisible join to first ch after initial 2-dc-bobble [8 bobbles + 16 ch]

Rnd 3: *{join yarn C in any ch-space, make your first stitch a standing stitch}* (2 sc in ch-space, sc in next 2-dc-bobble) repeat 8 times, fasten off with an invisible join to 2nd stitch [24]

Rnd 4: *{join yarn A in the back loop of any sc, make your first stitch a standing stitch. Work this round in BLO}* (3 dc in next st, crossed dc in previous st, skip 1 st) repeat 8 times, fasten off with an invisible join to 2nd stitch [48]

Rnd 5: *{join yarn B in the back loop of any dc, make your first stitch a standing stitch. Work this round in BLO}* BLO sc in all 48 st, slst in front loop of initial sc [48]

Rnd 6: *{work this round in FLO}* (skip 2 st, 2-dc-bobble + (ch 3 + 2-dc-bobble) repeat 4 times in same st, skip 2 st, slst in next st) repeat 7 times, skip 2 st, 2-dc-bobble + (ch 3 + 2-dc-bobble) repeat 4 times in same st, fasten off with an invisible join to initial 2-dc-bobble [8 petals]

Rnd 7: *{join yarn C in the leftover back loop of the central stitch of a petal, make your first stitch a standing stitch. this can be a bit tight, give your hook a little wriggle to work this stitch. Fold petals made in Rnd 6 forward and work into leftover back loops}* (dc in next 11 st, 2 dc in next st) repeat 4 times, slst in initial dc [52]

Rnd 8: ch 4 (count as tr), (htr + dc in next st, dc in next st, hdc in next 2 st, sc in next 4 st, hdc in next 2 st, dc in next st, dc + htr in next st, tr + ch 2 + tr in next st) repeat 3 times, htr + dc in next st, dc in next st, hdc in next 2 st, sc in next 4 st, hdc in next 2 st, dc in next st, dc + htr in next st, tr + ch 1 + sc in 4th ch of initial ch 4 [64 + 8 ch]

Rnd 9: *{work this round in BLO}* ch 3 (count as dc) + dc over joining sc in corner-space, (dc in next 16 st, 2 dc + ch 2 + 2 dc in corner-space) repeat 3 times, dc in next 16 st, 2 dc in initial corner-space, ch 1, sc in 3rd ch of initial ch 3 [80 + 8 ch]

Rnd 10: ch 2 (count as hdc) + 2 hdc over joining sc, [(FPdc around next st, BPdc around next st) repeat 10 times, 3 hdc + ch 2 + 3 hdc in corner-space] repeat 3 times, (FPdc around next st, BPdc around next st) repeat 10 times, 3 hdc + ch 2 in initial corner-space, fasten off with an invisible join in first true hdc [104 + 8 ch]

Embellishment (not in diagram): *{pull up a loop of yarn D from back to front in any stitch of Rnd 5 immediately outside the leftover front loop border made in Rnd 4. Work with right side facing you}* surface slst in next 47 st, fasten off with an invisible join to initial slst to form a final stitch [48]

Goldfingering or metallic yarns may not be the best choice if you want the result to be soft and cuddly. You might want to choose an alternative or leave out the embellishment, if you're making these squares into a baby blanket.

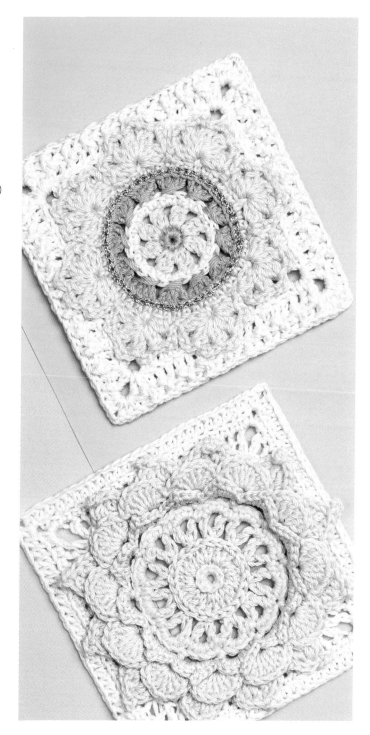

FLORAL SYMMETRY SQUARE 112 stitch square

Emmi Hai — Germany
⊗ www.emmihai.net

Skill level: Intermediate
Colors: Yarn A: Petroleum / Yarn B: Pistachio / Yarn C: Coral / Yarn D: Pearl
Special stitches: 3-dc-bobble (3 double crochet bobble) / **FPhdc** (Front post half double crochet) / **FPtr** (Front post treble crochet), **changing color mid-round**
Pattern-specific special stitch: 4-puff (Puff stitch with four long loops): (Yarn over and insert hook into indicated space, yarn over and pull up a long loop) repeat 4 times into the same space. Yarn over and pull through 8 loops. Yarn over again and pull through 2 loops to close the puff stitch.

INSTRUCTIONS

Rnd 1: *{start with yarn A}* start a magic ring with ch 3 (count as dc), 11 dc, slst in 3rd ch of initial ch 3 [12]

Rnd 2: ch 1, sc in same st, ch 2, sc in next 2 st, (sc in next st, ch 2, sc in next 2 st) repeat 3 times, fasten off with an invisible join to first ch after initial sc [12 + 8 ch]

Rnd 3: *{join yarn B in any ch-space, make your first stitch a standing stitch}* (3-dc-bobble + ch 3 + 3-dc-bobble in ch-space, ch 6) repeat 4 times, fasten off with an invisible join to first ch after initial 3-dc-bobble [8 + 36 ch]

Rnd 4: *{join yarn C in any ch-3-space, make your first stitch a standing stitch}* (7 tr in ch-3-space, ch 4) repeat 4 times, fasten off with an invisible join to 2nd stitch [28 + 16 ch]

Note: To change the color for stitches within Rnd 5, change the yarn while working the last stitch in the initial color. Work this stitch as normal until only the last two loops are left on the hook. Yarn over with the new color and pull through both loops on the hook.

Rnd 5: *{join yarn B in second tr of any 7-tr-group, make your first stitch a standing stitch}* [(sc in next st, ch 1) repeat 4 times, sc in next st *{change to yarn A}*, ch 2, 4 dc in next ch-space of Rnd 3 and 4 *{change to yarn B}*, ch 2, skip 1 tr] repeat 4 times, fasten off with an invisible join to first ch after initial sc [36 + 32 ch]

Rnd 6: *{join yarn A in ch-2-space between first sc and last dc of Rnd 5,*

make your first stitch a standing stitch} [2 sc in ch-2-space, ch 1, (2 sc in next ch-1-space, ch 1) repeat 4 times, 2 sc in next ch-2-space, sc in next 4 dc] repeat 4 times, fasten off with an invisible join to 2nd stitch [64 + 20 ch]

Rnd 7: *{join yarn D in first ch-space, make your first stitch a standing stitch}* [(4-puff in ch-space, ch 2 tightly) repeat 5 times, ch 6] repeat 4 times, fasten off with an invisible join to first ch after initial puff [20 + 64 ch]

Rnd 8: *{join yarn A around first puff, make your first stitch a standing stitch}* (FPhdc around next puff, 2 hdc in ch-2-space, FPhdc around next puff, 2 dc in ch-2-space, FPtr + ch 1 + FPtr around next puff, 2 dc in ch-2-space, FPhdc around next puff, 2 hdc in ch-2-space, FPhdc around next puff, dc in next 8 sc of Rnd 6) repeat 4 times, slst in initial FPhdc [88 + 4 ch]

Rnd 9: ch 1, sc in same st, sc in next 6 st, 2 sc + ch 1 + 2 sc in next ch-space, skip FPtr, (sc in next 21 st, 2 sc + ch 1 + 2 sc in next ch-space, skip FPtr) repeat 3 times, sc in next 14 st, fasten off with an invisible join to 2nd sc [100 + 4 ch]

Rnd 10: *{join yarn C in first sc of Rnd 9, make your first stitch a standing stitch}* [(sc in next st, ch 1, skip next st) repeat 4 times, sc in next st, ch 1, sc in next ch-space, ch 1, (sc in next st, ch 1, skip next st) repeat 8 times] repeat 4 times, fasten off with an invisible join to first ch after initial sc [56 + 56 ch]

Floral Symmetry Square is lovely when combined with any other open-shaped granny square, like Amber Square on page 82 or Rainbow Blossom Square on page 108.

ALPINE PINK SQUARE `112 stitch square`

Emmi Hai — Germany ⊕ www.emmihai.net

Skill level: Intermediate / Advanced
Colors: Yarn A: Cream / Yarn B: Antique pink / Yarn C: Graphite /
Yarn D: Lettuce
Special stitches: 2-dc-bobble (2 double crochet bobble stitch)
Pattern-specific special stitch: In this pattern we use two pattern-specific variants of the puff stitch.
4-puff (Puff stitch with four long loops): (Yarn over and insert hook into indicated stitch, yarn over and pull up a long loop) repeat 4 times into the same stitch. Yarn over and pull through 8 loops. Yarn over again and pull through 2 loops to close the puff stitch.
5-puff (Puff stitch with five long loops): (Yarn over and insert hook into indicated space, yarn over and pull up a long loop) repeat 5 times into the same space. Yarn over and pull through all 11 loops. Ch 1 to close the puff stitch (this chain is not counted as a stitch).

INSTRUCTIONS

Rnd 1: *{start with yarn A}* start a magic ring with 8 sc, fasten off with an invisible join to 2nd stitch [8]

Rnd 2: *{join yarn B in any sc, make your first stitch a standing stitch}* (4-puff, ch 1) repeat 8 times, slst in initial puff [8 + 8 ch]

Rnd 3: ch 1, sc in ch-space, ch 3, sc in next ch-space, ch 1, (sc in next ch-space, ch 3, sc in next ch-space, ch 1) repeat 3 times, fasten off with an invisible join to first ch after initial sc [8 + 16 ch]

Rnd 4: *{join yarn A in any ch-3-space, make your first stitch a standing stitch}* (2-dc-bobble + ch 2 + 2-dc-bobble + ch 2 + 2-dc-bobble in ch-3-space, ch 3) repeat 4 times, fasten off with an invisible join to first ch after initial 2-dc-bobble [12 + 28 ch]

Rnd 5: *{join yarn B in first ch-2-space between two 2-dc-bobbles, make your first stitch a standing stitch}* (5-puff in ch-2-space, ch 1, 5-puff in next ch-2-space, ch 6) repeat 4 times, fasten off with an invisible join to ch after initial puff [8 + 28 ch]

Rnd 6: *{continue working with yarn B, join in any ch-1-space between two 5-puffs, make your first stitch a standing stitch}* (5-puff in ch-1-space, ch 16) repeat 4 times, fasten off with an invisible join to first ch after initial puff [4 + 64 ch]

Rnd 7: *{join yarn C in any ch-space of Rnd 6, make your first stitch a standing stitch. Work only in the ch-spaces of Rnd 4, 5 and 6}* (5 sc in

Rnd 1-7

ch-space of Rnd 6, 2 dc in ch-spaces of Rnd 5 and 6, 2 dc in ch-spaces of Rnd 4 and 5, 2 dc in ch-spaces of Rnd 5 and 6, 5 sc in ch-space of Rnd 6) repeat 4 times, slst in initial sc [64] Do not fasten off. Put a stitch marker in the last loop to prevent it from unraveling. Pull out the Rnd 6 chains in the middle of each side, so you get 4 loops on the back side.

Rnd 8: {join yarn D in any loop you pulled out, make your first stitch a standing stitch} (6 tr + ch 3 + 6 tr in loop, ch 5) repeat 4 times, fasten off with an invisible join to 2nd stitch [48 + 32 ch] These four edges will form the leaves. Flip each leave to the back and pull through the matching space between the 2-dc-bobble-groups of Rnd 4.

Rnd 9: {put the yarn C loop at the end of Rnd 7 back on your hook} ch 3 (count as dc) + dc + ch 2 + 2 dc in first sc of Rnd 7, dc in next 15 st, (2 dc + ch 2 + 2 dc in next st, dc in next 15 st) repeat 3 times, slst in 3rd ch of initial ch 3 [76 + 8 ch]

Note: Attaching the petals in Rnd 10: Start dc by yarn over, insert hook into indicated stitch, yarn over and pull up a loop. Yarn over again and pull through two loops. Before completing the dc, put the ch-3-space of Rnd 8 over the hook, then yarn over and pull through all.

Rnd 8-11

Rnd 10: ch 3 (count as dc), dc in next st, 2 dc + ch 2 + 2 dc in next ch-space, dc in next 9 st, dc in next st and ch-3-space of Rnd 8 to join, (dc in next 9 st, 2 dc + ch 2 + 2 dc in next ch-space, dc in next 9 st, dc in next st and ch-3-space of Rnd 8 to join) repeat 3 times, dc in next 7 st, fasten off with an invisible join to first true dc [92 + 8 ch]

Rnd 11: {join yarn B in any ch-space, make your first stitch a standing stitch} [2 hdc + ch 2 + 2 hdc in ch-2-space, skip next st, (2 hdc in next st, skip next st) repeat 11 times] repeat 4 times, fasten off with an invisible join to 2nd stitch [104 + 8 ch]

NORDIC SERENITY SQUARE `112 stitch square`

Crochetedbytess (Therese Eghult) — Sweden
⊛ www.sistersinstitch.com

Skill level: Intermediate
Colors: Yarn A: Cream / Yarn B: Pearl / Yarn C: Fuchsia / Yarn D: Ecru / Yarn E: Peony Pink / Yarn F: Ice Blue
Special stitches: 6-puff (puff stitch with 6 loops) / v-stitch (dc + ch 2 + dc) / Long slst (long slip stitch) / Long 5-Puff (long puff stitch with 5 loops) / Dc-2tog (Double crochet 2 stitches together) / BPsc (Back post single crochet) / BPhdc (Back post half double crochet) / BPdc (Back post double crochet)

INSTRUCTIONS

Rnd 1: {start with yarn A} start a magic ring with (6-puff, ch 2, 6-puff, ch 3) repeat 4 times, fasten off with an invisible join to ch after initial puff [8 + 20 ch]

Rnd 2: {join yarn B in any ch-3-space, make your first stitch a standing stitch} (3 hdc + ch 1 + 3 hdc in ch-2-space) repeat 4 times, fasten off with an invisible join to 2nd stitch [24 + 4 ch]

Rnd 3: {join yarn C in any ch-space, make your first stitch a standing stitch} (2 dc + ch 1 + 2 dc in ch-space, hdc in next 2 st, sc in next st, long slst in the ch-2-space from Rnd 1, sc in next st, hdc in next 2 st) repeat 4 times, fasten off with an invisible join to 2nd stitch [44 + 4 ch]

Rnd 4: {join yarn D in any ch-space, make your first stitch a standing stitch} (sc in ch-space, ch 5, skip 4 st, BPdc around next sc, ch 1, BPdc around next sc, ch 5, skip 4 st) repeat 4 times, fasten off with an invisible join to first ch after initial sc [12 + 44 ch]

Rnd 5: {join yarn E in any ch-1-space, make your first stitch a standing stitch} (tr + 3 dc + ch 1 + 3 dc + tr in ch-1-space, skip 1 st, sc in the ch-space next to the sc from Rnd 4, ch 2, skip 1 st, sc in the ch-space on the other side of the sc, skip 1 st) repeat 4 times, fasten off with an invisible join to 2nd stitch [40 + 12 ch]

Rnd 6: {join yarn F in any ch-2-space, make your first stitch a standing stitch} (8 hdc in ch-2-space, skip 1 st, BPsc around next 4 st, 3 sc in next ch-space, BPsc around next 4 st, skip 1 st) repeat 4 times, fasten off with an invisible join to 2nd stitch [76]

Rnd 7: {join yarn A in any first hdc, make your first stitch a standing stitch} (BPhdc in next 4 st, sc in between the 4th and 5th hdc, BPhdc in next 4 st, ch 5, skip 5 st, sc in next st, ch 5, skip 5 st) repeat 4 times, fasten off with an invisible join to 2nd stitch [40 + 40 ch]

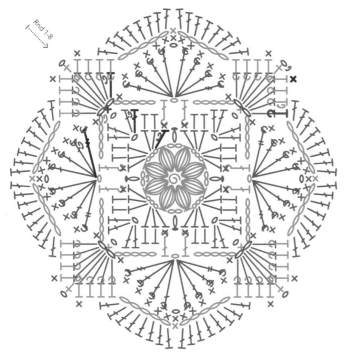

Rnd 1-8

Rnd 8: *{join yarn B in any fourth BPhdc, make your first stitch a standing stitch}* (sc in next st, ch 1, skip 1 st, sc in next st, skip 3 st, 8 dc in the next ch-space, skip 1 st, 8 dc in the next ch-space, skip 3 st) repeat 4 times, fasten off with an invisible join to ch after initial sc [72 + 4 ch]

Rnd 9: *{Join yarn A in any first dc after a sc, make your first stitch a standing stitch. In this round we will be working some stitches in front of our work and down to Rnd 7}* (BPhdc in next 8 st, long 5-puff down into the sc from Rnd 7, ch 1, BPhdc in next 8 st, skip 1 st, v-stitch over the ch1-space and into the sc from Rnd 7, skip 1 st) repeat 4 times, fasten off with an invisible join to 2nd stitch [76 + 12 ch]

Rnd 10: *{join yarn C around the middle ch-space of any v-stitch, make your first stitch a standing stitch}* [(2-dc-bobble + ch 2) repeat 3 times + 2-dc-bobble in v-stitch, skip 3 st *{the first skipped st is the last dc in the v-stitch}*, hdc in next 2 st, sc in next 4 st, slst between the BPhdc and the puff, skip puff, slst between the puff and the BPhdc, sc in next 4 st, hdc in next 2 st, ch 1, skip 3 st *{the last skipped st is the first dc in the v-stitch}*] repeat 4 times, fasten off with an invisible join to first ch after initial dc2tog [72 + 28 ch]

Rnd 11: *{join yarn A in any second ch-2-space, make your first stitch a standing stitch}* (2 dc + ch 2 + 2 dc in ch-space, dc in next st, 2 dc in next ch-2-space, dc in next 3 st, hdc in next 10 st, dc in next 2 st, dc2tog over next ch-1-space and the first 2-dc-bobble, 2 dc in next ch-2-space, dc in next st) repeat 4 times, fasten off with an invisible join to 2nd stitch [104 + 8 ch]

Rnd 9-11

PONDING LILY SQUARE `112 stitch square`

Crochetedbytess (Therese Eghult) — Sweden
⊕ www.sistersinstitch.com

Skill level: Intermediate
Colors: Yarn A: Golden Glow / Yarn B: Pearl / Yarn C: Pastel Pink /
Yarn D: Peony pink / Yarn E: Eucalyptus / Yarn F: Cream /
Yarn G: Nordic Blue
Special stitches: v-stitch (dc + ch 2 + dc) / **tall v-stitch** (tr + ch 2 + tr) /
FPhdc (Front post half double crochet) / BPhdc (Back post half double
crochet) / FPdc (Front post double crochet) / Sc2tog (Single crochet 2
stitches together) / **FP-2-tr-bobble** (Front post 2 treble bobble stitch) /
2-dc-bobble (2 double crochet bobble stitch)

INSTRUCTIONS

Rnd 1: {start with yarn A} start a magic ring with 6 sc, slst in initial sc [6]

Rnd 2: ch 3 (count as dc), dc in same st, 2 dc in next 5 st, fasten off with
an invisible join to first true dc [12]

Rnd 3: {join yarn B in any st, make your first stitch a standing stitch}
(2 sc in next st, FPhdc in next st) repeat 6 times, fasten off with an invisible
join to 2nd stitch [18]

Rnd 4: {join yarn C in any first sc, make your first stitch a standing
stitch} (BPhdc in next 2 st, FPv-stitch around the FPhdc) repeat 6 times,
fasten off with an invisible join to 2nd stitch [18]

Rnd 5: {join yarn D in any ch-space in a v-stitch, make your first stitch
a standing stitch. Skip all FPdc and BPhdc stitches} (7 dc in ch-space,
skip 2 st on Rnd 4, slst in second sc of Rnd 3, skip 2 st on Rnd 4) repeat
6 times, fasten off with an invisible join to 2nd stitch [42]

Rnd 6: {join yarn E in any first BPhdc from Rnd 4, make your first stitch
a standing stitch. Work behind the petals of Rnd 5, work only in the
BPhdc in Rnd 4} (3 dc in next BPhdc, 3 dc in next BPhdc) repeat 6 times,
slst in initial dc [36]

Rnd 7: ch 1 + hdc in same st, hdc in next 4 st, hdc + ch 1 + slst in next st,
(slst + ch 1 + hdc in next st, hdc in next 4 st, hdc + ch 1 + slst in next st)
repeat 5 times, fasten off with an invisible join to ch after initial slst
[64 + 12 ch]

Rnd 8: {join yarn F in the gap between any two petals, make your first

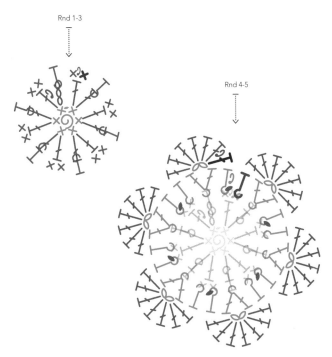

Rnd 1-3

Rnd 4-5

stitch a standing stitch. Work the tall v-stitch over and around the petals from Rnd 7 and 6} (tall v-stitch in gap between petals, ch 3, BLO sc in the fourth hdc of the leaf, ch 3) repeat 6 times, slst in initial tr [12 + 36 ch]

Note: in Rnd 9 you work a sc2tog over tall v-stitch tr-stitches and sc stitches from Rnd 8. Starting in the given ch-space before the stitch, begin as a normal sc (2 loops on the hook) and before doing the final yo, go under the next ch-space, yo and pull up a loop (3 loops on the hook), yo and pull through all 3 loops. You are never working in the stitches of Rnd 8 but the head of the decrease falls right on top of it, with one leg in each ch-space.

Rnd 9: slst in ch-2-space of the tall v-stitch, ch 1, 3 sc in same ch-space, sc2tog over the tall v-stitch treble stitch, 3 sc in next ch-space, sc2tog over the sc, 3 sc in next ch-space, sc2tog over the tall v-stitch treble stitch, (3 sc in next ch-space, sc2tog over the tall v-stitch treble stitch, 3 sc in next ch-space, sc2tog over the sc, 3 sc in next ch-space, sc2tog over the tall v-stitch treble stitch) repeat 5 times, fasten off with an invisible join to 2nd sc [72]

Rnd 10: *{join yarn G in any sc2tog, make your first stitch a standing stitch}* (v-stitch, skip 2 st) repeat 24 times, slst in initial dc [24]

Rnd 11: *{work in each dc and around each ch}* ch 1 + sc in same st, sc in next 15 st and ch, (skip 1 st, dc + ch 1 + dc + ch 1 + dc + ch 1 + dc in the ch-2-space of the v-stitch, skip 1 st, sc in next 20 st and ch) repeat 3 times, skip 1 st, (dc + ch 1 + dc + ch 1 + dc + ch 1 + dc in the ch-2-space of the v-stitch), skip 1 st, sc in next 4 st and ch, fasten off with an invisible join to 2nd sc [96 + 12 ch]

Rnd 12: *{join yarn F in any second ch-space, make your first stitch a standing stitch}* (dc + ch 3 + dc in second ch-space, FP-2-dc-bobble around the third dc, dc in the ch-space, FP-2-tr-bobble around the fourth dc, skip 2 st, hdc in next 4 st, sc in next 8 st, hdc in next 4 st, skip 2 st, FP-2-tr-bobble around the first dc, dc in the ch-space, FP-2-dc-bobble around the second dc) repeat 4 times, slst in initial dc [96 + 12 ch]

Rnd 13: (4 sc in next ch-3-space, sc in next st, sc in the gap between dc and 2-dc-bobble, skip 2-dc-bobble, sc in the gap between 2-dc-bobble and dc, sc in next dc, skip 2-tr-bobble, sc in the gap between 2-tr-bobble and hdc, skip hdc, sc in next 15 st, sc in the gap between hdc and 2-tr-bobble, skip 2-tr-bobble, sc in next dc, sc in the gap between dc and 2-dc-bobble, skip 2-dc-bobble, sc in next dc) repeat 4 times, fasten off with an invisible join to 2nd stitch [112]

Rnd 6-13

RANIA SQUARE `112 stitch square`

inas.craft (Inas Fadil Basymeleh) — Indonesia
@inas.craft www.inascraft.com

Skill level: Intermediate
Colors: Yarn A: Cream / Yarn B: Nordic Blue / Yarn C: Navy Blue /
Yarn D: Ice Blue
Special stitches: BPsc (Back post single crochet) / FPtr (Front post
treble crochet), **tall v-stitch** (tr + ch 2 + tr)

INSTRUCTIONS

Rnd 1: {*start with yarn A*} start a magic ring with (sc, ch 5) repeat 8 times, fasten off with an invisible join to first ch after initial sc [8 + 40 ch]

Rnd 2: {*join yarn A in any ch-space, make your first stitch a standing stitch*} (sc in ch-space, ch 3) repeat 8 times, fasten off with an invisible join to first ch after initial sc [8 + 24 ch]

Rnd 3: {*join yarn B in any ch-space, make your first stitch a standing stitch*} (slst + ch 2 + 2 dc + ch 2 + 2 dc + ch 2 + slst in ch-space) repeat 8 times, fasten off with an invisible join to first ch after initial slst [48 + 48 ch]

Rnd 4: {*join yarn A around any sc in Rnd 2, make your first stitch a standing stitch. Work behind Rnd 3*} (BPsc around sc in Rnd 2, ch 3) repeat 8 times, fasten off with an invisible join first ch after initial BPsc [8 + 24 ch]

Rnd 5: {*join yarn C in any Rnd 4 ch-space, make your first stitch a standing stitch*} (5 dc in ch-space, FPtr around sc in Rnd 2) repeat 8 times, slst in initial dc [48]

Rnd 6: ch 3 (count as dc), 2 dc in same st, sc in next ch-2-space of Rnd 3 (top of petal), skip next 3 st on Rnd 5, 3 dc in next st, tall v-stitch in next FPtr, (3 dc in next st, sc in ch-2-space in Rnd 3 (top of petal), skip next 3 st on Rnd 5, 3 dc in next st, tall v-stitch in next FPtr) repeat 7 times, fasten off with an invisible join to first true dc [72 + 16 ch]

Rnd 7: {*find the skipped 3 dc in Rnd 5 behind the petal, join yarn D in the second skipped dc, make your first stitch a standing stitch*} (sc in second skipped dc, ch 6) repeat 8 times, slst in initial sc [8 + 84 ch]

Rnd 8: ch 10 (count as tr + 6 ch) + tr in same st, ch 4, dc in next ch-6-space, ch 3, slst in ch-2-space of Rnd 6, ch 2, dc in same previous ch-6-space, ch 2, dc in next sc, ch 2, dc in next ch-6-space, ch 2, slst in ch-2-space of Rnd 6, ch 3, dc in same previous ch-6-space, ch 4, (tr + ch 6 + tr in next sc, ch 4, dc in next ch-6-space, ch 3, slst in ch-2 space of Rnd 6, ch 2, dc in same previous ch-6-space, ch 2, dc in next sc, ch 2, dc in next ch-6-space, ch 2, slst in ch-2-space of Rnd 6, ch 3, dc in same previous ch-6-space, ch 4) repeat 3 times, fasten off with an invisible join to 4th ch of initial ch 10 [36 + 112 ch]

Rnd 9: *{Join yarn A in any ch-6-space, make your first stitch a standing stitch}* (3 hdc + ch 2 + 3 hdc in ch-6-space, (2 hdc in next ch-space) repeat 8 times) repeat 4 times, fasten off with an invisible join to 2nd stitch [88 + 8 ch]

Rnd 10: *{Join yarn A in any ch-2-corner-space, make your first stitch a standing stitch}* (2 dc + ch 2 + 2 dc in ch-2-space, dc in next 22 st) repeat 4 times, fasten off with an invisible join to 2nd stitch [104 + 8 ch]

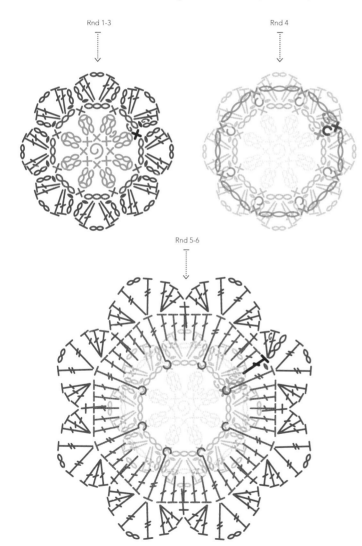

Rnd 1-3

Rnd 4

Rnd 5-6

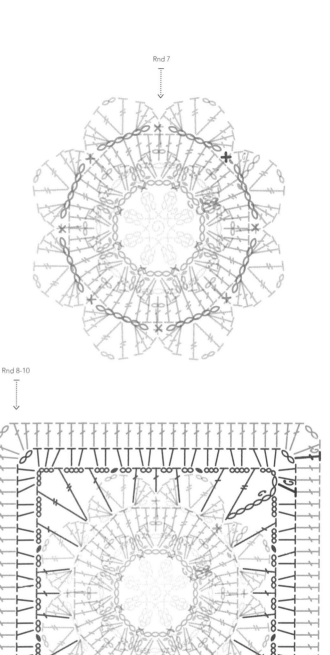

Rnd 7

Rnd 8-10

Rania Square — 153

OH I ADORE SQUARE 112 stitch square

Crochetedbytess (Therese Eghult) — Sweden
⊕ www.sistersinstitch.com

Skill level: Intermediate / Advanced
Colors: Yarn A: Cream / Yarn B: Ice Blue / Yarn C: Limestone /
Yarn D: Pearl / Yarn E: Cream / Yarn F: Jade Gravel
Special stitches: 4-dc-pc (4 double crochet popcorn stitch) /
3-dc-bobble (3 double crochet bobble stitch) / sc2tog (single crochet
2 stitches together)
Pattern-specific special stitch: starting 4-dc-pc: standing dc + 3 dc or
ch 2 + 3 dc, closes as a normal popcorn.

INSTRUCTIONS

Rnd 1: *{start with yarn A}* start a magic ring with 6 sc, slst in initial sc [6]

Rnd 2: starting 4-dc-pc, ch 2, (4-dc-pc, ch 2) repeat 5 times, slst in initial
pc [6 + 6 ch]

Rnd 3: *{Work exclusively in the ch-spaces between the pc stitches}* slst
in ch-space, starting 4-dc-pc + ch 2 + 4-dc-pc + ch 2 in the same
ch-space, (4-dc-pc + ch 2 + 4-dc-pc + ch 2 in next ch-space) repeat 5
times, slst in initial 4-dc-pc [12 + 12 ch]

Rnd 4: *{Work exclusively in the pc stitches}* (ch 8, slst in next pc) repeat
12 times, fasten off with an invisible join to 2nd ch [12 + 96 ch]

Rnd 5: *{join yarn B around the chain between any set of pc increases in
Rnd 3, make your first stitch a standing stitch. Work the pc stitches in
front of the ch-8-spaces which you fold to the back, and in the ch-space
between the pc increases from Rnd 3}* (4-dc-pc + ch 1 in ch-space of
Rnd 3, 6 hdc + dc + ch 2 + dc + 6 hdc in next ch-8-space) repeat 6 times,
fasten off with an invisible join to 2nd stitch [90 + 12 ch, 6 petals]

Rnd 6: *{join yarn C in a leftover ch-2-space between any 2 pc stitches
from Rnd 3, make your first stitch a standing stitch. Fold the petal
back and work in front of it}* (4-dc-pc + ch 2 + 4-dc-pc + ch 3 in ch-space
between 2 pc stitches from Rnd 3, 4 hdc + dc + ch 2 + dc + 4 hdc in the
leftover ch-8-space behind the pc from Rnd 5, ch 2) repeat 6 times, fasten
off with an invisible join to first ch after initial pc [56 + 24 ch]

Rnd 7: *{join yarn D in any of the top ch-2-spaces of Rnd 6, make
your first stitch a standing stitch}* (sc in ch-2-space of Rnd 6, ch 6, sc in
ch-2-space of Rnd 5, ch 6) repeat 6 times, slst in initial sc [12 + 72 ch]

Rnd 1-5

Note: in Rnd 8 you work a decrease over sc from Rnd 7. Starting in the given ch-space, begin as a normal sc (2 loops on the hook) and before doing the final yo, go under the next ch-space, yo and pull up a loop (3 loops on the hook), yo and pull through all 3 loops. You are never working in the sc of Rnd 8 but the head of the decrease falls right on top of it, with one leg in each ch-space.

Rnd 8: slst in next ch-space, ch 1, (8 sc in next ch-space, sc2tog over the sc from Rnd 7 connecting 2 ch-spaces) repeat 12 times, fasten off with an invisible join to first ch after initial slst [108]

Rnd 9: *{join yarn E in any sc2tog stitch from Rnd 8, make your first stitch a standing stitch}* (3-dc-bobble + ch 3 + 3-dc-bobble + ch 3 + 3-dc-bobble + ch 3 + 3-dc-bobble in sc2tog from Rnd 8, ch 3, skip 8 st, sc in next sc2tog, ch 7, sc in next sc2tog, ch 3, skip 8 st) repeat 4 times, fasten off with an invisible join to first ch after dc-3-bobble [24 + 88 ch]

Rnd 10: *{join yarn F in any ch-3-space between a second and third 3-dc-bobble from Rnd 9, make your first stitch a standing stitch}* (2 dc + ch 3 + 2 dc in ch-3-space between the second and third 3-dc-bobble, skip 3-dc-bobble, 2 sc in next ch-space, ch 1, skip 3-dc-bobble, 3 hdc in next ch-space, ch 1, skip 1 st, 3 hdc + ch 1 + 3 hdc in next ch-space, ch 1, skip 1 st, 3 hdc in next ch-space, ch 1, skip 3-dc-bobble, 2 sc in the next ch-space, skip 3-dc-bobble) repeat 4 times, fasten off with an invisible join to 2nd stitch [80 + 32 ch]

Rnd 6-10

IN LIKE A LAMB - OUT LIKE A LION SQUARE   `112 stitch square`

Designs By Muggins (Margaret MacInnis) — Canada
mugginsquilts **f** DesignsbyMuggins 🌐 www.designsbymuggins.com

Skill level: Intermediate / Advanced
Colors: Yarn A: Pearl / Yarn B: Peony Pink / Yarn C: Glass /
Yarn D: Sunflower
Special stitches: FPdc (Front post double crochet) / FPtr (Front post treble crochet) / FPdtr (Front post double treble crochet)
Pattern-specific special stitch:
Special Decrease: worked over 3 stitches as follows:
Stitch 1: yarn over, insert hook in BLO of 6th dc on petal, yarn over, pull through first loop, yarn over, pull through 2 loops,
Stitch 2: yarn over 2 times, insert hook into skipped hdc on Rnd 1 and work around the space between two petals, yarn over, pull loop through, (yarn over, pull through 2 loops) repeat 2 times (3 loops on hook)
Stitch 3: yarn over, insert hook in back loop of chain of next dc of next petal, yarn over, pull loop through, yarn over, pull through 2 loops (4 loops on hook); yarn over, pull through 4 loops on hook

INSTRUCTIONS

Note: We use a smaller hook for Rnd 3, one size smaller than the one used for the main work
Note: Pay special attention to the distinction between working in the back bump of a chain, working in BLO, and working in both loops of a stitch to achieve the right stitch definition and texture.

Rnd 1: *{start with yarn D}* start a magic ring with ch 2 (count as hdc), 11 hdc, fasten off with an invisible join to first true hdc [12]

Rnd 2: *{join yarn A in FLO of any hdc, make your first stitch a standing stitch}* (FLO slst in next hdc, ch 8, BLO dc in 3rd ch from hook, BLO dc in next 5 ch, FLO slst in same st as beginning slst, skip next hdc) repeat 6 times, fasten off with an invisible join to first ch after initial slst [6 petals]

Rnd 3: *{Use a smaller hook for this round. Join yarn B in second ch at the tip of a petal, make your first stitch a standing stitch. Count down from the back bumps on the chains on the next tip to determine where to finish the special decrease stitch}* (sc in back bump of second ch, BLO sc in next 5 dc, work Special Decrease, sc in back bump at base of next 5 dc, sc in back bump of first ch, ch 2) repeat 6 times, fasten off with an invisible join to 2nd stitch [6 petals]

Rnd 4: *{Use your normal hook for this round. Join yarn C in fourth sc*

Rnd 1-3
|- - - - - >

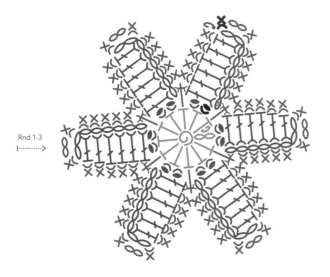

after any petal tip, make your first stitch a standing stitch. Work this entire round in BLO except for the FP stitches} (sc in next 2 st, skip 1 st, FPtr around center post of Special Decrease st, skip 1 st, sc in next 3 st, ch 4, place ch 4 behind the petal tip, skip to third sc left side of petal tip, sc in this stitch) repeat 6 times, slst in initial sc [42 + 24 ch]

Rnd 5: *{Work this entire round in both loops}* ch 2 (count as hdc), hdc in next st, (FPdc around FPtr, hdc in next 3 st, 5 dc in ch-4-space, hdc in next 3 st) repeat 5 times, FPdc around FPtr, hdc in next 3 st, 5 dc in ch-4-space, hdc in next st, fasten off with an invisible join to first true hdc [72]

Rnd 6: *{Join yarn B in 1st dc of any 5-dc-group, make your first stitch a standing stitch}* (sc in next 2 st, hdc in third dc of 5-dc-group enclosing ch-2 tip from Rnd 3 petal, sc in next 2 st, skip 3 st, 2 tr + FPdtr + 2 tr in next FPdc *{work these last 2 tr in the same st but slightly behind the post st}* skip 3 st) repeat 6 times, fasten off with an invisible join to 2nd stitch [60]

Rnd 7: *{Join yarn A in any Fpdtr, make your first stitch a standing stitch}* (sc in next 2 st, 2 hdc in next st, dc in next 2 st, tr in next 2 st, 2 tr + ch 2 + 2 tr in next st, tr in next 2 st, dc in next 2 st, 2 hdc in next st, sc in next 2 st) repeat 4 times, fasten off with an invisible join to 2nd stitch [80 + 8 ch]

Rnd 8: *{Join yarn C in any corner-space, make your first stitch a standing stitch}* [hdc + ch 1 + dc + ch 2 + dc + ch 1 + hdc + ch 1 in corner-space, skip 2 st, (hdc in next st, ch 1, skip next st) repeat 9 times] repeat 4 times, fasten off with an invisible join to first ch after initial hdc [52 + 56 ch]

Rnd 9: *{Join yarn B in first hdc of any corner, make your first stitch a standing stitch. All sc in this round are worked in Rnd 8, all other stitches are worked in Rnd 7}* [sc in next hdc, dc in corner-space of Rnd 7 behind ch-1-space of Rnd 8, sc in next dc, sc in corner-space, tr behind corner-space and into corner-space of Rnd 8, sc in same corner-space, sc in dc, dc in corner-space of Rnd 7 and behind ch-1-space of Rnd 8, sc in next hdc, dc in second skipped st below and behind ch-1-space (sc in next hdc, dc in next skipped st below and behind ch-1-space) repeat 9 times] repeat 4 times, fasten off with an invisible join to 2nd stitch [112]

"In like a lamb, out like a lion" is an English proverb describing March weather. The month of March starts with cold, winter weather, but ends mild and pleasant when spring starts.

Rnd 4-5

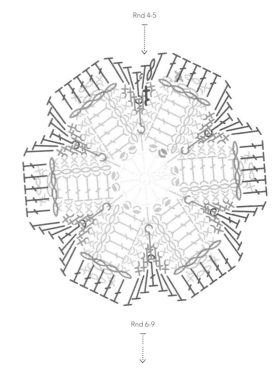

Rnd 6-9

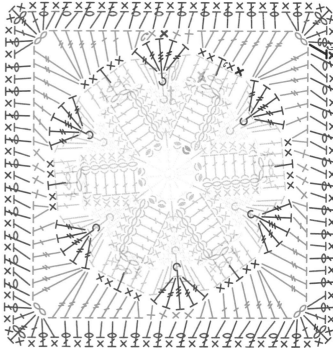

KITTEN'S CLAW SQUARE `112 stitch square`

Designs By Muggins (Margaret MacInnis) — Canada
© mugginsquilts f DesignsbyMuggins ⊕ www.designsbymuggins.com

Skill level: Intermediate
Colors: Yarn A: Cream / Yarn B: Jade gravel / Yarn C: Glass / Yarn D: Riverside / Yarn E: Cantaloupe / Yarn F: Sorbet
Special stitches: FPdc (Front post double crochet) / FPtr (Front post treble crochet) / FPdtr (Front post double treble crochet) / FPtrtr (Front post triple treble crochet)

INSTRUCTIONS

Note: Make sure you have a set of stitch markers at hand. Counting, marking, and figuring out where to put posts: this pattern goes down as far as three rows prior and it's important to mark those stitches to track stitch placement. This is crucial to the balance of the final work.

Rnd 1: {start with yarn A} start a magic ring with ch 3 (count as dc), 2 dc, ch 2, (3 dc, ch 2) repeat 3 times, fasten off with an invisible join to first true dc [12 + 8 ch]

Rnd 2: {join yarn B in any ch-space, make your first stitch a standing stitch} 2 dc in ch-space, (dc in next 3 st, 2 dc + ch 2 + 2 dc in ch-space) repeat 3 times, dc in next 3 st, 2 dc + ch 2 in initial ch-space, fasten off with an invisible join to 2nd stitch [28 + 8 ch]
Place a stitch marker around the post of the center dc stitches of each side.

Rnd 3: {join yarn C in first dc following corner ch-space, make your first stitch a standing stitch} (dc in next 7 st, 2 dc + ch 2 + 2 dc in ch-space) repeat 4 times, slst in initial dc [44 + 8 ch]
Place a stitch marker around the post of the fourth dc stitch before and after the ch-2-space of each side.

Rnd 4: ch 3 (count as dc), dc in next 8 st, 2 dc + ch 2 + 2 dc in ch-space, (dc in next 11 st, 2 dc + ch 2 + 2 dc in next ch-space) repeat 3 times, dc in next 2 st, fasten off with an invisible join to first true dc [60 + 8 ch]
Place a stitch marker around the post of the fourth dc stitch before and after the ch-2-space of each side.

Rnd 5: {join yarn D in any corner-space, make your first stitch a standing stitch} (2 dc + ch 2 + 2 dc in next ch-space, dc in next 15 st) repeat 4 times, fasten off with an invisible join to 1st true dc [76 + 8 ch]
Place a stitch marker around the post of the fourth dc stitch before and

after the ch-2-space of each side.

Note: in Rnd 6 we'll work a series of post stitches around the marked stitches of the previous 4 rounds. Each subsequent post stitch will be longer, and then gradate back up to form a "V". Skip the stitches behind the post stitches on Rnd 6. Remove the markers as you work. Work the post stitches very loosely.

Rnd 6: *{join yarn A in the first stitch after a corner-space, make your first stitch a standing stitch}* (sc in next 3 st, FPdc around post of marked stitch of Rnd 5, sc in next st, FPtr around post of marked stitch of Rnd 4, sc in next st, FPdtr around post of marked stitch of Rnd 3, sc in next st, FPtrtr around post of marked stitch of Rnd 2, sc in next st, FPdtr around post of marked stitch of Rnd 3, sc in next st, FPtr around post of marked stitch of Rnd 4, sc in next st, FPdc around post of marked stitch of Rnd 5, sc in next 3 st, sc + ch 2 + sc in ch-space) repeat 4 times, slst in initial sc [84 + 8 ch]

Option 1 Rnd 7: *{This is a regular round for those who find their sides already even. The total stitch count is the same}* sc in same st, sc in next 19 st, 3 sc in next ch-space, (sc in next 21 st, 3 sc in next ch-space) repeat 3 times, sc in next st, invisible join to 2nd stitch [96]

Option 2 Rnd 7 (not in diagram): *{This is the even up round, which will smooth out the kite effect of the previous round if you get a large dip in the sides. The total stitch count is the same}* ch 1, (sc in next st, hdc in next 4 st, dc in next 3 st, tr in next 3 st, dc in next 3 st, hdc in next 4 st, sc in next 2 st, 3 sc in ch-space, sc in next st) repeat 4 times, invisible join to 2nd stitch [96]

Rnd 8: *{join yarn E in a middle corner sc, make your first stitch a standing stitch}* [sc + ch 2 + sc in middle corner sc, (ch 1, skip next st, sc in next st) repeat 11 times, ch 1, skip next st] repeat 4 times, fasten off with an invisible join to 1st ch after initial sc [52 + 56 ch]

Rnd 9: *{join yarn F in a corner-space, make your first stitch a standing stitch}* [sc + ch 2 + sc in corner-space, (skip next st, 2 long sc in next Rnd 7 skipped stitch enclosing Rnd 8 ch-1-space) repeat 12 times, skip next st] repeat 4 times, fasten off with an invisible join to 1st ch after initial sc [104 + 8 ch]

Kitten's Claw Square shows its features best when choosing high contrasting colors for yarn A versus yarns C and D.

BEAUTY IN EXCELLENCE SQUARE `112 stitch square`

Designs By Muggins (Margaret MacInnis) — Canada
mugginsquilts DesignsbyMuggins www.designsbymuggins.com

Skill level: Advanced
Colors: Yarn A: Petrol Blue / **Yarn B:** Old Pink / **Yarn C:** Birch
Special stitches: 2-dc-bobble (2 double crochet bobble stitch) /
FPsc (Front post single crochet) / FPdc (Front post double crochet)
Pattern-specific special stitch:
Beginning-2-dc-bobble: join with a slst, ch 2, yo, insert hook, (yo, pull through 2 loops) repeat 2 times
Bobble Group: 2-dc-bobble + ch 1 + 2-dc-bobble + ch 1 + 2-dc-bobble in same stitch or space
Make X: skip to space following next sc and before bobble-group, dc in this space, ch 1, *lay dc just made on top of sc skipped, dc into space to the right of the same sc (enclosing both the dc just laid down and the space).
Beginning X: start with slst in space following sc, ch 4 (count as dc + ch 1), finish X as in Make X from *.

INSTRUCTIONS

Rnd 1: *{start with yarn A}* work a magic ring with ch 3 (count as dc), dc, (ch 3 + 3 dc) repeat 3 times, ch 3, dc, slst in 3rd ch of initial ch 3 [12 + 12 ch]

Rnd 2: ch 3 (count as dc), dc in next st, (5 dc in next ch-space, dc in next 3 st) repeat 3 times, 5 dc in next ch-space, dc in next st, fasten off with an invisible join to first true dc [32]

Rnd 3: *{join yarn B in the last dc of any 5-dc-group in a corner, make your first stitch a standing stitch}* sc in next 5 st, (3 sc in middle corner st, sc in next 7 st) repeat 3 times, 3 sc in middle corner st, sc in next st, slst in initial sc (40)
Put a stitch maker in your yarn B loop to prevent it from unraveling. Keep yarn and loop to the back while you work Rnd 4.

Rnd 4: *{Join yarn C with a slst in second sc of any corner}* Beginning-2-dc-bobble, finish bobble-group in same st, (ch 1, skip 1 st, sc in next st, skip 2 st, bobble-group in next st, skip 2 st, sc in next st, ch 1, skip 1 st, bobble-group in next st) repeat 3 times, ch 1, skip 1 st, sc in next st, skip 2 st, bobble-group in next st, skip 2 st, sc in next st, ch 1, skip 1 st, slst in initial bobble [32 + 24 ch]
Put a stitch maker in your yarn C loop to prevent it from unraveling. Keep yarn and loop to the back while you work Rnd 5.

Rnd 5: *{put yarn B at the end of Rnd 3 back on your hook, slst in next gap after the sc}* Beginning-X, sc in top of middle bobble in next bobble-group, ch 1, Make X over next sc, (sc in ch-1-space between first two bobble of corner bobble-group, ch 3, sc in ch-1-space between second and third bobble of bobble-group, ch 1, Make X over next sc, sc in middle bobble of next bobble-group, ch 1, Make X over next sc) repeat 3 times, sc in ch-1-space between first two bobble of corner bobble-group, ch 3, sc in ch-1-space between second and third bobble of bobble-group, ch 1, slst over the ch in initial X [12 + 20 ch + 8 X]
Put a stitch maker in your yarn B loop to prevent it from unraveling. Keep yarn and loop to the back while you work Rnd 6.

Rnd 6: *{put yarn C at the end of Rnd 4 back on your hook, slst in next ch-3-space}* Beginning-2-dc-bobble, finish bobble-group in same ch-space, ch 1, (FPsc around next sc, bobble-group in center of next X, FPsc around next st, bobble-group in center of next X, FPsc around next sc, ch 1, bobble-group in corner-space, ch 1) repeat 3 times, FPsc around next sc, bobble-group in center of next X, FPsc around next sc, bobble-group in center of next X, FPsc around next sc, ch 1, slst in initial bobble [48 + 32 ch]
Fasten off.

Rnd 7: *{put yarn B at the end of Rnd 5 back on your hook, slst at the left of closest FPsc}* Beginning-X, ch 1, (sc in top of middle bobble of next bobble-group, ch 1, Make X, ch 1+ sc + ch 1 in top of middle bobble of next bobble-group, Make X, ch 1, sc in ch-space between first and second bobble of next bobble-group, ch 3, sc in ch-space between second and third bobble of bobble-group, ch 1, Make X, ch 1) repeat 3 times, sc in top of middle bobble of next bobble-group, ch 1, Make X, ch1 + sc + ch 1 in top of middle bobble of next bobble-group, Make X, sc in ch-space between first and second bobble of next bobble-group, ch 3, sc in ch-space between second and third bobble of bobble group, ch 1, slst over post of right hand side of X [40 + 48 ch]

Rnd 8: *{use the final slst over the post in Rnd 7 as the start of a FPdc}* ch 2 [FPdc around first dc of first X of side, (hdc in center ch-1-space of X, FPdc around second dc of X, hdc in space between X and next sc, FPdc around next sc, hdc in space between sc and next X, FPdc around first dc of next X) repeat 2 times, hdc in center ch-1-space of X, FPdc around second dc of X, hdc in space between X and next sc, FPdc around next sc, 5 dc in next ch-3-space, FPdc around next sc, hdc in space between sc and next X] repeat 4 times, fasten off with an invisible join to 2nd stitch [96]

Rnd 9: *{join yarn A in any third dc of a 5-dc-group (in a corner), make your first stitch a standing stitch}* (2 dc + ch 1 + 2 dc in third dc of 5-dc-group, hdc in next 8 st, sc in next 7 st, hdc in next 8 st) repeat 4 times, fasten off with an invisible join to first true dc [108 + 4 ch]

THUMBELINA SQUARE `80 stitch square`

Crochetedbytess (Therese Eghult) — Sweden
🌐 www.sistersinstitch.com

Skill level: Advanced
Colors: Yarn A: Golden Glow / Yarn B: Pearl / Yarn C: Eucalyptus /
Yarn D: Cream / Yarn E: Old Pink
Special stitches: Work in the third loop / spike-sc (spike single crochet)

INSTRUCTIONS

Rnd 1: *{start with Yarn A}* start a magic ring with 8 sc, slst in initial sc [8]
Do not tighten the magic ring yet.

Rnd 2: ch 1, 16 spike-sc over Rnd 1 in the center of the magic ring,
tighten the magic ring, fasten off with an invisible join to 2nd stitch [16]

Rnd 3: *{join yarn B in any st, make your first stitch a standing stitch}*
sc in first st, (ch 3, skip 2 st *{mark the first skipped st}*, sc in next st, turn,
with the wrong side facing you: 8 hdc in the ch-space you just made,
turn, with the right side facing you: sc in the 2nd skipped st) repeat 7
times, ch 3, working behind the first petal, sc in marked skipped st of first
repeat, turn, 8 hdc in the ch-space you just made, turn, slst around the
legs of the first sc stitch of the round, fasten off with an invisible join to
first sc [8 petals]

Rnd 4: *{Join Yarn C in the third loop of any sc of Rnd 2, make your
first stitch a standing stitch. Work all stitches in the third loop of the
sc stitches of Rnd 2}* (sc in next st, ch 3, skip 1 st) repeat 8 times, slst in
initial sc [8 + 24 ch]

Rnd 5: slst in ch-space, ch 2 (count as hdc) + 3 hdc in same ch-space,
skip 1 st, (4 hdc in next ch-space, skip 1 st) repeat 7 times, slst in 2nd ch
of initial ch 2 [32]

Rnd 6: ch 1, sc in same st, ch 4, skip 2 st, sc in next st, turn, with the
wrong side facing you, 3 sc + 2 hdc + 5 dc in the ch-space you just
made, turn, with the right side facing you, sc in the 2nd skipped sc,
(ch 4, skip next 3 st, sc in next st, turn, with the wrong side facing you,
3 sc + 2 hdc + 5 dc in the ch-space you just made, turn, with the right
side facing you, sc in the 2nd skipped sc) repeat 9 times, ch 4, skip next
2 st, slst in initial sc, turn, with the wrong side facing you, 3 sc + 2 hdc
+ 5 dc in the ch-space you just made, turn, with the right side facing you,
slst in initial sc [11 petals]

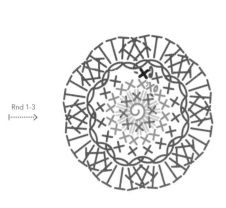

Rnd 1-3
|·········>

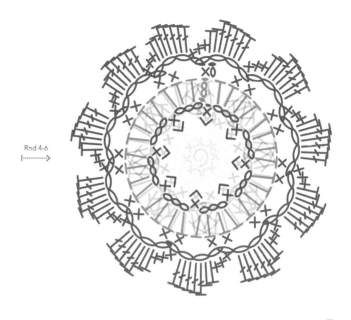

Rnd 4-6
|·········>

Rnd 7-11

Note: Shape the petals with your fingers before continuing.

Rnd 7: *{work behind the petals, in the leftover skipped sc stitches of Rnd 6}* (slst in next st, ch 4) repeat 11 times, fasten off with an invisible join to first ch after initial slst [11 + 44 ch]

Rnd 8: *{Join Yarn D in any ch-space, make your first stitch a standing stitch}* 4 hdc in all 11 ch-spaces, slst in initial hdc [44]

Rnd 9: ch 3 (count as dc), dc in same st, hdc in next 2 st, sc in next 5 st, hdc in next 2 st, 2 dc + ch 2 in next st, (2 dc in next st, hdc in next 2 st, sc in next 5 st, hdc in next 2 st, 2 dc + ch 2 in next st) repeat 3 times, fasten off with an invisible join to first true dc [52 + 8 ch]

Rnd 10: *{Join Yarn B in any ch-space, make your first stitch a standing stitch}* (2 dc + ch 2 + 2 dc in ch-space, skip 1 st, hdc in next 12 st) repeat 4 times, fasten off with an invisible join to 2nd stitch [64 + 8 ch]

Rnd 11: *{Join Yarn E in any ch-space, make your first stitch a standing stitch}* (2 sc + ch 1 + 2 sc in ch-space, skip 1 st, sc in next 15 st) repeat 4 times, fasten off with an invisible join to 2nd stitch [76 + 4 ch]

ALCHEMY GARDEN SQUARE `112 stitch square` `80 stitch square`

CatsWhiskers Crochet (Christine Bateman) — United Kingdom
 ChrisLudlow @ludlowsophie

Skill level: Advanced
Colors: Yarn A: Peridot / Yarn B: Pastel Pink / Yarn C: Cream /
Yarn D: Old Pink / Yarn E: Plum / Yarn F: Grape
Special stitches: Crossed stitch (worked in previous stitch) /
edc (extended double crochet) / etr (extended treble crochet) /
Work in third loop / FPtr (Front post treble crochet) / FPdc (Front post
double crochet) / FPsc (Front post single crochet) / BPsc (Back post
single crochet) / 4-tr-bobble (4 treble crochet bobble)

Note: This square is available in two sizes, finishing at Rnd 9 for an
80-stitch square or continuing up to Rnd 13 for a 112 stitch square.

INSTRUCTIONS

Rnd 1: *{start with yarn A}* start a magic ring with ch 6 (count as tr + ch 2),
(tr, 2 dc, tr, ch 2) repeat 3 times, tr, 2 dc, fasten off with an invisible join to
4th ch of initial ch 6 [16 + 8 ch]

Rnd 2: *{join yarn B in any ch-space, make your first stitch a standing
stitch}* (sc + ch 2 + sc in ch-space, skip 1 (hidden) st, sc in next 3 st) repeat
4 times, fasten off with an invisible join to first ch after initial sc [20 + 8 ch]

Rnd 3: *{join yarn C in any ch-space, make your first stitch a standing
stitch. Place a stitch marker in the standing stitch and in each sc in the
ch-spaces to follow}* (sc in ch-space, sc in next st, hdc in next st, dc + ch 2
+ dc in next st, hdc in next st, sc in next st) repeat 4 times, remembering
to attach a stitch marker on each side, fasten off with an invisible join to
2nd stitch [28 + 8 ch]

Rnd 4: *{join yarn B in any ch-2-space, make your first stitch a standing
stitch}* (2 dc + ch 2 + 2 dc in corner-space, skip next (hidden) dc, hdc in next
2 st, FPtr around first of 2 tr in Rnd 1 below, ch 1, FPtr around 2nd of 2 tr in
Rnd 1 below, place a stitch marker in the ch-space just made, skip 2 st on
Rnd 3, hdc in next 2 st) repeat 4 times, remembering to attach a stitch marker on each side, fasten off with an invisible join to 2nd stitch [40 + 12 ch]

Rnd 5: *{join yarn D in any corner-space, make your first stitch a standing
stitch}* (sc + ch 2 + sc in corner-space, hdc in next 2 st, FPdc around first
FPtr, skip 1 st, hdc in next st behind FPdc, hdc in the top of the same FPtr
you just worked around, skip next ch-space, hdc in next FPtr, hdc in next
st, crossed FPdc around FPtr you just worked into, skip 1 st, hdc in next

Rnd 1-5

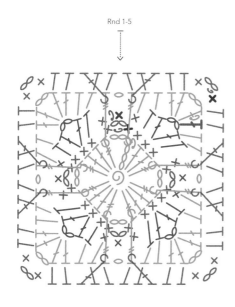

Rnd 6-9

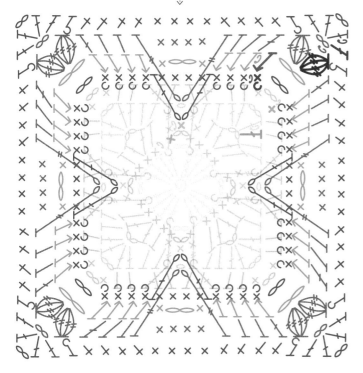

2 st) repeat 4 times, fasten off with an invisible join to first ch after initial sc [48 + 8 ch]

Note: When working edc in Rnd 6, make sure not to skip the stitch behind the edc when you continue crocheting.

Rnd 6: *{join yarn E in the first st after a corner-space, make your first stitch a standing stitch}* (BPsc around next 4 st, working in front of Rnd 4 and 5, edc in marked st in Rnd 3 *{remove the stitch marker, don't skip the stitch behind the edc}*, sc in next 4 st, working in front of Rnd 4 and 5, edc in same st as previous edc, *{don't skip the stitch behind the edc}* BPsc around next 4 st, ch 2, skip corner-space) repeat 4 times, fasten off with an invisible join to 2nd stitch [56 + 8 ch]

Rnd 7: *{join yarn F in the third loop of first st after a corner-space, make your first stitch a standing stitch}* (hdc in third loop of next 4 st, skip 1 edc, sc in both loops of next st, ch 2, skip next 2 st, sc in both loops of next st, skip next edc, hdc in third loop of next 4 st, ch 2, skip corner-space) repeat 4 times, fasten off with an invisible join to 2nd stitch [40 + 16 ch]

Note: the corners may curl in Rnd 8 but the next round will even them out and bring out the texture. When working etr in Rnd 8, make sure not to skip the stitch behind the etr when you continue crocheting, unless specifically mentioned.

Rnd 8: *{join yarn A in any corner-space, make your first stitch a standing stitch}* (4-tr-bobble + ch 2 + 4-tr-bobble in corner-space, skip 1 (hidden) st, dc in next st, hdc in next 2 st, etr in the marked ch-space in Rnd 4, *{work over the top of Rnd 5, 6 and 7. Remove the stitch marker, don't skip the stitch behind the etr}* sc in next st, 2 sc in next ch-space, sc in next st, etr in same ch-space as previous etr, skip next st behind the etr, hdc in next 2 st, dc in next st) repeat 4 times, fasten off with an invisible join to first ch after initial 4-tr-bobble [56 + 8 ch]

Rnd 9: *{join yarn C in any corner-space, make your first stitch a standing stitch}* (2 dc + 2 ch + 2 dc in corner-space, FPhdc around 4-tr-bobble, sc in next 12 st *{the first is hidden}*, FPhdc around 4-tr-bobble) repeat 4 times, fasten off with an invisible join to 2nd stitch [72 + 8 ch]

Note: Finish here for the 80 stitch square. Continue for the 112 stitch square.

Rnd 10: *{join yarn F in any corner-space, make your first stitch a standing stitch}* (sc + ch 2 + sc in corner-space, sc in third loop of next 18 st) repeat 4 times, fasten off with an invisible join to first ch after initial sc [80 + 8 ch]

Rnd 10-13

Rnd 11: *{Join yarn B in any corner-space, make your first stitch a standing stitch}* [sc in corner-space, skip 1 (hidden) st, sc in next st, slst in next st, (3 dc in next st, slst in next st) repeat 8 times, sc in next st] repeat 4 times, fasten off with an invisible join to 2nd stitch [144]

Note: Rnd 11 will make your square looked ruffled but the next round will pull it back in and create a pleasing dimpled texture.

Rnd 12: *{join yarn E in any corner sc, make your first stitch a standing stitch}* [3 dc + ch 2 + 3 dc in corner sc, skip 1 st, (dc in next slst, skip 1 st, FPsc around middle dc of a 3-dc-group, skip 1 st) repeat 8 times, dc in next st, skip 1 st] repeat 4 times, fasten off with an invisible join to 2nd stitch [92 + 8 ch]

Rnd 13: *{join yarn F in any corner-space, make your first stitch a standing stitch}* (2 hdc + ch 2 + 2 hdc in corner-space, skip 1 (hidden) st, BLO hdc in next 22 st) repeat 4 times, fasten off with an invisible join to 2nd stitch [104 + 8 ch]

WINDMILLS SQUARE

112 stitch square

Madelenón (Soledad Iglesias Silva) — Argentina

⊕ www.madelenon.com ⦿ @handmadelenon 𝐟 madelenonface

Skill level: Advanced

Colors: Yarn A: Pastel Pink / **Yarn B:** Peony Pink / **Yarn C:** Antique Pink / **Yarn D:** Fuchsia / **Yarn E:** Plum / **Yarn F:** Lavender

INSTRUCTIONS

Rnd 1: *{start with yarn A}* start a magic ring with ch 3 (count as dc), 15 dc, slst in initial dc [16]

Rnd 2: (ch 21, slst in next 2 st) repeat 8 times [8 petals]

Rnd 3: (sc in next 10 ch, 3 sc in next ch, sc in next 10 ch) repeat 8 times, fasten off with an invisible join to 2nd stitch [8 petals]

Rnd 4: *{join yarn B in any first sc of a petal, make your first stitch a standing stitch}* (sc in next 11 st, 3 sc in next st, sc in next 11 st) repeat 8 times, fasten off with an invisible join to 2nd stitch [8 petals]

Rnd 5: *{join yarn C in any first sc of a petal, make your first stitch a standing stitch}* (sc in next 12 st, 3 sc in next st, sc in next 12 st) repeat 8 times, fasten off with an invisible join to 2nd stitch [8 petals]
Twist the top of each individual petal sideways and tuck it behind its main part, so the wrong side of the top faces forward.

Rnd 6: *{locate the center stitch of any petal, count 5 stitches backwards, join yarn D in this st, make your first stitch a standing stitch. Continue crocheting around the twisted petals as if they were in 1 line}* (sc in next 5 st, 3 sc in next st, sc in next 5 st, jump to the next petal) repeat 8 times, fasten off with an invisible join to 2nd stitch [8 petals]

Rnd 7: *{join yarn E in the middle sc of the 3-sc-group in any petal tip, make your first stitch a standing stitch}* (slst in next st, sc in next 2 st, hdc in next 2 st, dc in next 4 st, hdc in next 2 st, sc in next 2 st, slst in next st, 4 dtr in the gap between next 2 petals, ch 3, 4 dtr in same gap) repeat 4 times, fasten off with an invisible join to 2nd stitch [88 + 12 ch]

Rnd 8: *{join yarn F in any ch-space, make your first stitch a standing stitch}* (2 hdc + ch 2 + 2 hdc in ch-space, hdc in next 4 st, sc in next 14 st, hdc in next 4 st) repeat 4 times, fasten off with an invisible join to second stitch [104 + 8 ch]

TINY STAR SQUARE `112 stitch square`

Vivid Kreations (Mikaela Bates) — Australia
🌐 www.vividkreations.com.au 📷 @vividkreations **f** VK.VividKreations

Skill level: Advanced
Colors: Yarn A: Cream / Yarn B: Ice Blue / Yarn C: Navy /
Yarn D: Pacific Blue / Yarn E: Lavender / Yarn F: Purple Bordeaux /
Yarn G: Girly Pink / Yarn H: Salmon
Special stitches: FPsc (Front post single crochet) / FPdc (Front post double crochet)
Pattern-specific special stitch:
First star st (into a dc): Insert hook into bar just below top of dc, pull up a loop (2 loops on hook), insert hook under the 2 bars on the bottom left of the dc, pull up a loop (3 loops on hook), insert hook into BLO of the same sc as the dc, pull up a loop (4 loops on hook), insert hook into the BLO of the next sc, pull up a loop (pull this loop a little higher, 5 loops on hook), insert hook into the blo of the next sc, pull up a loop (pull this loop up a little higher, 6 loops on hook), yo and pull through all 6 loops, ch 1.
Star st: insert hook into the circle created by the ch 1, pull up a loop (2 loops on hook), insert hook under the 2 bars of the last spike of the previous star stitch, pull up a loop (3 loops on hook), insert hook into BLO of the same sc as the last spike of the previous star stitch, pull up a loop (4 loops on hook), insert hook into the BLO of the next sc, pull up a loop (pull this loop a little higher, 5 loops on hook), insert hook into the BLO of the next sc, pull up a loop (pull this loop a little higher, 6 loops on hook), yo and pull through all 6 loops, ch 1.
Mod tr2tog: yo 2 times, insert hook into the first st, yo pull up a loop (4 loops on hook), yo and pull through 2 loops (3 loops on hook), yo and insert hook into the next st, yo and pull up a loop (5 loops on hook), yo and pull through 2 loops (4 loops on hook), yo and pull through 2 loops (3 loops on hook), yo and pull through 2 loops (2 loops on hook), yo and pull through the last 2 loops on the hook.

INSTRUCTIONS

Note: This pattern is worked in 2 hook sizes.
Note: take this pattern one stitch at a time, it's worth your patience.

Rnd 1: {start with yarn A} start a magic ring with (sc, dc, ch 2, dc) repeat 5 times, fasten off with an invisible join to 2nd stitch [15 + 10 ch]

Rnd 2: {join yarn B in any sc, make your first stitch a standing stitch} (BLO dc in next st, ch 2, skip 1 st, sc in ch-space, ch 2, skip 1 st) repeat 4 times, skip 1 st, sc in ch-space, ch 2, fasten off with an invisible join to first ch after initial BLO dc [10 + 20 ch]

Rnd 3: {join yarn C in any BLO dc, make your first stitch a standing stitch} (FPdc around dc, 3 hdc in next ch-space, FPdc around sc, 3 hdc in next ch-space) repeat 5 times, slst in initial FPdc [40]

Note: work to the FPdc of Rnd 3 two times: start with a hdc in the top, followed by a FPdc around the post of the same stitch.

Rnd 4: ch 1, FPdc around FPdc, (hdc in the next 4 st, FPdc around same st as last hdc) repeat 9 times, hdc in the next 3 st, hdc over the initial ch 1 and into the top of the st the first FPdc goes around, fasten off with an invisible join to 2nd stitch [50]

Rnd 5: {join yarn D in any FPdc, make your first stitch a standing stitch} sc in all 50 st, slst in initial sc [50]

Rnd 6: {work this round in BLO} sc in same st as slst join, sc in next 6 st, 2 sc in next st, sc in next 9 st, 2 sc in next st, sc in next 7 st, 2 sc in next st, sc in next 7 st, 2 sc in next st, sc in next 7 st, 2 sc in next st, sc in next 8 st, 2 sc in next st, fasten off with an invisible join to 2nd stitch [56]

Rnd 7: {Join yarn E in any sc above a FPdc, make your first stitch a standing stitch, work this round in BLO} (hdc in next 2 st, dc in next 2 st, ch 2, mod tr2tog, ch 2, dc in next 2 st, hdc in next 2 st, sc in next 4 st) repeat 4 times, slst in initial hdc [52 + 16 ch]

Rnd 8: ch 2 (count as hdc), hdc in next 3 st, (2 hdc + dc in ch-space, ch 1, FPdc around mod tr2tog, ch 1, dc + 2 hdc in ch-space, hdc in next 12 st) repeat 3 times, 2 hdc + dc in ch-space, ch 1, FPdc around mod tr2tog, ch 1, dc + 2 hdc in ch-space, hdc in next 8 st, fasten off with an invisible join to first true hdc [72 + 12 ch]

Rnd 9: {join yarn F in any first corner ch-space, make your first stitch a standing stitch} (2 sc in ch-space, ch 2, skip FPdc, 2 sc in next ch-space, skip 1 st, BLO sc in next 17 st) repeat 4 times, fasten off with an invisible join to 2nd stitch [84 ch]

Note: Work Rnd 10 with a hook 1 size larger.
Note: Make the dc stitches in the corner-space a little bit taller so they are the same height as the other stitches in this round.

Rnd 10: {join yarn G in BLO of the second sc after any corner, make your first stitch a standing stitch} [BLO dc in second sc after a corner, first star st in BLO over next 2 st, (star st in BLO over next 2 st) repeat 8 times, BLO dc in next st, 2 dc + ch 2 + 2 dc in next ch-space, skip 1 st] repeat 4 times, fasten off with an invisible join in 2nd stitch [60 + 8 ch - where star stitch counts as 1 st]

Note: Continue working with your regular hook size.

Rnd 11: {join yarn H in first dc after a corner, make your first stitch a standing stitch. In this round you switch back and forth between BLO and both loops} [BLO sc in first st, (BLO sc in top of star st, sc in circle made by ch 1 of star st) repeat 9 times, BLO sc in next st, FPsc around next 2 st, sc + ch 2 + sc in ch-space, FPsc around next 2 st] repeat 4 times, fasten off with an invisible join to 2nd stitch [104 + 8 ch]

ROSETTE SQUARE `112 stitch square`

Spincushions (Shelley Husband) — Australia
🌐 www.spincushions.com 📷 @spincushions 🅕 Spincushions

Skill level: Advanced
Colors: **Yarn A:** Blue Lake / **Yarn B:** Turquoise / **Yarn C:** Opaline Glass /
Yarn D: Cream
Special stitches: **FPdc** (Front post double crochet) / **BPsc** (Back post
single crochet) / **5-dc-pc** (5 double crochet popcorn stitch) / **dc2tog**
(double crochet 2 stitches together)

INSTRUCTIONS

Rnd 1: {start with yarn A} start a magic ring with ch 3 (count as dc),
11 dc, slst in 3rd ch of initial ch 3 [12]

Rnd 2: ch 3 (count as dc), dc in same st as slst, 2 dc in next 11 st, slst in
3rd ch of initial ch 3 [24]

Rnd 3: ch 3 (count as dc), (FPdc around next st, dc in next st) repeat
11 times, FPdc around next st, fasten off with an invisible join to first
true FPdc [24]

Note: You'll notice that Rnd 3 is intentionally cupped.

Rnd 4: {join yarn B around a regular dc, not a FPdc. Make your first
stitch a standing stitch. Work double crochet stitches in the leftover
stitches of Rnd 2, behind the FPdc of Rnd 3. Bpsc stitches are worked
in Rnd 3} (BPsc around dc, 2 dc in next st in Rnd 2, skip 1 st, 2 dc in next
st in Rnd 2) repeat 6 times, slst in initial BPsc [30]

Rnd 5: ch 3 (count as dc), dc in next st, (dc + ch 2 + slst in next st, slst +
ch 2 + dc in next st, dc in next 3 st) repeat 5 times, dc + ch 2 + slst in next
st, slst + ch 2 + dc in next st, dc in next st, slst in 3rd ch of initial ch 3 [42
+ 24 ch]

Rnd 6: ch 3 (count as dc), (dc2tog, ch 4, skip ch-space, sc in gap between
stitches in Rnd 4 below, ch 4, skip ch-space, dc2tog, dc in next st) repeat
5 times, dc2tog, ch 4, skip ch-space, sc in gap between stitches on Rnd 4
below, ch 4, skip ch-space, dc2tog, slst in 3rd ch of initial ch 3 [24 + 48 ch]

Note: Chain loosely in Rnd 7, if it feels tight.

Rnd 7: ch 3 (count as dc) + 4 dc in same st as last slst, form first pc with
these 5 st, (ch 10, skip 1 st + ch-4-space + 1 st + ch-4-space + 1 st, 5-dc-pc
in next st) repeat 5 times, ch 10, skip 1 st + ch-4-space + 1 st + ch-4-space
+ 1 st, fasten off with an invisible join in first ch after initial pc [6 pc + 60 ch]

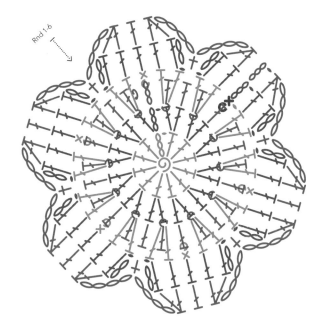

Rnd 1-6

Rnd 8: *{join yarn C in top of any pc, make your first stitch a standing stitch}* sc in pc, (12 sc in ch-space, 2 sc in pc) repeat 5 times, 12 sc in ch-space, sc in same pc as first st, slst in initial sc [84]

Rnd 9: ch 3 (count as dc), 4 dc in same st as slst, (skip 3 st, sc in next 14 st, skip 3 st, 5 dc in next st) repeat 3 times, skip 3 st, sc in next 14 st, skip 3 st, fasten off with an invisible join to first true dc [76]

Rnd 10: *{join yarn D to the middle dc of a 5-dc corner, make your first stitch a standing stitch}* (2 dc + ch 2 + 2 dc in next st, 2 dc in next 2 st, dc in next st, hdc in next st, sc in next 10 st, hdc in next st, dc in next st, 2 dc in next 2 st,) repeat 4 times, fasten off with an invisible join to 2nd stitch [104 + 8 ch]

Designer Spincushions looks out at the sea every day and loves the dreamy calm blues. Rosette Square looks gorgeous in her favorite turquoise-blue color scheme, but of course you can use any color combination you like.

Rnd 7-10

MACEY ANN SQUARE `112 stitch square`

A Yarn of Serendipity (Pam Knighton-Haener) — USA
℗ PKnightonHaener ⊛ www.pknightonhaener.wordpress.com
f A Yarn of Serendipity

Skill level: Advanced
Colors: Yarn A: Golden Glow / Yarn B: Raspberry / Yarn C: Olive /
Yarn D: Sunflower / Yarn E: Cream
Special stitches: trtr (Triple treble crochet) / **Long hdc** (Long half
double crochet) / **Long dc** (Long double crochet) / **Long tr** (Long treble
crochet) / **FPsc** (Front post single crochet) / **FPhdc** (Front post half
double crochet) / **2-dc-bobble** (2 double crochet bobble) / **4-dc-pc**
(Popcorn stitch with 4 dc) / **ch-3-picot** (Picot stitch)
Pattern-specific special stitch: Back-stitch: Identify the designated
stitch one row below and fold the work toward you. Insert your hook
vertically into the tip of the inverted "v" of the stitch, come out at the
base of the stitch and complete the stitch as usual.

INSTRUCTIONS

Rnd 1: {start with yarn A} start a magic ring with ch 5 (count as dc + ch 2),
(dc, ch 2) repeat 7 times, invisible join to 4th ch of initial ch 5 [8 + 16 ch]

Rnd 2: {join yarn B in any ch-2-space, make your first stitch a standing
stitch} (sc + ch 4 + sc in ch-space, skip next dc) repeat 8 times, slst in
initial sc [16 + 32 ch]

Rnd 3: slst in ch-4-space, ch 1 (count as sc) + 3 hdc + dc + tr + ch-3-picot
+ tr + dc + 3 hdc + sc in ch-4-space, skip 1 st, slst in next st {put a stitch
marker in this slst}, (sc + 3 hdc + dc + tr + ch-3-picot + tr + dc + 3 hdc +
sc in ch-space, skip 1 st, slst in next st {put a stitch marker in this slst})
repeat 7 times, fasten off with an invisible join to first hdc [112]

Rnd 4: {join yarn C in the slst between petals of Rnd 3, make your first
stitch a standing stitch} (trtr in slst of Rnd 3 {remove stitch marker},
ch 4, sc + ch 1 + sc in the top of next ch-3-picot, ch 4) repeat 8 times,
fasten off with an invisible join to first ch after initial trtr [24 + 72 ch]

Rnd 5: {join yarn D in any ch-1-space, make your first stitch a standing
stitch} (sc + ch 2 + sc in ch-1-space, ch 4, skip 4 ch, 4-dc-pc in next trtr,
ch 4, skip 4 ch, sc in next ch-1-space, ch 4, skip 4 ch, 4-dc-pc in next trtr,
ch 4, skip 4 ch) repeat 4 times, fasten off with an invisible join to first ch
after initial sc [20 + 72 ch]

Rnd 6: {join yarn E in any ch-2-space, make your first stitch a standing

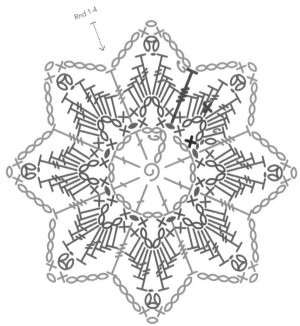

Rnd 1-4

stitch} [dc + ch 1 + dc + ch 2 + dc + ch 1 + dc in ch-2-space, skip 1 st, 2-dc-bobble in ch-4-space of Rnd 5 + long dc around ch 4 from Rnd 4 and ch 4 of Rnd 5 + 2-dc-bobble in ch 4 space of Rnd 5, FPhdc around pc, in next ch-4-space: (hdc in ch-4-space of Rnd 5 + long hdc around ch 4 of Rnd 4 and ch 4 of Rnd 5 + sc in ch-4-space of Rnd 5), FPsc around sc, sc in ch-4-space + long hdc around ch 4 from Rnd 4 and ch 4 of Rnd 5 + hdc in ch-4-space of Rnd 5, FPhdc around pc, 2-dc-cluster in ch-4-space of Rnd 5 + long dc around ch 4 from Rnd 4 and ch 4 of Rnd 5 + 2-dc-bobble in ch-4-space of Rnd 5, skip 1 st] repeat 4 times, slst in initial dc [76 + 16 ch]

Rnd 7: slst in ch-1-space, slst in dc, slst in corner-space, ch 2 (count as hdc) + hdc + ch 2 + 2 hdc in ch-2-corner-space, hdc in next st, hdc in next ch-1-space, hdc in next 17 st, hdc in next ch-1-space, hdc in next st, (2 hdc + ch 2 + 2 hdc in corner-space, hdc in next st, hdc in next ch-1-space, hdc in next 17 st, hdc in next ch-1-space, hdc in next st) repeat 3 times, fasten off with an invisible join to first true hdc [100 + 8 ch]

Rnd 8: {join yarn A in any ch-2-corner-space, make your first stitch a standing stitch} [sc + ch 2 + sc in ch-2-corner-space, skip 1 st, (hdc in next st, hdc back-stitch in next st) repeat 12 times] repeat 4 times, fasten off with an invisible join to first ch after initial sc [104 + 8 ch]

Rnd 5-8

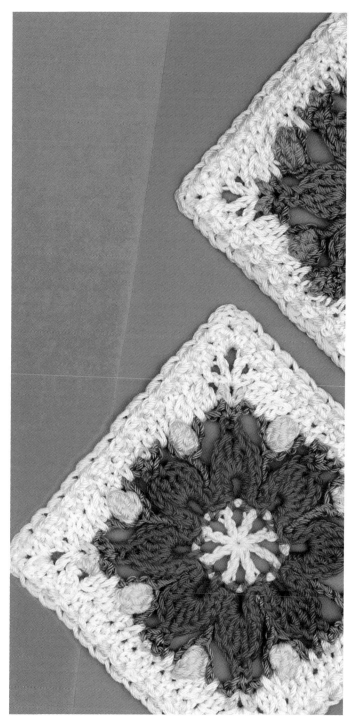

JACKFIELD TILE MINI SQUARE
112 stitch square 80 stitch square

CatsWhiskers Crochet (Christine Bateman) — United Kingdom
© ChrisLudlow 🅾 @ludlowsophie

Skill level: Advanced
Colors: Yarn A: Pistachio / Yarn B: Peridot / Yarn C: Forest /
Yarn D: Cream / Yarn E: Mustard / Yarn F: Chestnut
Special stitches: edc (Extended double crochet) / Work in third loop /
FPsc (Front post single crochet) / BPsc (Back post single crochet)

Note: This square is available in two sizes, finishing at Rnd 9 for an
80-stitch square or continuing up to Rnd 14 for a 112 stitch square.

The 80-stitch square generally turns out smaller than other 80-stitch
squares in this book. You might want to use a bigger hook size to make
sizes match if you're planning to combine squares in a project.

INSTRUCTIONS

Rnd 1: *{start with yarn A}* start a magic ring with 8 sc, fasten off with an
invisible join to 2nd stitch [8]

Rnd 2: *{join yarn B in any st, make your first stitch a standing stitch}*
2 sc in all 8 st, fasten off with an invisible join to 2nd stitch [16]

Rnd 3: *{join yarn C in any st, make your first stitch a standing stitch}*
(3 BLO dc in next st, skip 1st st, ch 1) repeat 8 times, fasten off with an
invisible join to 2nd stitch [24 + 8 ch]

Rnd 4: *{join yarn D in any first dc of a 3-dc-group, make your first stitch
a standing stitch}* sc in first dc of a 3-dc-group, sc in next 2 st, working in
front of Rnd 3, BLO edc in skipped st of Rnd 2, skip ch-space behind edc)
repeat 8 times, fasten off with an invisible join in 2nd stitch [32]

Rnd 5: *{join yarn E in the first st after edc, make your first stitch a stand-ing stitch}* (sc in next st, 3 dc in next st, sc in next st, ch 1, skip 1st st) repeat
8 times, fasten off with an invisible join to 2nd stitch [40 + 8 ch]

Note: In Rnd 6 and 8 various stitches are worked in the third loop.
This is not essential, they can be worked in BLO instead, but working
in third loop will give better definition.

Rnd 6: *{join yarn F in any ch-space, make your first stitch a standing stitch}*
(dc + tr + ch 2 + tr + dc in ch-space, skip 1st st, hdc in third loop of next st,
sc in third loop of next 2 st, hdc in third loop of next st, skip next ch-space,

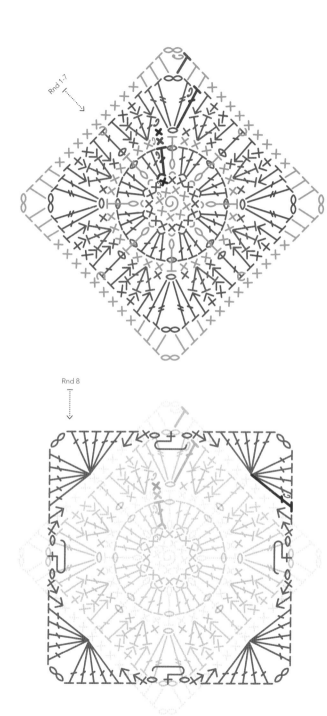

Rnd 1-7

Rnd 8

working in front of Rnd 5, dc in the skipped st in Rnd 4 below, hdc in third loop of next st, sc in third loop of next 2 st, hdc in third loop of next st, skip 1 st) repeat 4 times, fasten off with an invisible join to 2nd stitch [52 + 8 ch]

Rnd 7: *{join yarn D in any corner-space, make your first stitch a standing stitch}* (hdc + ch 2 + hdc in corner-space, hdc in next 2 st, sc in next 4 st, FPsc around next st, sc in next 4 st, hdc in next 2 st) repeat 4 times, fasten off with an invisible join to first ch after initial hdc [60 + 8 ch]

Rnd 8: *{join yarn A in any FPsc in the center of a side, make your first stitch a standing stitch}* (5 dc + ch 2 + 5 dc in FPsc, skip 2 st, hdc in third loop of next st, sc in third loop of next st, continue working behind the corner, ch 1, BPsc around both tr in Rnd 6 below, skip next 8 st of corner, ch 1, sc in third loop of 4th st (first sc) on the next side, hdc in third loop of next st, skip next 2 st) repeat 4 times, fasten off with an invisible join to 2nd stitch [60 + 16 ch]

Note: the ch-spaces between the two 5-dc-groups now form the corners of the square.

Note: There are two variants of Rnd 9, one for the 80 stitch square and one for the 112 stitch square.

Rnd 9 (80 stitch square): *{join yarn C in any corner-space, make your first stitch a standing stitch}* (dc + ch 2 + dc in corner-space, skip 1 (hidden) st, dc in next 6 st, dc in next ch-space, sc in ch-space at apex of Rnd 7, skip 1 st (the BPsc behind the apex), dc in next ch-space, dc in next 7 st) repeat 4 times, fasten off with an invisible join to first ch after initial dc [72 + 8 ch]

Note: Finish here for the 80 stitch square. Continue for the 112 stitch square.

Rnd 9 (112 stitch square): *{join yarn C in any corner-space, make your first stitch a standing stitch}* (sc + ch 2 + sc in corner-space, skip 1 (hidden) st, sc in next 6 st, sc in next ch-space, sc in next st, sc in next ch-space, skip 1 st, sc in next 6 st) repeat 4 times, fasten off with an invisible join to first ch after initial sc [68 + 8 ch]

Rnd 10: *{join yarn D in any corner-space, make your first stitch a standing stitch}* [2 dc + ch 2 + 2 dc in corner-space, skip 1 (hidden) st, dc in next st, (skip 1 st, 2 dc in next st) repeat 3 times, sc in ch-space (the apex) of Rnd 7 below, skip 2 st, (2 dc in next st, skip 1 st) repeat 3 times, dc in next st] repeat 4 times, fasten off with an invisible join to 2nd stitch [76 + 8 ch]

Rnd 11: *{join yarn F in any corner-space, make your first stitch a standing stitch}* [sc + ch 2 + sc in corner-space, skip 1 (hidden) st, sc in next 2 st, (dc in skipped st of Rnd 9 just below, skip 1 st behind dc just worked, sc in next st) repeat 2 times, dc in skipped st of Rnd 9 just below, don't skip st behind dc just worked, sc in next 5 st, (dc in skipped st of Rnd 9 just below, skip 1 st behind dc just worked, sc in next st) repeat 3 times, sc in next st] repeat 4 times, fasten off with an invisible join to first ch after initial sc [84 + 8 ch]

Rnd 12: *{join yarn E in any corner-space, make your first stitch a standing stitch}* [sc in corner-space, BLO sc in next 2 st, (BLO sc in next st, FPsc around next st) repeat 3 times, BLO sc in next 5 st, (FPsc around next st, BLO sc in next st) repeat 3 times, BLO sc in next 2 st] repeat 4 times, fasten off with an invisible join to 2nd stitch [88]

Rnd 13: *{join yarn C in the first stitch after any corner sc, make your first stitch a standing stitch}* (BLO sc in next 21 st, ch 2, skip next st) repeat 4 times, fasten off with an invisible join to 2nd stitch [84 + 8 ch]

Rnd 14: *{join yarn B in the second stitch after a corner-space, make your first stitch a standing stitch}* (BLO sc in next 20 st, 3 dc + ch 2 + 3 dc in corner sc of Rnd 12 (working over Rnd 13), skip next st) repeat 4 times, fasten off with an invisible join to 2nd stitch [104 + 8 ch]

Rnd 9 (80-stitch square)

Rnd 9-14 (112-stitch square)

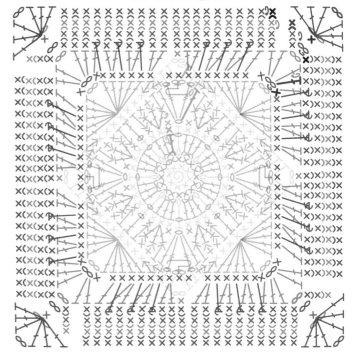

RAINY DAY PUDDLES SQUARE 80 stitch square

Yarn Blossom Boutique (Melissa Bradley) — USA
@yarnblossomboutique f yarnblossomboutique

Skill level: Intermediate
Colors: Yarn A: Denim / Yarn B: Cream / Yarn C: Jade Gravel
Special stitches: FPtr (Front post treble crochet) / FPdc (Front post double crochet)

INSTRUCTIONS

Rnd 1: *{start with yarn A}* start a magic ring with ch 4 (count as dc + ch 1), (dc, ch 1) repeat 7 times, slst in 3rd ch of initial ch 3 [16]

Rnd 2: ch 2 (count as hdc) + 2 hdc in next ch-space, 3 hdc in next 7 ch-spaces, fasten off with an invisible join in first true hdc [24]

Rnd 3: *{join Yarn B in any first hdc of a 3-hdc-group, make your first stitch a standing stitch}* (dc in next 3 st, FPtr around dc from Rnd 1) repeat 8 times, fasten off with an invisible join in 2nd stitch [32]

Rnd 4: *{join Yarn C in any second dc of a 3-dc-group, make your first stitch a standing stitch}* (sc in next st, skip next st, FPtr + ch 2 + FPtr around next FPtr, skip next st) repeat 8 times, slst in initial sc [24 + 16 ch]

Rnd 5: sc in same st, 5 dc in next ch-space, (sc in next st, 5 dc in next ch-space) repeat 7 times, fasten off with an invisible join to first dc [48]

Rnd 6: *{join Yarn B in any 3rd dc of a 5-dc-group, make your first stitch a standing stitch}* (sc in next st, ch 3, skip 3 st, FPdc around both of the two tr below from Rnd 4 to join them together, ch 3, skip 2 st) repeat 8 times, fasten off with an invisible join to first ch after initial sc [16 + 48 ch]

Rnd 7: *{join Yarn A in any ch-space after a FPdc, make your first stitch a standing stitch}* (3 sc in ch-space, sc + hdc + dc in next ch-space, FPtr + ch 1 + FPtr around next FPdc, dc + hdc + sc in next ch-space, 3 sc in next ch-space, FPdc around next FPdc) repeat 4 times, fasten off with an invisible join to 2nd stitch [60 + 4 ch]

Rnd 8: *{join Yarn B in any dc after a FPtr, make your first stitch a standing stitch}* (dc in next 14 st, 2 dc + ch 2 + 2 dc in next ch-space, skip next st) repeat 4 times, fasten off with an invisible join to 2nd stitch [72 + 8 ch]

L.A. SUNFLOWER SQUARE `112 stitch square`

Crochetedbytess (Therese Eghult) — Sweden
⊕ www.sistersinstitch.com

Skill level: Advanced
Colors: Yarn A: Golden Glow / Yarn B: Pastel Pink / Yarn C: Peony Pink / Yarn D: Raspberry / Yarn E: Cream / Yarn F: Lavender
Special stitches: ch-3-picot (picot stitch) / FPsc (Front post single crochet) / 2-dc-bobble (2 double crochet bobble) / long slst (long slip stitch)

INSTRUCTIONS

Rnd 1: *{start with yarn A}* start a magic ring with 8 sc [8]

Rnd 2: (slst + ch 4 + slst in next st) repeat 8 times, fasten off with an invisible join to first ch after initial slst [16 + 32 ch]

Rnd 3: *{join yarn B in any ch-space, make your first stitch a standing stitch}* (3 dc + ch 1 + 3 dc in ch-space, FPsc around next 2 slst from Rnd 2) repeat 8 times, fasten off with an invisible join to 2nd stitch [56 + 8 ch]

Rnd 4: *{turn your flower backwards and find the 2 lines that were made by the FPsc from Rnd 3. Hold the flower with the right side facing and Join Yarn C in any set of those, make your first stitch a standing stitch}* slst + ch 3 in next 8 st, slst in initial slst [8 + 24 ch]

Rnd 5: slst in ch-space, ch 1, 5 sc in ch-space, skip 1 slst, (5 sc in next ch-space, skip 1 slst) repeat 7 times [40]

Rnd 6: (slst + 2-dc-bobble in next st, 2-dc-bobble in next st, ch 2, slst in the ch-1-space of Rnd 3, ch 2, skip 1 st, 2-dc-bobble in next st, 2-dc-bobble + slst in next st) repeat 8 times, fasten off with an invisible join to 2nd stitch [56 + 32 ch]

Rnd 7: *{join yarn D in any first ch-2-space, make your first stitch a standing stitch}* (3 hdc in ch-space, ch-3-picot, skip 1 slst, 3 hdc in next ch-space, 2 hdc in next st, slst in next st, skip 1 slst, long slst down into the gap between the 5-sc-group from Rnd 5, skip 1 slst, slst in next st, 2 hdc in next st) repeat 8 times, fasten off with an invisible join to 2nd stitch [104 + 8 picots]

Rnd 8: *{join yarn E in the center space of any picot from Rnd 7, make your first stitch a standing stitch. Work only in the picots}* (sc + ch 6 in next picot, sc + ch 1 + sc + ch 6 in next picot) repeat 4 times, slst in initial sc [12 + 52 ch]

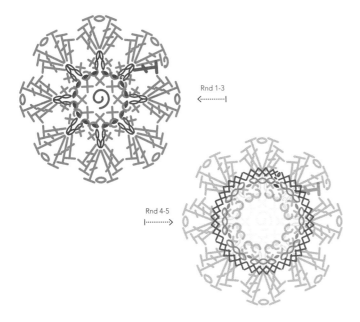

Rnd 1-3
⟵·············|

Rnd 4-5
|·············⟶

Rnd 9: sc in next st, (10 sc in the ch-6-space, sc in next st, sc + ch 2 + sc in the ch-1-space, sc in next st, 10 sc in the ch-6-space, sc in next st) repeat 4 times, fasten off with an invisible join to 2nd stitch [100 + 8 ch]

Rnd 10: *{join yarn F in any ch-space, make your first stitch a standing stitch}* [sc in ch-space, ch 5, skip 6 st, sc in next st, skip 5 st, (tr + ch 1) repeat 4 times + tr in next st, skip 5 st, sc in next st, ch 5, skip 6 st] repeat 4 times, slst in initial sc [32 + 56 ch]

Rnd 11: (5 sc in next ch-space, hdc in next st, hdc in the gap between the sc and tr stitch from Rnd 10, skip next tr, 2 sc in next ch-1-space, skip next tr, 2 sc in next ch-1-space, sc + ch 1 + sc in next st, 2 sc in next ch-1-space, skip next tr, 2 sc in next ch-1-space, skip next tr, hdc in the gap between the tr and sc from Rnd 10, hdc in next st, 5 sc in next ch-space, sc in next st) repeat 4 times, fasten off with an invisible join to 2nd stitch [100 + 4 ch]

Rnd 12: *{join yarn E in any ch-1-space, make your first stitch a standing stitch}* (2 hdc + ch 1 + 2 hdc in ch-1-space, skip 1 st, hdc in next 6 st, sc in next 11 st, hdc in next 6 st, skip 1 st) repeat 4 times, fasten off with an invisible join to 2nd stitch [108 + 4 ch]

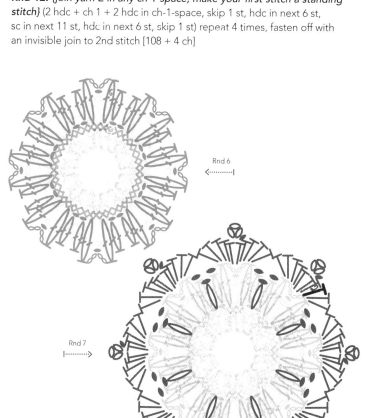

Rnd 6

Rnd 7

Rnd 8-12

OMBRÉ ROSE SQUARE `112 stitch square`

Crochet Road (Joy Clements) — Australia
@crochetroad Crochet Road Crochet Road

Skill level: Advanced
Colors: Yarn A: Golden glow / Yarn B: Antique pink / Yarn C: Old pink / Yarn D: Pearl / Yarn E: Lettuce / Yarn F: Cream
Special stitches: BPsc (Back post single crochet stitch)

INSTRUCTIONS

Rnd 1: *{start with yarn A}* start a magic ring with ch 2 (count as hdc), 15 hdc, slst in 2nd ch of initial ch 2 [16]

Rnd 2: (ch 3, skip 1 st, sc in next st) repeat 7 times, ch 3, skip 1 st, slst in first ch of initial ch 3 [8 + 24 ch] Mark this round with a stitch marker so you can easily detect it later.

Note: The next round is worked into the skipped stitches of Rnd 1. Work in front of the Rnd 2 chains. Fold the chains away from you to make it easier to work this round.

Rnd 3: *{Work in skipped stitches of Rnd 1}* ch 1, (slst in next hdc from Rnd 1, skip 1 st, FLO 5 dc in next st, skip 1 st) repeat 4 times, fasten off with an invisible join to first slst [4 petals]

Rnd 4: *{Join yarn B in a ch-3-space from Rnd 2 that is behind the central dc of the 5-dc-group made in Rnd 3, make your first stitch a standing stitch}* (slst in next ch-space, 5 dc in next ch-space) repeat 4 times, fasten off with an invisible join to first slst [4 petals]

Rnd 5: *{Join yarn C to the post of a sc made in Rnd 2, immediately preceding a petal from Rnd 4, make your first stitch a standing stitch. Work behind petals of Rnd 4, with the right side of the flower facing you}* (BPsc around sc from Rnd 2, ch 3) repeat 8 times, slst in top of initial BPsc [8 + 24 ch]

Rnd 6: (slst in next ch-space, 7 dc in next ch-space) repeat 4 times, slst in initial slst [4 petals]

Rnd 7: *{work behind petals of Rnd 6, with the right side of the flower facing you}* ch 1, (BPsc around next BPsc in Rnd 5, ch 3) repeat 8 times, slst in top of initial BPsc [8 + 24 ch]

Rnd 8: *{ruffled petals round. Squish up your stitches as you work, so you can fit them all in each ch-space}* sc + 9 dc + sc in all 8 ch-spaces, fasten off with an invisible join to first sc [8 petals]

Rnd 1-2
|··········>

Rnd 3-4
|··········>

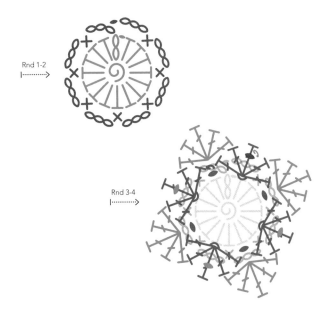

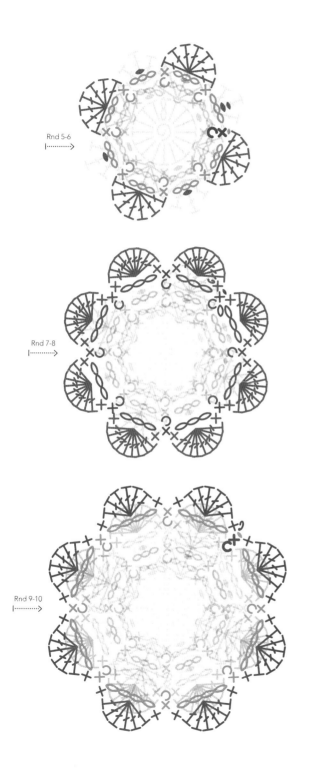

Rnd 5-6
|·············>

Rnd 7-8
|·············>

Rnd 9-10
|·············>

Rnd 9: {Join yarn D in any BPsc from Rnd 7, make your first stitch a standing stitch. Work behind petals of Rnd 8, with the right side of the flower facing you. Fold petals forward to make it easier to work each BPsc} (BPsc around next BPsc in Rnd 7, ch 4) repeat 8 times, slst in top of first BPsc [8 + 32 ch]

Rnd 10: sc + 6 dc + sc in all 8 ch-spaces, fasten off with an invisible join to first sc [8 petals]

Rnd 11: {Join yarn E in any BPsc from Rnd 9, make your first stitch a standing stitch} (BPsc around next BPsc in Rnd 9, ch 4, BPsc around next BPsc in Rnd 9, ch 7, slst in FLO and around post of BPsc just completed, ch 4) repeat 4 times, slst in initial BPsc [8 ch-4-spaces, 4 ch-7-loops]

Rnd 12: (2 sc in next ch-4-space, 9 dc + ch 3 + 9 dc in next ch-7-space, 2 sc in next ch-4-space) repeat 4 times, fasten off with an invisible join to 2nd sc [4 leaves]

Rnd 13: {Join yarn F in a BPsc from Rnd 11, in the middle between 2 leaves, make your first stitch a standing stitch. Work behind leaves of Rnd 12, with the right side of the flower facing you} (BPsc around BPsc, ch 5) repeat 8 times, slst in initial BPsc [8 + 40 ch]

Rnd 14: slst in next 3 ch, sc in same ch-space, (ch 7, sc in next ch-space, ch 5, sc in next ch-space) repeat 3 times, ch 7, sc in next ch-space, ch 5, slst in initial sc [8 + 48 ch]

Rnd 15: slst in next 4 ch, 6 sc in remainder of same ch-7-space, 5 sc in ch-5-space, (10 sc in ch-7-space, 5 sc in ch-5-space) repeat 3 times, 4 sc over initial 4 slst, slst in initial sc [60]

Rnd 16: ch 2 (count as hdc), hdc in next 14 st, (hdc + ch 2 + hdc in next st, hdc in next 14 st) repeat 3 times, hdc in same st as initial ch 2, ch 1, sc in 2nd ch of initial ch 2 [64 + 8 ch]

Note: in Rnd 17, you will catch the leaves in place as follows: when the pattern says 'catch leaf' you will: yarn over, insert hook into BLO of 10th dc of leaf, then complete 1st BLO dc of the side as instructed. In the last st of this side before the corner is made, repeat this process for the next leaf - yarn over, insert hook into 9th dc of leaf, then complete BLO dc. Make the corner as directed. Repeat on each side around.

Rnd 17: {work this round in BLO} ch 3 (count as dc), BLO dc in next st (catch leaf), BLO dc in next 15 st (catch leaf in last dc), (dc + ch 2 + dc in ch-space, BLO dc in next st (catch leaf), BLO dc in next 15 st (catch leaf in last dc)) repeat 3 times, dc in initial ch-space, ch 2, fasten off with an invisible join to first true dc [72 + 8 ch]

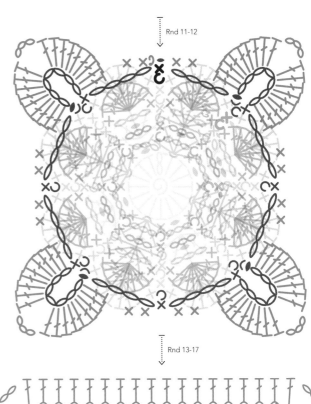

Rnd 11-12

Rnd 13-17

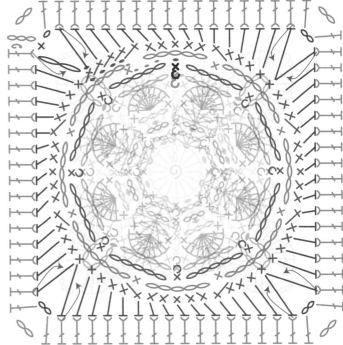

HANEEN'S LOVELY SQUARE `112 stitch square`

inas.craft (Inas Fadil Basymeleh) — Indonesia
@inas.craft ⊕ www.inascraft.com

Skill level: Intermediate
Colors: Yarn A: Cream / Yarn B: Pastel Pink / Yarn C: Peony Pink
Special stitches: 5-dc-pc (5 double crochet popcorn stitch) /
FPtr (Front post treble crochet)

INSTRUCTIONS

Rnd 1: {start with yarn A} start a magic ring with (ch 6, slst) repeat
8 times, fasten off with an invisible join to 2nd ch [8 petals]

Rnd 2: {continue with yarn A, join yarn in any ch-space, make your first
stitch a standing stitch} (sc in ch-space, ch 3) repeat 8 times, fasten off
with an invisible join to first ch after initial sc [8 loops]

Rnd 3: {join yarn B in any ch-space, make your first stitch a standing
stitch} (5-dc-pc + ch 4 + 5-dc-pc in ch-space, ch 2) repeat 8 times, fasten
off with an invisible join to first ch after initial pc [16 + 48 ch]

Rnd 4: {join yarn C in any ch-4-space, make your first stitch a standing
stitch} (3 dc + ch 3 + slst + ch 3 + 3 dc in ch-4 space, FPtr around sc in
Rnd 2, skip next ch-2 space) repeat 8 times, fasten off with an invisible join
to 2nd stitch [64 + 48 ch]

Note: the flower now has 8 petals and each petal has 2 sides (right-side
and left-side).

Rnd 5: {join yarn A in top ch in any right-side petal, make your first
stitch a standing stitch} (hdc in top ch of right-side petal, ch 2, dc in top
ch of left-side petal, ch 1, 2 dtr + ch 4 + 2 dtr in next FPtr, ch 1, dc in next
top ch of right side petal, ch 2, hdc in top ch of next left-side petal, ch 1,
2 tr in next FPtr, ch 1) repeat 4 times, fasten off with an invisible join to first
ch after initial hdc [40 + 48 ch]

Rnd 6: {join yarn B in any ch-4-space, make your first stitch a standing
stitch} [2 sc + ch 2 + 2 sc in ch-4 space, (sc in next 2 st, sc in next
ch-1 space, sc in next st, 2 sc in next ch-2 space, sc in next st, sc in
next ch-1 space) repeat 2 times, sc in next 2 st] repeat 4 times, fasten
off with an invisible join to 2nd stitch [88 + 8 ch]

Rnd 7: {join yarn C in any ch-space, make your first stitch a standing
stitch} (2 dc + ch 2 + 2 dc in ch-space, dc in next 22 st) repeat 4 times,
fasten off with an invisible join to 2nd stitch [104 + 8 ch]

DARLING PUFF SQUARE `112 stitch square`

Crochetedbytess (Therese Eghult) — Sweden
🌐 www.sistersinstitch.com

Skill level: Advanced
Colors: Yarn A: Golden Glow / Yarn B: Pastel Pink / Yarn C: Peony Pink / Yarn D: Cream / Yarn E: Antique Pink / Yarn F: Mustard
Special stitches: 4-puff (puff stitch with 4 loops) / Long 6-puff (Long puff stitch with 6 loops) / 3-puff (puff stitch with 3 loops) / 4-dc-pc (popcorn stitch with 4 dc) / FPv-stitch (front post v stitch: {FPdc, ch 2, FPdc}) / 3-dc-bobble (3 double crochet bobble) / FPsc (Front post single crochet) / FPdc (Front post double crochet) / BPhdc (Back post half double crochet) / BPdc (Back post double crochet)

INSTRUCTIONS

Rnd 1: {start with yarn A} start a magic ring with 8 sc, fasten off with an invisible join to 2nd stitch [8]

Rnd 2: {join yarn B in any st, make your first stitch a standing stitch. You work both around and in each stitch so this round might feel a bit tight and crowded while working} BPdc around next st, ch 1, (4-puff + ch 2 in next st, reverse BPdc around the sc you worked the puff in, ch 1) repeat 7 times, 4-puff in same st you worked the first BPdc around, ch 2, fasten off with an invisible join to first ch after initial BPdc [16 + 24 ch]

Rnd 3: {join Yarn C in any puff st, make your first stitch a standing stitch. Work this round only in the puff stitches} (3-dc-bobble in next puff + ch 6) repeat 8 times, fasten off with an invisible join to first ch after initial 3-dc-bobble [8 + 48 ch]

Rnd 4: {join Yarn D in any st, make your first stitch a standing stitch. Work this round in front of the ch-6-spaces of Rnd 3} (FPv-stitch around the BPdc from Rnd 2, FPsc around the 3-dc-bobble from Rnd 3) repeat 8 times, fasten off with an invisible join to first ch after initial FPdc [16] Gently pull all the ch-6-spaces from Rnd 3 upwards to make sure that they are not tangled under the FPsc just made.

Rnd 5: {join yarn E in any FPv-stitch, make your first stitch a standing stitch. Work around the ch-6-spaces of Rnd 3 and the ch-2-spaces of Rnd 4} (7 dc in next ch-space, ch 1, skip next FPsc) repeat 8 times, fasten off with an invisible join to 2nd stitch [56 + 8 ch]

Rnd 6: {join yarn D in any first dc, make your first stitch a standing stitch. Work in front of the ch-spaces of Rnd 5} (BPhdc in next 7 st, skip next ch, 4-dc-pc + ch 2 + 4-dc-pc + ch 1 in the FPsc of Rnd 4) repeat 8 times, fasten off with an invisible join to 2nd stitch [72 + 8 ch]

Rnd 7: {join yarn F in any first BPhdc, make your first stitch a standing stitch} (BPhdc in next 7 st, FPsc around pc, ch 1, skip 1 ch, FPsc around pc) repeat 8 times, fasten off with an invisible join to 2nd stitch [72 + 8 ch]

Rnd 8: {join yarn E in any first BPhdc, make your first stitch a standing stitch. Please note that the long puffs are worked between the 2 pc from Rnd 6 and around all ch-1-spaces from Rnd 5, 6 and 7} (BPhdc in next 7 st, skip 1 FPsc, long 6-puff down around the ch-space from Rnd 5, skip 1 FPsc) repeat 8 times, fasten off with an invisible join to 2nd stitch [64]

Rnd 9: {join yarn D in any first BPhdc, make your first stitch a standing stitch} (dc in next 2 st, hdc in next 3 st, sc in next 2 st, skip 1 puff, sc in next 2 st, hdc in next 3 st, dc in next 2 st, FPv-stitch around the long 6-puff) repeat 4 times, fasten off with an invisible join to 2nd stitch [60]

Rnd 10: {join yarn C in any ch-space of a FPv-stitch, make your first stitch a standing stitch} (2 dc + ch 2 + 2 dc in next st, FPdc around next st, skip 1 st, 3-puff + ch 1 in next 12 st, skip 1 st, FPdc around next st) repeat 4 times, fasten off with an invisible join to 2nd stitch [72 + 56 ch]

Rnd 11: {join yarn D in any ch-space, make your first stitch a standing stitch} (2 hdc + ch 1 + 2 hdc in next ch-space, hdc + FPdc around next 2 st, FPdc around next st, hdc in the gap between the FPdc and the puff, hdc in next 11 gaps between the puffs, hdc in the gap between the puff and the FPdc, FPdc around next st, FPdc + hdc in next 2 st, fasten off with an invisible join to 2nd stitch [108 + 4 ch]

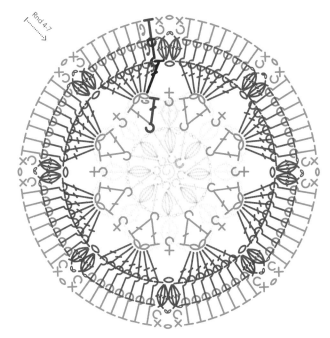

Rnd 4-7

Rnd 8-11

Rnd 1-3

IRIS SQUARE `112 stitch square`

Designs By Muggins (Margaret MacInnis) — Canada
© mugginsquilts f DesignsbyMuggins ⊗ www.designsbymuggins.com

Skill level: Advanced
Colors: Yarn A: Eucalyptus / Yarn B: Denim / Yarn C: Old Pink /
Yarn D: Pearl / Yarn E: Riverside
Special stitches: **4-puff** (puff stitch with 4 loops) / **4-dc-pc** (4 double
crochet popcorn stitch) / **FPhdc** (front post half double crochet) /
FPdc (front post double crochet)
Pattern-specific special stitch:
Two variants of the v-stitch:
   V-2: dc + ch 2 + dc in same space or stitch.
   V-3: dc + ch 3 + dc in same space or stitch.
Beginning V-2: ch 3 (count as dc) + ch 2 + 2 dc in same space or stitch.
Fan: 2 dc + ch 2 + 2 dc in same space or stitch;
Beginning-fan: ch 3 (count as dc) + dc + ch 2 + 2 dc in same space or stitch.
SPtrtr (Special triple treble): yo 4 times, insert hook, work in front of
previous rounds, work off as usual 2 loops at a time, enclosing the
ch-1-space in Rnd 3 below with the last draw through only.

INSTRUCTIONS

Rnd 1: {start with yarn A} start a magic ring with ch 3 (count as dc), 15 dc,
slst in initial dc [16] Place a stitch marker in yarn A loop and hold the loop
and the yarn to the front of your work.

Rnd 2: {join yarn B in the stitch after the join in Rnd 1, make your first
stitch a standing stitch} (V-2 in next st, ch 1, skip 1 st) repeat 8 times, slst in
initial dc [16 + 24 ch]

Rnd 3: slst in ch-2-space, beginning-fan in same ch-space, (ch 1, V-3 in next
ch-2-space, ch 1, fan in next ch-2-space) repeat 3 times, ch 1, V-3 in next
ch-2-space, ch 1, fasten off with an invisible join to first true dc [24 + 28 ch]

*Note: In Rnd 4 you work a FLO slst in all stitches (dc and ch-stitches)
except in each ch-1. In the ch-1, you work a SPtrtr in front of Rnd 2
and 3.*

Rnd 4: {pick up the yarn A loop, work in front of Rnd 2 and 3} ch 5, work
the 5th ch over the ch-1-space in Rnd 3 (count as SPtrtr), (FLO slst in next
6 st and chains, SPtrtr in next skipped dc in Rnd 1, FLO slst in next 5 st and
chains, SPtrtr in next skipped dc in Rnd 1) repeat 3 times, FLO slst in next
6 st and chains, SPtrtr in next skipped dc in Rnd 1, FLO slst next 5 st and
chains, fasten off with an invisible join to first slst after initial ch 5 [52]

Rnd 1-4
|············>

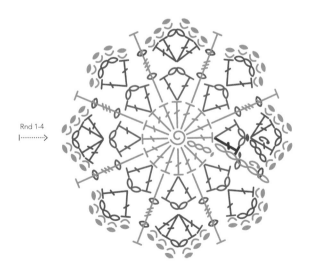

Note: In Rnd 5 you work treble stitches in the ch-2-space of Rnd 2 in front of Rnd 3 V-3 and Rnd 4 slst.

Rnd 5: *{join yarn C in any ch-2-space of Rnd 2, make your first stitch a standing stitch}* (5 tr in ch-2-space of Rnd 2, ch 1, FPhdc around SPtrtr, ch 3, 4-puff in ch-space of Rnd 3 enclosing the slst, ch 3, FPhdc around SPtrtr, ch 1) repeat 4 times, fasten off with an invisible join to 2nd stitch [32 + 32 ch]

Rnd 6: *{join yarn E in any ch-1-space before a 5-tr-group, make your first stitch a standing stitch}* (2 sc in ch-1-space, ch 5, skip 5-tr-group, 2 sc in next ch-1-space, FPhdc around FPhdc, 3 sc in next ch-3-space, FPhdc around top of puff, 3 sc in next ch-3-space, FPhdc around next FPhdc) repeat 4 times, fasten off with an invisible join to 2nd stitch [52 + 20 ch]

Rnd 7: *{join yarn D in any first tr of a 5-tr-group of Rnd 5, make your first stitch a standing stitch. Work all treble stitches over the ch-5-space of Rnd 6, in the treble stitches of Rnd 5}* (2 tr in first tr, 2 tr in next tr, tr + ch 3 + tr in next tr, 2 tr in next 2 tr, ch 3, skip 6 st, V-2 in Rnd 6 FPhdc over the puff, ch 3, skip 6 st) repeat 4 times, slst around initial tr [48 + 44 ch]

Rnd 8: ch 2 (count as FPdc), FPdc around next 4 tr, 5 hdc in ch-3-space, FPdc around next 5 tr, 3 sc in next ch-3-space, FPhdc around next dc, 3 sc in next ch-2-space, FPhdc around next dc, 3 sc in next ch-3-space, (FPdc around next 5 tr, 5 hdc in ch-3-space, FPdc around next 5 tr, 3 sc in next ch-3-space, FPhdc around next dc, 3 sc in next ch-2-space, FPhdc around next dc, 3 sc in next ch-3-space) repeat 3 times, fasten off with an invisible join to first true FPdc [104]

Rnd 9: *{join yarn B in any first hdc of 5 hdc in ch-3-space, make your first stitch a standing stitch. Work in stitches of Rnd 8 unless otherwise mentioned}* (sc in next 5 hdc, fold the front layer forward, hdc in next 5 tr of Rnd 7 (the ones with FP, work behind the FP stitches), sc in next 4 st, ch 1, 4-dc-pc in top of Rnd 6 FPhdc, ch 1, skip 3 st, sc in next 4 st, hdc in next 5 tr of Rnd 7) repeat 4 times, fasten off with an invisible join to 2nd stitch [96 + 8 ch]

Rnd 10: *{join yarn A in any ch-space following a pc, make your first stitch a standing stitch}* (sc in ch-space, sc in next 4 st, hdc in next 7 st, 2 hdc + ch 1 + hdc in next st, hdc in next 7 st, sc in next 4 st, skip next ch-space, FPhdc around pc) repeat 4 times, invisible join to 2nd stitch [108 + 4 ch]

Rnd 5-8

Rnd 9-10

CHAMPA SQUARE `112 stitch square`

IrShCrochet (Irana Shintarani) — Indonesia
f IrShCrochet ○ iranashintarani

Skill level: Advanced
Colors: Yarn A: Navy Blue / Yarn B: Green Ice / Yarn C: Sunflower / Yarn D: Chestnut
Special stitches: FPdc (Front post double crochet) / hdc3tog (half double crochet 3 stitches together) / sc2tog (single crochet 2 stitches together) / 3-dc-bobble (3 double crochet bobble) / 3-tr-bobble (3 treble crochet bobble)

INSTRUCTIONS

Rnd 1: *{start with yarn A}* start a magic ring with 8 sc, fasten off with an invisible join to 2nd stitch [8]

Rnd 2: *{join yarn B in any st, make your first stitch a standing stitch. Work this round in BLO}* 2 sc in all 8 st, fasten off with an invisible join to 2nd stitch [16]

Rnd 3: *{join yarn C in any st, make your first stitch a standing stitch. Work this round in BLO}* (sc in next st, 2 sc in next st) repeat 8 times, fasten off with an invisible join to 2nd stitch [24]

Rnd 4: *{join yarn A in second sc of any 2 sc increase, make your first stitch a standing stitch}* (BLO sc in next 3 st, FLO tr in leftover front loop of Rnd 1 below, *{don't skip the stitch behind the FLO tr}*) repeat 8 times, fasten off with an invisible join to 2nd stitch [32]

Rnd 5: *{join yarn B in any tr stitch, make your first stitch a standing stitch. Work this round in BLO}* (sc in next 2 st, 2 sc in next st, sc in next st) repeat 8 times, fasten off with an invisible join to 2nd stitch [40]

Rnd 6: *{join yarn A in first sc stitch of any 2 sc increase, make your first stitch a standing stitch}* (BLO sc in next 3 st, FPdc around tr of Rnd 4, *{don't skip the stitch behind the FPdc}*, BLO sc in next 2 st) repeat 8 times, fasten off with an invisible join to 2nd stitch [48]

Rnd 7: *{join yarn C in any FPdc, make your first stitch a standing stitch}* (sc in next 3 st, FLO 2 tr in middle sc of Rnd 4 below, skip 1 st (behind FLO 2 tr), sc in next 2 st) repeat 8 times, fasten off with an invisible join to 2nd stitch [56]

Note: In Rnd 8 the first leg of the first hdc3tog will be in the same stitch as the last leg of the last dc3tog.

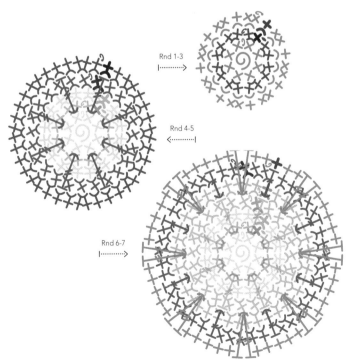

Rnd 1-3

Rnd 4-5

Rnd 6-7

Rnd 8: {join yarn D in any sc above a FPdc of Rnd 6, make your first stitch a standing stitch} hdc3tog, ch 5, FLO sc in Rnd 4 sc between 2 tr of Rnd 7, ch 5, skip 2 FLO tr, hdc3tog, ch 3, (hdc3tog starting in the same st as the last leg of the previous hdc3tog, ch 5, FLO sc in Rnd 4 sc between 2 tr of Rnd 7, ch 5, skip 2 FLO tr, hdc3tog, ch 3) repeat 7 times, fasten off with an invisible join to first ch after initial hdc3tog [24 + 104 ch]

Rnd 9: {join yarn B in any first hdc3tog of Rnd 8, make your first stitch a standing stitch} (sc in hdc3tog, 3 dc in Rnd 7 st holding the 2 legs of each tog st {in front of ch 3 of Rnd 8}, sc in next hdc3tog, ch 2, sc2tog in skipped tr of Rnd 7 behind Rnd 8 chains, ch 2) repeat 8 times, fasten off with an invisible join to 2nd stitch [88]

Rnd 10: {join yarn C in any sc2tog, make your first stitch a standing stitch} (sc in sc2tog, ch 4, skip ch 2, dc5tog {over sc + 3 dc + sc}, ch 5, skip ch 2) repeat 8 times, fasten off with an invisible join to first ch after initial sc [70 + 72 ch]

Rnd 11: {join yarn B in any first ch-5-space, make your first stitch a standing stitch} (5 sc in ch-5-space, sc2tog over both ch-spaces of Rnd 10 enclosing both ch-2-spaces of Rnd 9 {skipping the sc in the middle}, 5 sc in next ch-4-space, ch 1, skip dc5tog) repeat 8 times, fasten off with an invisible join to 2nd stitch [80 + 8 ch]

Rnd 12: {in this round we create 4 sides of the square. Join yarn A in any ch-1-space, make your first stitch a standing stitch} (2 sc in next st, sc in next 2 st, skip 3 st, 3 dc in next sc2tog, skip 3 st, sc in next 2 st, 2 sc in next ch-1-space, sc in next 2 st, ch 1, skip 3 st, 3-dc-bobble + ch 2 + 3-tr-bobble + ch 2 + 3-dc-bobble in next sc2tog, ch 1, skip 3 st, sc in next 2 st) repeat 4 times, fasten off with an invisible join to 2nd stitch [72 + 24 ch]

Rnd 13: {join yarn D in any last ch-2-space, make your first stitch a standing stitch} (3 dc in ch-2-space, FPdc around next 3-dc-bobble, dc in next ch-1-space, dc in next st, hdc in next st, sc in next 11 st, hdc in next st, dc in next st, dc in next ch-1-space, FPdc around next 3 dc-bobble, 3 dc in next ch-2-space, ch 2, skip 3-tr-bobble) repeat 4 times, fasten off with an invisible join to 2nd stitch [100 + 8 ch]

Rnd 14: {join yarn A in any ch-2-corner-space, make your first stitch a standing stitch} (sc + ch 1 + sc in ch-space, sc in next 25 st) repeat 4 times, fasten off with an invisible join to first ch after initial sc [108 + 4 ch]

Rnd 8-10

⊢·········>

Rnd 11-14

A LITTLE SOMETHING SQUARE 112 stitch square

Crochetedbytess (Therese Eghult) — Sweden
⊕ www.sistersinstitch.com

Skill level: Advanced
Colors: Yarn A: Mustard / Yarn B: Pearl / Yarn C: Cream / Yarn D: clay /
Yarn E: Pastel Pink / Yarn F: Birch / Yarn G: Antique Pink
Special stitches: 5-dc-pc (5 double crochet popcorn stitch) / **broom
stitch** / **long sc** (long single crochet) / **long dc** (long double crochet) /
BPsc (Back post single crochet) / **FPhdc** (Front post half double crochet)

INSTRUCTIONS

Rnd 1: *{start with yarn A}* start a magic ring with 10 sc, slst in initial sc [10]
Do not tighten the magic ring yet.

Rnd 2: *{work this entire round over the previous round, in the center
of the magic circle}* 16 long sc, tighten the magic ring, fasten off with an
invisible join to 2nd stitch [16]

Rnd 3: *{join yarn B in any st, make your first stitch a standing stitch}*
(sc + ch 2 in next st, sc in next st) repeat 8 times, fasten off with an
invisible join to first ch after initial sc [16 + 16 ch]

Rnd 4: *{join yarn B in any ch-space, make your first stitch a standing
stitch}* (3 dc + ch 1 + 3 dc in ch-space, slst in gap between the 2 sc
stitches from Rnd 3) repeat 8 times, fasten off with an invisible join to 2nd
stitch [8 petals + 8 slst]

Rnd 5: *{join yarn C in any ch-space make your first stitch a standing
stitch. Work only in the ch-spaces}* (sc in ch-space, ch 5) repeat 8 times,
slst in first sc [8 loops]

*Note: To decrease over the single crochet from Rnd 5, you start in
the given ch-space, begin as a normal sc (2 loops on the hook) and
before doing the final yarn over, you insert your hook in the next
ch-space, yarn over and pull up a loop (3 loops on the hook). Yarn
over and pull through all 3 loops. You are never working in the sc of
Rnd 5 but the head of the decrease stitch falls right on top of it.*

Rnd 6: slst + 5 sc in next ch-space, dec over the sc from Rnd 5, (5 sc in
next ch-space, dec over the sc from Rnd 5) repeat 7 times, fasten off with
an invisible join to 2nd stitch [48]

Rnd 1-9

Note: If you know yourself to crochet tightly, loosen your tension while working the treble crochet stitches in Rnd 7 or try to work the first and last one in each combination as a triple treble crochet stitch instead.

Rnd 7: *{join yarn D in any decrease stitch, make your first stitch a standing stitch}* (sc + ch 1 + sc in next st, skip 5 st, 10 tr in next st, skip 5 st) repeat 4 times, fasten off with an invisible join to first ch after initial sc [48 + 4 ch]

Rnd 8: *{join yarn E in any ch-space, make your first stitch a standing stitch}* (5-dc-pc + ch 2 + 5-dc-pc + ch 3 in ch-space, skip 1 st, BPsc around next 10 st, ch 2, skip 1 st) repeat 4 times, fasten off with an invisible join to first ch after initial pc [48 + 20 ch]

Rnd 9: *{join yarn F in any ch-space before a first pc stitch, make your first stitch a standing stitch}* (hdc + 5 dc in ch-space, sc in 5-dc-pc, ch 1, sc in 5-dc-pc, 5 dc + hdc in next ch-space, slst in next st, broom stitch in next 8 st, slst in next st) repeat 4 times, fasten off with an invisible join to 2nd stitch [96 + 4 ch]

Rnd 10: *{join yarn C in any corner-space between the pc from Rnd 8, working around the ch 1 from previous round. Make your first stitch a standing stitch}* (2 long dc + ch 2 + 2 long dc in corner-space in Rnd 8, skip 1 st, BPsc around next 6 st, skip 1 slst, sc in next 8 loops, skip 1 slst,

Rnd 10-12

BPsc around next 6 st) repeat 4 times, fasten off with an invisible join to 2nd stitch [96 + 8 ch]

Rnd 11: *{join yarn C in any ch-space, make your first stitch a standing stitch}* (hdc + ch 2 + hdc in ch-space, FPhdc in next 2 st, sc in next 20 st, FPhdc in next 2 st) repeat 4 times, fasten off with an invisible join to first ch after initial hdc [104 + 8 ch]

Rnd 12: *{join yarn G in any ch-2-space, make your first stitch a standing stitch}* (3 sc in ch-2-space, sc in next st, hdc in next 24 st, sc in next st) repeat 4 times, fasten off with an invisible join to 2nd stitch [112]

KAMALA SQUARE `112 stitch square`

IrShCrochet (Irana Shintarani) — Indonesia
f IrShCrochet ⬡ iranashintarani

Skill level: Advanced
Colors: Yarn A: Satay / Yarn B: Peridot / Yarn C: Mustard /
Yarn D: Limestone
Special stitches: 3-tr-bobble (3 treble crochet bobble stitch) / FPsc
(Front post single crochet) / FPdtr (Front post double treble crochet)

INSTRUCTIONS

Rnd 1: *{start with yarn A}* start a magic ring with 8 sc, fasten off with an invisible join to 2nd stitch [8]

Rnd 2: *{join yarn B in any st, make your first stitch a standing stitch. Work this round in BLO}* 2 sc in all 8 st, slst in initial sc [16]

Rnd 3: ch 1, sc in same st, 2 sc in next st, (sc in next st, 2 sc in next st) repeat 7 times, fasten off with an invisible join to 2nd stitch [24]

Rnd 4: *{join yarn C in any single sc, make your first stitch a standing stitch}* (BLO sc in next 3 st, FLO 3-tr-bobble in leftover front loop of Rnd 1 below, *{don't skip the stitch behind the FLO 3-tr-bobble}*) repeat 8 times, fasten off with an invisible join to 2nd stitch [32]

Rnd 5: *{join yarn B in any first sc after 3-tr-bobble, make your first stitch a standing stitch}* (BLO sc in next st, BLO 2 sc in next st, BLO sc in next st, FPsc around 3-tr-bobble) repeat 8 times, fasten off with an invisible join to 2nd stitch [40]

Rnd 6: *{join yarn A in any FPsc, make your first stitch a standing stitch. Work this round in BLO}* (2 sc in next st, sc in next 4 st) repeat 8 times, fasten off with an invisible join to 2nd stitch [48]

Rnd 7: *{join yarn D in any second sc of a 2 sc increase, make your first stitch a standing stitch}* (sc in next st, FLO 3-tr-bobble in first sc after 3-tr-bobble of Rnd 4, ch 3, skip 1 st of Rnd 4, FLO 3-tr-bobble in next st of Rnd 4, skip 4 st of Rnd 6, sc in next st of Rnd 6) repeat 8 times, fasten off with an invisible join to 2nd stitch [32 + 24 ch]

Rnd 8: *{join yarn B in any 3-tr-bobble after a ch space, make your first stitch a standing stitch, all dc are worked behind the ch 3 from Rnd 7}* (sc in next 3-dc-bobble, sc in next 2 st, sc in next 3-dc-bobble, dc in next 4 skipped st of Rnd 6) repeat 8 times, fasten off with an invisible join to 2nd stitch [64]

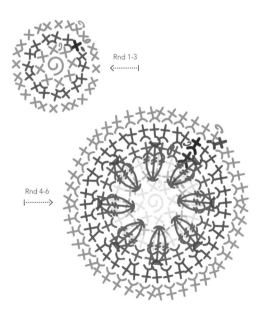

Rnd 1-3
←·········|

Rnd 4-6
|·········→

Rnd 9: {join yarn A in any ch-3-space of Rnd 7, make your first stitch a standing stitch} (sc + hdc + 3 dc + hdc + sc in ch-3-space, FLO tr in FPsc of Rnd 5) repeat 8 times, fasten off with an invisible join to 2nd stitch [64]

Rnd 10: {join yarn C in any second dc of a 3-dc-group, make your first stitch a standing stitch} (3 sc in next st, sc in next 7 st) repeat 8 times, fasten off with an invisible join to 2nd stitch [80]

Rnd 11: {join yarn B in any first sc of a 3-sc-group, make your first stitch a standing stitch} (sc in next 3 st, hdc in next 3 st, hdc + ch 3 + hdc in next st, hdc in next 3 st, sc in next 3 st, hdc in next 2 st, dc in next 3 st, hdc in next 2 st) repeat 4 times, fasten off with an invisible join to 2nd stitch [80 + 12 ch]

Rnd 12: {join yarn D in any ch-3-space, make your first stitch a standing stitch} (2 dtr + 2 tr + ch 3 + 2 tr + 2 dtr in ch-3-space, skip 5 st, sc in next 11 st, skip 5 st) repeat 4 times, fasten off with an invisible join to 2nd stitch [76 + 12 ch]

Rnd 13: {join yarn C in any ch-3-space of Rnd 11, make your first stitch a standing stitch} (3 tr + ch 2 + 3 tr in ch-3-space of Rnd 11 in the center between tr of Rnd 12, sc in next 8 st of Rnd 12, FPdtr in sc of Rnd 10 which is above tr of Rnd 9, skip 1 st, sc in next st, reverse FPdtr in same sc of Rnd 10, skip 1 st, sc in next 8 st) repeat 4 times, fasten off with an invisible join to 2nd stitch [100 + 8 ch]

Rnd 14: {join yarn A in any ch-2-space, make your first stitch a standing stitch} (sc + ch 1 + sc in ch-2 space, sc in next 25 st) repeat 4 times, fasten off with an invisible join in first ch after initial sc [108 + 4 ch]

Rnd 9-12

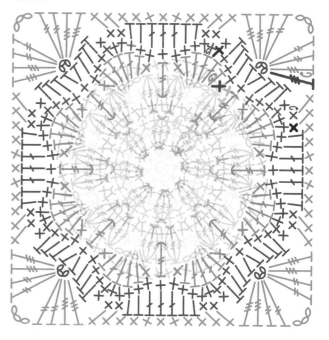

Rnd 13-14

Rnd 7-8

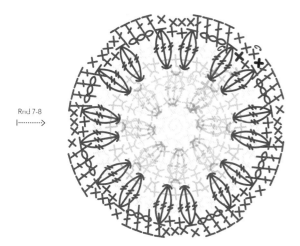

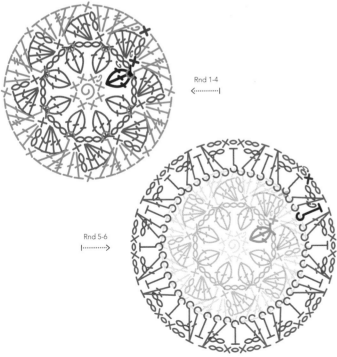

Rnd 1-4
<··············|

Rnd 5-6
|··············>

AMEERA LUBNA SQUARE `112 stitch square`

inas.craft (Inas Fadil Basymeleh) — Indonesia
@inas.craft   www.inascraft.com

Skill level: Advanced
Colors: Yarn A: Cream / Yarn B: Peony Pink / Yarn C: Pastel Pink / Yarn D: Pearl
Special stitches: FPhdc (Front post half double crochet) / FPdc (Front post double crochet) / FPtr (Front post treble crochet) / 5-dc-pc (5 double crochet popcorn stitch) / Changing color mid-round

INSTRUCTIONS

Rnd 1: *{start with yarn A}* start a magic ring with 8 sc, fasten off with an invisible join to 2nd stitch [8]

Rnd 2: *{join yarn B in any st, make your first stitch a standing stitch}* (5-dc-pc in next st + ch 3) repeat 8 times, fasten off with an invisible join to first ch after initial pc [8 + 24 ch]

Rnd 3: *{join yarn C in any ch-3 space, make your first stitch a standing stitch}* (sc + ch 2 + 4 dc in ch-space, skip pc) repeat 8 times, fasten off with an invisible join to first ch after initial sc [40 + 16 ch]

Rnd 4: *{join yarn A in any first dc after ch 2, make your first stitch a standing stitch}* (sc in first dc after ch 2, skip 3 dc, 2 dc in next sc, FPtr around pc in Rnd 2, 2 dc in same previous sc) repeat 8 times, fasten off with an invisible join to 2nd stitch [48]

Rnd 5: *{join yarn D around any FPtr, make your first stitch a standing stitch}* (FPhdc around FPtr, skip 2 st, ch 2, FPhdc around next sc, skip 2 st, ch 2) repeat 8 times, fasten off with an invisible join to first ch after initial FPhdc [16 + 32 ch]

Rnd 6: *{join yarn A in any ch-space before FPhdc around sc, make your first stitch a standing stitch}* (sc in ch-space, ch 1, sc in next ch-space, ch 2, FPdc2tog around next 2 dc before FPtr in Rnd 4, FPdc2tog around next 2 dc after FPtr in Rnd 4, ch 2) repeat 8 times, fasten off with an invisible join to first ch after initial sc [32 + 40 ch]

Rnd 7: *{join yarn B in any ch-1-space, make your first stitch a standing stitch}* (3 dc + ch 2 + 3 dc in ch-1-space, FPtr around same previous FPhdc in Rnd 5, FPdc around both FPdc2tog in Rnd 6, *{change to yarn D}* FPtr around next FPhdc in Rnd 5, dc + 4 hdc + dc in ch-1-space, FPtr around same previous FPhdc in Rnd 5, *{change to yarn B}* FPdc around both FPdc2tog in Rnd 6, FPtr around next FPhdc in Rnd 5) repeat 4 times, slst in initial dc [72 + 8 ch]

Rnd 8: ch 3 (count as dc), dc in next 2 st, 2 dc + ch 2 + 2 dc in ch-2-space, dc in next 3 st, FPdc around FPtr, dc in next st, *{change to yarn D}* FPdc around FPtr, sc in next 2 st, ch 2, skip 2 st, sc in next 2 st, FPdc around FPtr, *{change to yarn B}* dc in next st, FPdc around FPtr, (dc in next 3 st, 2 dc + ch 2 + 2 dc in ch-2-space, dc in next 3 st, FPdc around FPtr, dc in next st, *{change to yarn D}* FPdc around FPtr, sc in next 2 st, ch 2, skip 2 st, sc in next 2 st, FPdc around FPtr, *{change to yarn B}* dc in next st, FPdc around FPtr) repeat 3 times, fasten off both yarns, invisible join to first true dc [80 + 16 ch]

Rnd 9: *{join yarn A in any corner-space, make your first stitch a standing stitch}* (2 dc + ch 2 + 2 dc in corner-space, dc in next 10 st, skip 2 ch, FPtr around 2nd skipped dc in Rnd 7, reverse FPtr around first skipped dc in Rnd 7, dc in next 10 st) repeat 4 times, fasten off with an invisible join to 2nd stitch [104 + 8 ch]

> *Did you know Ameera means "Princess, leader" in Arabic? Lubna means "Styrax tree", a tree which yields an aromatic resin used in perfume and medicine.*

Rnd 7-9

TWISTED LILY SQUARE 112 stitch square

Crochetedbytess (Therese Eghult) — Sweden
⊕ www.sistersinstitch.com

Skill level: Extra advanced
Colors: Yarn A: Vanilla / **Yarn B:** Pastel Pink / **Yarn C:** Peony Pink / **Yarn D:** Antique Pink / **Yarn E:** Peridot / **Yarn F:** Pistachio
Special stitches: ch-2-picot (Picot stitch) / **FPtr** (Front post treble crochet) / **FPhdc** (Front post half double crochet) / **3-tr-bobble** (3 treble crochet bobble stitch)

INSTRUCTIONS

Note: For the petal rounds where you work slst in slst (9, 12 and 15) you can also choose to work the slst in BLO to make it a bit easier.

Rnd 1: *{start with yarn A}* start a magic ring with 8 sc, slst in initial sc [8]

Note: the final slst of Rnd 1 counts as the first stitch of Rnd 2.

Rnd 2: *{work this round in FLO}* (slst in next st, ch 2, slst in second ch from hook, slst back into base st, slst in next st, ch 3, slst in second ch from hook, slst in next ch, slst back into base st) repeat 4 times, slst in final slst of Rnd 1 [28 + 20 ch]

Rnd 3: *{work this round in leftover back loops of Rnd 1}* ch 1, 2 sc in next 8 st, slst in initial sc [16]

Note: the final slst of Rnd 3 counts as the first stitch of Rnd 4.

Rnd 4: *{work this round in FLO}* (slst in next st, ch 4, slst in second ch from hook, slst in next 2 ch, slst back into base st) repeat 16 times, slst in final slst of Rnd 3 [80 + 64 ch]

Rnd 5: *{work this round in leftover back loops of Rnd 3}* ch 1, (sc in next st, 2 sc in next st) repeat 8 times, slst in initial sc [24]

Note: the final slst of Rnd 5 counts as the first stitch of Rnd 6.

Rnd 6: *{work this round in FLO}* (slst in next st, ch 10, slst in same st) repeat 24 times, fasten off with an invisible join to 1st ch [48 + 240 ch]

Rnd 7: *{join yarn B in any st, make your first stitch a standing stitch. Work this round in leftover back loops of Rnd 6}* (sc in next 2 st, 2 sc in next st) repeat 8 times, slst in initial sc *{place a stitch marker in this stitch}* [32]

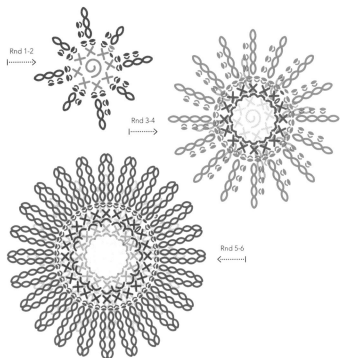

Rnd 1-2 |┈┈┈┈┈>

Rnd 3-4 |┈┈┈┈┈>

Rnd 5-6 <┈┈┈┈┈|

Note: the final slst of Rnd 7 counts as the first stitch of Rnd 8.

Rnd 8: *{work this round in FLO}* (slst in next st, ch 3, slst in same st, slst in next 3 st) repeat 8 times, slst in final slst of Rnd 7 [40 + 24 ch]

Rnd 9: (slst + ch 3 + 2 dc + ch-2-picot + 2 dc + ch 3 + slst in ch-space, skip slst below ch-3 eyelet of Rnd 8, slst in next 3 st, skip 1 st) repeat 8 times, fasten off with an invisible join to first ch after initial slst [60 + 48 ch]

Rnd 10: *{join yarn C in the stitch marked in Rnd 7, make your first stitch a standing stitch. Work this round in the back loops of Rnd 7}* (sc in next 3 st, 2 sc in next st) repeat 8 times, slst in initial sc *{place a stitch marker in the back loop of this stitch}* [40]

Note: for Rnd 11 and 14 the ch 4-spaces (which hold the petals) should line up in between the ones from the previous petal rounds.

Rnd 11: *{work this round in FLO}* (slst in next 4 st, slst in next st, ch 4, slst in same st) repeat 8 times [48 + 32 ch]

Rnd 12: (slst in next 4 st, skip 1 st below ch-4-eyelet, slst + ch 4 + 2 tr + ch-2-picot + 2 tr + ch 4 + slst in next ch-space, skip 1 st) repeat 8 times, fasten off with an invisible join to 2nd slst [88 + 64 ch]

Rnd 13: *{join yarn D in the stitch marked in Rnd 10, make your first stitch a standing stitch. Work this round in back loops of Rnd 10}* (sc in next 4 st, 2 sc in next st) repeat 8 times, FLO slst in initial sc *{place a stitch marker in the back loop of this stitch}* [48]

Note: the final slst of Rnd 13 counts as the first stitch of Rnd 14.

Rnd 14: *{work this round in FLO}* slst in next 2 st (slst in next st, ch 4, slst in same st, slst in next 5 st) repeat 7 times, slst in next st, ch 4, slst in same st, slst in next 3 st [56 + 32 ch]

Rnd 15: (slst in next 2 st, skip 1 st below ch-4-eyelet, slst + ch 5 + 2 dtr + ch-2-picot + 2 dtr + ch 5 + slst in next ch-space, skip 1 st below ch-4-eyelet, slst in next 3 st) repeat 8 times, fasten off with an invisible join to first ch after initial slst [96 + 80 ch]

Rnd 16: *{Join yarn E in the stitch marked in Rnd 13, make your first stitch a standing stitch}* (sc in next 5 st, 2 sc in next st) repeat 8 times, slst in initial sc [56]

Rnd 17: ch 3 (counts as dc) + dc in same st, ch 2, (2 dc in next st, dc in next st, hdc in next 3 st, sc in next 4 st, hdc in next 3 st, dc in next st, 2 dc in next st, ch 2) repeat 3 times, 2 dc in next st, dc in next st, hdc in next 3 st, sc in next 4 st, hdc in next 3 st, dc in next st, fasten off with an invisible join to the first true dc [64 + 8 ch]

Rnd 7-9

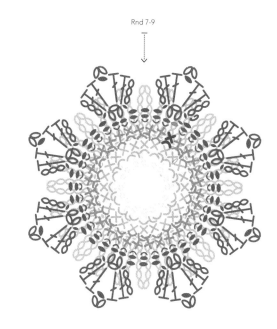

Rnd 10-12

Rnd 18: {join yarn E in any ch 2-space, make your first stitch a standing stitch} (3-tr-bobble + ch 5 + 3-tr-bobble + ch 1 in next ch-space, skip next 2 st, tr in next st, skip next 4 st, 3-tr-bobble + ch 3 + 3-tr-bobble + ch 3 + 3-tr-bobble in the gap between the 2nd and 3rd sc from Rnd 17, skip 5 st, tr + ch 1 in next st, skip next 2 st) repeat 4 times, slst in the top of the initial bobble [56 + 52 ch]

Rnd 19: ch 1, sc in same st, [7 sc in next ch-5-space, sc in next st, sc in next ch-1-space, sc in next st, sc in gap between tr and next 3-tr-bobble, sc in next st, (3 sc in next ch-3-space, sc in next st) repeat 2 times, sc in gap between tr and next 3-tr-bobble, sc in next st, sc in next ch-1-space, sc in next st] repeat 3 times, 7 sc in next ch-5-space, sc in next st, sc in next ch-1-space, sc in next st, sc in gap between tr and next 3-tr-bobble, sc in next st, (3 sc in next ch-3-space, sc in next st) repeat 2 times, sc in gap between tr and next 3-tr-bobble, sc in next st, sc in next ch-1-space, fasten off with an invisible join to 2nd stitch [96]

Rnd 20: {join yarn F in the 4th sc of any 7-sc corner-sequence, make your first stitch a standing stitch} (2 dc + ch 1 + 2 dc in next st, dc in next 3 st, FPtr around 3-tr-bobble from Rnd 18, skip next st behind FPtr, dc in next 3 st, FPtr around 3-tr-bobble from Rnd 18, skip next st behind FPtr, hdc in next st, sc in next 2 st, FPhdc around 3-tr-bobble from Rnd 18, skip next st behind FPhdc, sc in next 2 st, hdc in next st, FPtr around 3-tr-bobble from Rnd 18, skip next st behind FPtr, dc in next 3 st, FPtr around 3-tr-bobble from Rnd 18, skip next st behind FPtr, dc in next 3 st) repeat 4 times, fasten off with an invisible join to 2nd stitch [108 + 4 ch]

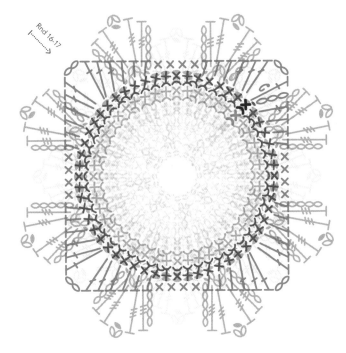

Rnd 16-17

Rnd 18-20

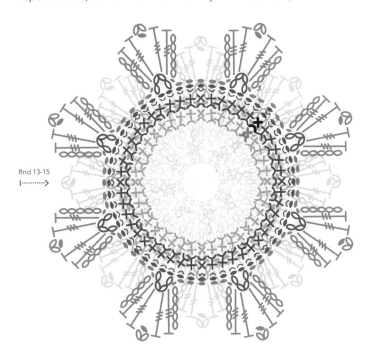

Rnd 13-15

CHANGE OF HEART SQUARE 112 stitch square

Designs By Muggins (Margaret MacInnis) — Canada
 mugginsquilts f DesignsbyMuggins www.designsbymuggins.com

Skill level: Extra advanced
Colors: Yarn A: Sorbus / Yarn B: Cream / Yarn C: Petrol Blue
Special stitches: FPdc (Front post double crochet) / FPtr (Front post treble crochet) / spike-dc (spike double crochet) / FLhdc (Front loop half double crochet) / FLdc (Front loop double crochet) / FLtr (Front loop treble crochet) / FLhdc2tog (work 2 hdc stitches together in the front loops only)
Pattern-specific special stitch: beginning elongated loop: extend the loop a little longer than you normally would

INSTRUCTIONS

Note: Work progresses as a grid in the Navajo blanket-style with FLhdc/FLdc/FLtr over a previously made stitch, worked in the previously worked round below.

Note: All stitches in all rounds are worked in BLO, except when working over corner chains or when working FLhdc/FLdc/FLtr.

Note: The first sc continuity line is best maintained by not making an actual sc. Pull up a beginning elongated loop from the Drop Loop and ch 1 loosely. When working the slst at the end, slst into both loops of the beginning elongated loop. When working into the st afterwards, work into the slst portion instead of the other side of the st, being careful not to work the same stitch two times. Occasionally, you will need the help of your yarn needle to elongate an access point.

Rnd 1: {start with yarn A} start a magic ring with 8 sc, fasten off with an invisible join to 2nd stitch [8]

Rnd 2: {join yarn B in any st, make your first stitch a standing stitch. Work this round and all other rounds in BLO unless otherwise noted} (sc + ch 2 + sc in next st, sc in next st) repeat 4 times, slst in both loops of initial sc [12 + 8 ch] Put a stitch maker in your yarn B loop to prevent it from unraveling. Keep yarn and loop to the back while you work Rnd 3.

Note: Pull a section of yarn for each round before you begin. While working the following rounds, it is helpful to have one color on your right side, and one color on your left side. Before you pick up the loop each round, untwist the work (not the yarn) so the yarn travels from the square without twisting.

Rnd 3: {*join yarn C in BLO of the second sc of a corner, make your first stitch a standing stitch*} (sc in next 3 st, sc + ch 2 + sc in next ch-space) repeat 4 times, slst in both loops of initial sc [20 + 8 ch]
Put a stitch marker in your yarn C loop to prevent it from unraveling.
Keep yarn and loop to the back while you work Rnd 4.

Rnd 4: {*pick up the yarn B loop in BLO of the stitch after the ch-space*} begin with an elongated loop, ch 1 loosely, sc in next st, (FLdc in next st, sc in next 2 st, sc + ch 2 + sc in next ch-space, sc in next 2 st) repeat 3 times, FLdc in next st, sc in next 2 st, sc + ch 2 + sc in next ch-space, slst in both loops of initial elongated loop [28 + 8 ch]
Put a stitch maker in your yarn B loop to prevent it from unraveling.
Keep yarn and loop to the back while you work Rnd 5.

Rnd 5: {*mark the first sc after a corner as you work, to make counting easier. Pick up yarn C in BLO of the first stitch after the center FLdc of a side*} begin with an elongated loop, ch 1 loosely, sc in next 2 st, (3 spike-dc in ch-2-space of Rnd 3 enclosing ch-space of Rnd 4, sc in next 7 st) repeat 3 times, 3 spike-dc in ch-2-space of Rnd 3 enclosing ch-space of Rnd 4, sc in next 4 st, slst in both loops of beginning elongated loop [40]
Put a stitch maker in your yarn C loop to prevent it from unraveling. Keep yarn and loop to the back while you work Rnd 6.

Rnd 6: {*pick up yarn B loop in BLO in 2nd stitch before Fpdc of Rnd 4*} begin with an elongated loop, ch 1 loosely, (FLdc in next st, sc in next st {*this should be the middle st*} FLdc in next st, sc in next 3 st, sc + ch 2 + sc in middle spike-dc, sc in next 3 st) repeat 3 times, FLdc in next st, sc in next st {*this should be the middle st*}, FLdc in next st, sc in next 3 st, sc + ch 2 + sc in middle spike-dc, sc in next 2 st, slst in both loops of beginning elongated loop [44 + 8 ch]
Put a stitch maker in your yarn B loop to prevent it from unraveling. Keep yarn and loop to the back while you work Rnd 7.

Rnd 7: {*pick up yarn C loop in BLO of 2nd stitch after middle sc*} begin with an elongated loop, ch 1 loosely, sc in next st, (FLdc in next 2 st of Rnd 5, fold the corner away from you, FLdc + FLtr + FLdc in middle spike-dc of Rnd 5, FLdc in next 2 st of Rnd 5, skip 2 st underneath on Rnd 6, sc in next 3 st, FLdc in center st of side, sc in next 3 st) repeat 3 times, FLdc in next 2 st of Rnd 5, fold the corner away from you, FLdc + FLtr + FLdc in middle spike-dc of Rnd 5, FLdc in next 2 st of Rnd 5, skip 2 st underneath on Rnd 6, sc in next 3 st, FLdc in center st of side, sc in next st, slst in both loops of beginning elongated loop [56]
Put a stitch maker in your yarn C loop to prevent it from unraveling.
Keep yarn and loop to the back while you work Rnd 8.

Odd rounds

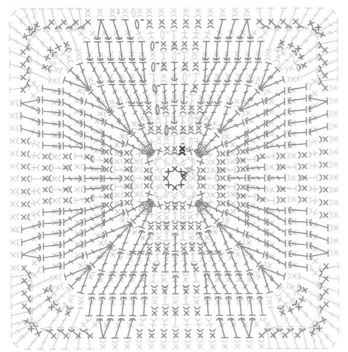

Even rounds

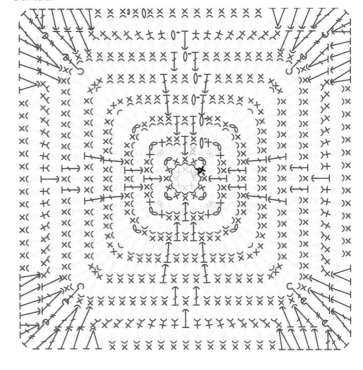

Rnd 8: {pick up yarn B loop in BLO of stitch before middle stitch} begin with an elongated loop, ch 1 loosely, sc in next 2 st, (FLdc in next st, sc in next 4 st, 3 sc in next tr, sc in next 4 st, FLdc in next st, sc in next 3 st) repeat 3 times, FLdc in next st, sc in next 4 st, sc + ch 2 + sc in next tr, sc in next 4 st, FLdc in next st, slst in both loops of beginning elongated loop [64]
Put a stitch maker in your yarn B loop to prevent it from unraveling. Keep yarn and loop to the back while you work Rnd 9.

Rnd 9: {Pick up yarn C loop in BLO of 2nd stitch after center st} begin with an elongated loop, ch 1 loosely, (FLdc in next 4 st, FLdc + FLtr + FLdc in corner st of Rnd 7, FLdc in next 4 st, sc in the next FLdc of Rnd 8, FLdc in next 3 center st, sc in next FLdc of Rnd 8) repeat 3 times, FLdc in next 4 st, FLdc + FLtr + FLdc in corner st of Rnd 7, FLdc in next 4 st, sc in next FLdc of Rnd 8, FLdc in next 3 center st, slst in both loops of beginning elongated loop [64]
Put a stitch maker in your yarn C loop to prevent it from unraveling. Keep yarn and loop to the back while you work Rnd 10.

Rnd 10: {Pick up yarn B loop in BLO of stitch before middle stitch} begin with an elongated loop, ch 1 loosely, sc in next 2 st, (FLdc in next st, sc in next 5 st, BLO 3 sc in next tr, sc in next 5 st, FLdc in next st, sc in next 3 st) repeat 3 times, FLdc in next st, sc in next 5 st, BLO 3 sc in next tr, sc in next 5 st, FLdc in next st, slst in both loops of beginning elongated loop [72]
Put a stitch maker in your yarn B loop to prevent it from unraveling. Keep yarn and loop to the back while you work Rnd 11.

Rnd 11: {pick up yarn C loop in BLO of next Rnd 10 FLdc following middle stitch} begin with an elongated loop, ch 1 loosely, (2 FLdc in first FLdc, FLdc in next 4 FLdc, FLdc + FLtr + FLdc in tr of Rnd 9, FLdc in next 4 FLdc, 2 FLdc in next FLdc, sc in next FLdc of Rnd 10, sc in next sc of Rnd 10, FLdc in next st, sc in next st, sc in next FLdc of Rnd 10) repeat 3 times, 2 FLdc in first FLdc, FLdc in next 4 FLdc, FLdc + FLtr + FLdc in tr of Rnd 9, FLdc in next 4 FLdc, 2 FLdc in next FLdc, sc in next 2 st, FLdc in next st, sc in next st, slst in both loops of beginning elongated loop [80]
Put a stitch maker in your yarn C loop to prevent it from unraveling. Keep yarn and loop to the back while you work Rnd 12.

Note: In rounds 12, 13 and 14 a number of stitches are worked FP instead of FL. Please note this difference as it defines the dip in the corners of the hearts.

Rnd 12: {Pick up Yarn B loop in BLO of middle stitch} begin with an elongated loop, ch 1 loosely, (FLdc in next st, sc in next 8 st, BLO sc + FPdc + BLO sc in next tr, sc in next 8 st, FLdc in next st, sc in next st *{this should be the center of the side}*) repeat 3 times, FLdc in next st, sc in next 8 st, BLO sc in next tr + FPdc around same tr + BLO sc in other side of same tr, sc in next 8 st, FLdc in next st, slst in both loops of beginning elongated loop [88]
Put a stitch maker in your yarn B loop to prevent it from unraveling.

Keep yarn and loop to the back while you work Rnd 13.

Rnd 13: {pick up yarn C loop in BLO of 2nd stitch following middle stitch} begin with an elongated loop, ch 1 loosely, (FLhdc in first 6 FLdc of Rnd 11, skip last FLdc, sc in next st, BLO 3 sc in FPdc, sc in next st, skip 1 st, FLhdc in next 6 FLdc, sc in next 5 st *{3rd sc is worked in center st}*) repeat 3 times, FLhdc in next 6 FLdc, sc in next st, BLO 3 sc in FPdc, sc in next st, skip first st, FLhdc in next 6 st, sc in next 4 st, slst in both loops of beginning elongated loop [88] Put a stitch maker in your yarn C loop to prevent it from unraveling. Keep yarn and loop to the back while you work Rnd 14.

Rnd 14: {pick up yarn B in BLO of stitch after middle st} begin with an elongated loop, ch 1 loosely, sc in next 7 st, (FLhdc in next st, 2 FLdc in next st, working in front of corner, FPtr around next FPdc, 2 FLdc in next st, FLhdc in next st, sc in next 8 st, FLhdc in middle st, sc in next 8 st) repeat 3 times, FLhdc in next st, 2 FLdc in next st, working in front of corner, FPtr around next FPdc, 2 FLdc in next st, FLhdc in next st, sc in next 8 st, FLhdc in next st, slst in both loops of beginning elongated loop [96]
Put a stitch maker in your yarn B loop to prevent it from unraveling. Keep yarn and loop to the back while you work Rnd 15.

Rnd 15: {pick up yarn C loop in BLO of 3rd stitch after middle st} begin with an elongated loop, ch 1 loosely, (starting in second FLhdc, FLhdc in next 2 st, FLhdc2tog over next 2 st, skip 4 st behind FL stitches just made, sc in next 4 st, 3 sc in FPtr, sc in next 4 st, skip first FLhdc, FLhdc2tog over next 2 st, FLhdc in next 2 st, skip 4 st behind FL stitches just made, sc in next 7 st) repeat 3 times, starting in second FLhdc, FLhdc in next 2 st, FLhdc2tog over next 2 st, skip 4 st behind FL stitches just made, sc in next 4 st, 3 sc in FPtr, sc in next 4 st, skip first FLhdc, FLhdc2tog over next 2 st, FLhdc in next 2 st, skip 4 st behind FL stitches just made, sc in next 6 st, fasten off, invisible join in 1st FLhdc [96]

Rnd 16: {pick up yarn B loop in both loops of third stitch after middle stitch, work through both loops unless otherwise noted} begin with an elongated loop, ch 1 loosely, (sc in next 3 FL stitches, sc in next st, 2 FLhdc in sc of Rnd 14, FLhdc in next 3 st, 2 FLdc in corner FPtr enclosing both loops of Rnd 15 sc, FPtr around FPtr, 2 FLdc in next st enclosing both loops of Rnd 15 sc, FLhdc in next 2 st, 2 FLhdc in next sc of Rnd 14, sc in next 3 FL stitches, sc in next 7 st) repeat 4 times, working the final sc in the initial elongated loop, fasten off with an invisible join in 2nd stitch [112]

Embellishment: top slst around Rnd 16 in Yarn A, fasten off.

Change Of Heart Square works best when using high contrasting colors for yarns B and C.

WAVY SQUARE 112 stitch square

Madelenón (Soledad Iglesias Silva) — Argentina
🌐 www.madelenon.com 📷 @handmadelenon f madelenonface

Skill level: Extra advanced
Colors: Yarn A: Peach / Yarn B: Green Ice

INSTRUCTIONS

Note: Odd rounds in this pattern create a foundation chain over which we work the even rounds.

Rnd 1: {start with yarn A} ch 7, join with a slst to form a ring [7]

Rnd 2: {work all stitches in the ring, not in the chain stitches} ch 3 (count as dc), dc, ch 1, 2 dc, (2 dc, ch 1, 2 dc) repeat 3 times, slst in 3rd ch of initial ch 3 [16 + 4 ch]
cCh 3, put a stitch maker in the last chain to prevent it from unraveling.

Rnd 3: {join yarn B with a slst around the Rnd 1 chain, between the last and first stitches of Rnd 2. Insert the hook in the center circle, from front to back, and come out between 2 dc stitches. Pull up a loop and make a slst} (ch 6, skip 4 dc, sc around the Rnd 1 chain between the two middle dc of a 4-dc-group in Rnd 2) repeat 3 times, ch 3, tr in initial slst [4 loops]

Rnd 4: {with the loop on your hook, Insert the hook in the current ch-6-space of Rnd 3 and ch-1-space of Rnd 2 at the same time} slst, ch 3 (count as dc) + dc + ch 1 + 2 dc in same ch-space {the ch 3 you left on hold in Rnd 2 is at the front side of the work}, (2 dc + ch 1 + 4 dc + ch 1 + 2 dc in next ch-6-space of Rnd 3 and ch-1-space of Rnd 2) repeat 3 times, 2 dc + ch 1 + 2 dc in the initial ch-space, slst in 3rd ch of initial ch 3 [32 + 8 ch]
Ch 3, put a stitch maker in this last chain to prevent it from unraveling.

Rnd 5: {put yarn A at the end of Rnd 2 back in the hook} ch 3 {6 ch in total}, sc in the ch-6-space of Rnd 3 centered between the 4 dc of Rnd 4, ch 6, sc in the gap between dc of Rnd 2, (ch 6, sc in the ch-6-space of Rnd 3 centered between the 4 dc of Rnd 4, ch 6, sc in the gap between dc of Rnd 2) repeat 2 times, ch 6, sc in the ch-6-space of Rnd 3 centered between the 4 dc of Rnd 4, ch 3, tr in same st as final slst of Rnd 2 [8 loops]

Rnd 6: {with the loop on your hook, Insert the hook in the current ch-6-space of Rnd 5 and ch-1-space of Rnd 4 at the same time} slst, ch 3 (count as dc) + dc + ch 1 + 2 dc in same ch-space, {the ch 3 you left on hold in Rnd 4 is at the front side of the work} 2 dc + ch 1 + 2 dc in next ch-6-space of Rnd 5 and ch-1-space of Rnd 4, 2 dc + ch 1 + 2 dc in the gap between two middle dc of a 4-dc-group in Rnd 4, [(2 dc + ch 1 + 2 dc in next ch-6-space of Rnd 5 and ch-1-space of Rnd 4 at the same time) repeat

Odd rounds

2 times, 2 dc + ch 1 + 2 dc in the gap between two middle dc of a 4-dc-group in Rnd 4] repeat 3 times, slst in 3rd ch of initial ch 3 [48 + 12 ch] Ch 3, put a stitch maker in this last chain to prevent it from unraveling.

Rnd 7: *{put yarn B at the end of Rnd 4 back on the hook}* ch 3 *{6 ch in total}*, sc in the gap between dc-groups of Rnd 4, (ch 6, sc in the gap between unworked dc of Rnd 4) repeat 2 times [ch 6, sc in the gap between dc-groups of Rnd 4 (ch 6, sc in the gap between unworked dc of Rnd 4) repeat 2 times] repeat 2 times, ch 6, sc in the gap between dc-groups of Rnd 4, ch 6, sc in the gap between unworked dc of Rnd 4, ch 3, tr in same st as final slst of Rnd 4 [12 loops]

Rnd 8: *{with the loop on your hook, Insert the hook in the current ch-6-space of Rnd 7 and ch-1-space of Rnd 6 at the same time}* slst, ch 3 (count as dc), dc + ch 1 + 2 dc in same ch-space *{the ch 3 you left on hold in Rnd 6 is at the front side of the work}* (2 dc + ch 1 + 2 dc in next ch-6-space of Rnd 7 and ch-1-space of Rnd 6 at the same time) repeat 2 times, 2 dc + ch 1 + 4 dc + ch 1 + 2 dc in next ch-space, [(2 dc + ch 1 + 2 dc in next ch-6-space of Rnd 7 and ch-1-space of Rnd 6 at the same time) repeat 2 times, 2 dc + ch 1 + 4 dc + ch 1 + 2 dc in next ch-space] repeat 2 times, (2 dc + ch 1 + 2 dc in next ch-6-space of Rnd 7 and ch-1-space of Rnd 6 at the same time) repeat 2 times, 2 dc + ch 1 + 2 dc in the initial ch-space, slst in 3rd ch of initial ch 3 [64 + 16 ch]
Ch 3, put a stitch maker in this last chain to prevent it from unraveling.

Rnd 9: *{put yarn A at the end of Rnd 6 back in the hook}* ch 3 *{6 ch in total}*, sc in the gap between dc-groups of Rnd 6, ch 6, sc in the gap between unworked dc of Rnd 6, ch 6, sc in next ch-space between dc of Rnd 8, [(ch 6, sc in the gap between dc-groups of Rnd 6) repeat 3 times, ch 6, sc in next ch-space between dc of Rnd 8] repeat 3 times, ch 3, tr in same st as final slst of Rnd 6 [16 loops]

Rnd 10: *{with the loop on your hook, Insert the hook in the current ch-6-space of Rnd 9 and ch-1-space of Rnd 8 at the same time}* slst, ch 3 (count as dc) + dc + ch 1 + 2 dc in the same ch-space, *{the ch 3 you left on hold in Rnd 8 is at the front side of the work}* (2 dc + ch 1 + 2 dc in next ch-6-space of Rnd 9 and ch-1-space of Rnd 8 at the same time) repeat 3 times, 2 dc + ch 1 + 2 dc in the gap between center dc of Rnd 8, [(2 dc + ch 1 + 2 dc in next ch-6-space of Rnd 9 and ch-1-space of Rnd 8 at the same time) repeat 4 times, 2 dc + ch 1 + 2 dc in the gap between center dc of Rnd 8] repeat 3 times, slst in 3rd ch of initial ch 3 [80 + 20 ch] Fasten off.

Rnd 11: *{Put yarn B at the end of Rnd 8 back on the hook}* ch 3 *{6 ch in total}*, sc in next gap between dc-groups of Rnd 8, (ch 6, sc in next gap between dc-groups of Rnd 8) repeat 2 times, (ch 6, sc in gap between unworked dc of Rnd 8) repeat 2 times, [[(ch 6, sc in next gap between dc-groups of Rnd 8) repeat 3 times (ch 6, sc in gap between unworked dc of Rnd 8) repeat 2 times] repeat 2 times, (ch 6, sc in gap between dc-groups of Rnd 8) repeat 3 times, ch 6, sc in gap between unworked dc of Rnd 8, ch 3, tr in same st as final slst of Rnd 8 [20 loops]

Rnd 12: *{With the loop on your hook, Insert the hook in the current ch-6-space of Rnd 11 and ch-1-space of Rnd 10 at the same time}* slst, ch 3 (counts as dc), 2 dc in the same ch-space, [4 dc in next ch-6-space of Rnd 11 and ch-1-space of Rnd 10 at the same time, (5 dc in next ch-6-space of Rnd 11 and ch-1-space of Rnd 10 at the same time) repeat 2 times, 4 dc in next ch-6-space of Rnd 11 and ch-1-space of Rnd 10 at the same time, 3 dc + ch 3 + 3 dc in next ch-6-space of Rnd 11 and ch-1-space of Rnd 10 at the same time] repeat 3 times, 4 dc in the ch-6-space of Rnd 11 and ch-1-space of Rnd 10 at the same time, (5 dc in next ch-6-space of Rnd 11 and ch-1-space of Rnd 10 at the same time) repeat 2 times, 4 dc in next ch-6-space of Rnd 11 and ch-1-space of Rnd 10 at the same time, 3 dc in next ch-6-space of Rnd 11 and ch-1-space of Rnd 10 at the same time, ch 3, slst in 3rd ch of initial ch 3 [96 + 12 ch] Fasten off.

Rnd 13: *{Join yarn A with a standing stitch in any first st after a corner-space}* (sc in next 24 st, sc + ch 2 + sc in next ch-space) repeat 4 times, fasten off with an invisible join to 2nd stitch [104 + 8 ch]

Even rounds

COTTON CANDY SQUARE `112 stitch square`

Crochetedbytess (Therese Eghult) — Sweden
⊕ www.sistersinstitch.com

Skill level: Advanced
Colors: Color A: Cream / Color B: Old Pink / Color C: Eucalyptus / Color D: Pearl / Color E: Birch
Special stitches: 5-dc-pc (5 double crochet popcorn stitch) / 4-puff (puff stitch with 4 loops) / FP-4-tr-bobble (Front Post 4 treble Bobble) / BPhdc (Back post half double crochet)

INSTRUCTIONS

Rnd 1: {start with yarn A} start a magic ring with (4-puff, ch 3) repeat 6 times, slst in closing chain of initial puff [6 + 12 ch]

Rnd 2: (FPsc around puff, 3 sc in next ch-space) repeat 6 times, fasten off with an invisible join to 2nd stitch [24]

Note: the final 2 sc stitches of Rnd 3 are worked in the stitches behind the first FP-4-tr-bobble stitch.

Rnd 3: {join yarn B in any FPsc, make your first stitch a standing stitch} FP-4-tr-bobble around next FPsc, ch 1, skip 4 st, sc in next 2 st, (reverse FP-4-tr-bobble around the FPsc you just skipped, ch 1, skip 2 st, sc in next 2 st) repeat 5 times, fasten off with an invisible join to first ch after initial FP-4-tr-bobble [18 + 6 ch]

Rnd 4: {join yarn C in any ch-space, make your first stitch a standing stitch} (sc + ch 2 + sc in ch-space, ch 4, skip 3 st) repeat 6 times, slst in initial sc [12 + 36 ch]

Rnd 5: slst in next ch-space, ch 3 (count as dc) + 4 dc, form first pc with these 5 st + ch 2 + 5-dc-pc + ch 1 in ch-2-space, skip 1 st, 6 sc in next ch-4-space, skip 1 st, (5-dc-pc + ch 2 + 5-dc-pc + ch 1 in ch-2-space, skip 1 st, 6 sc in next ch-4-space, skip 1 st) repeat 6 times, slst in initial pc [48 + 6 ch]

Rnd 6: {Work only in the pc from Rnd 5} sc in same st, ch 3, skip ch-space, sc in next st, ch 5, skip 6 st, (sc in next st, ch 3, skip ch-space, sc in next st, ch 5, skip 6 st) repeat 5 times, fasten off with an invisible join in initial sc [12 + 48 ch]

Rnd 7: {join yarn A in any ch-5-space, make your first stitch a standing stitch} (10 dc in ch-5-space, skip sc, skip first ch, slst in second ch, skip third ch, skip sc) repeat 6 times, fasten off with an invisible join to 2nd stitch [66]

Note: Next, we make the 6 flower heads on top, in between 2 pc of Rnd 5.

Flower heads: *{join yarn D in any ch-1-space between 2 pc of Rnd 5, make your first stitch a standing stitch. You only work in the ch-1-spaces and in ch-3-spaces from Rnd 5 and 6}* sc + 2 hdc + 3 dc in ch-1-space of Rnd 5, continue working in ch-3-space of Rnd 6 and on the left side of the slst of Rnd 7. With the wrong side facing, fold the 10 dc stitches back, 2 dc around ch-3-space, skip slst, 3 dc around same ch-3-space, fasten off with an invisible join to initial sc [11 per flower head] Repeat between all pc-stitches [6 flower heads]

Rnd 8: *{join yarn E in any first dc of Rnd 7, make your first stitch a standing stitch}* (10 BPhdc, skip 1 st) repeat 6 times, slst in initial BPhdc [60]

Rnd 9: *{work this round in FLO}* ch 3 (count as dc) + 4 dc in next st, 5 dc in next 59 st, fasten off with an invisible join to first true dc [300]

Note: When working in BLO in Rnd 10 make sure to work in the third chain as well to make sure the construction stays firm.

Rnd 10: *{join yarn A in any BLO BPhdc of Rnd 8, make your first stitch a standing stitch. Tilt the ruffle towards you to make crocheting a bit*

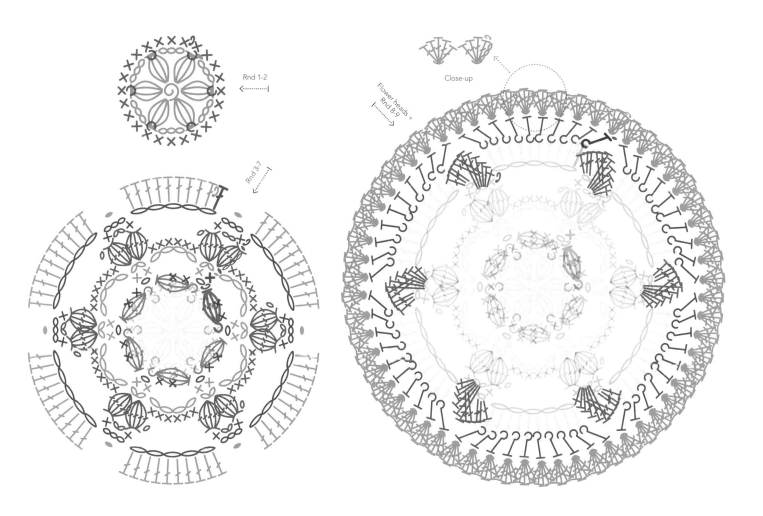

Rnd 1-2

Rnd 3-7

Close-up

Flower heads +
Rnd 8-9

easier, work the entire round in BLO} (2 hdc + ch 2 + 2 hdc in next st, hdc in next 14 st) repeat 4 times, slst in initial hdc [72 + 8 ch]

Rnd 11: slst in next st, slst in ch-space, [2 hdc + ch 1 + 2 hdc in ch-space, hdc in next 3 st, (ch 1, skip 1 st, sc in next st) repeat 3 times, sc in next st, (ch 1, skip 1 st, sc in next st) repeat 2 times, ch 1, skip 1 st, hdc in next 3 st] repeat 4 times, fasten off with an invisible join to 2nd hdc [68 + 28 ch]

Rnd 12: *{join yarn E in any corner-space, make your first stitch a standing stitch}* [2 dc + ch 2 + 2 dc in ch-space, skip 1 st, hdc in next 4 st, (4-puff + ch 1 in next st, hdc in next st) repeat 3 times, hdc in next st, (4-puff + ch 1 in next st, hdc in next st) repeat 2 times, 4-puff + ch 1 in next st, skip 1 st, hdc in next 4 st] repeat 4 times, fasten off with an invisible join [96 + 8 ch]

Rnd 13: *{join yarn E in any ch-1-space, make your first stitch a standing stitch. Make sure to make the sc in the puff stitches and not the closing chains}* [2 sc + ch 1 + 2 sc in ch-space, skip 1 st, sc in next 5 st, (sc in puff, skip closing ch, sc in next hdc) repeat 3 times, sc in next hdc, (sc in puff, skip closing ch, sc in next hdc) repeat 3 times, sc in next 5 st] repeat 4 times, fasten off with an invisible join to 2nd stitch [112]

Rnd 10-13